The Book of Fire

Also by Steven Forrest

The Inner Sky

The Changing Sky

The Night Speaks

The Book of Pluto

Measuring the Night (with Jeffrey Wolf Green)

Measuring the Night Vol. 2 (with Jeffrey Wolf Green)

Stalking Anubis

Skymates (with Jodie Forrest)

Skymates II (with Jodie Forrest)

Yesterday's Sky

The Book of the Moon

The Book of Fire

The Life-Givers

by Steven Forrest

Seven Paws Press, Inc.
Borrego Springs, CA

Published in 2019 by Seven Paws Press, Inc.
PO Box 82
Borrego Springs, CA 92004
www.sevenpaws.com

Copyright © 2019 by Steven Forrest

All rights reserved. No part of this publication may be reproduced or transmitted in any form or by any means, electronic or mechanical, including mimeographing, recording, taping, scanning, via Internet download, or by any information storage and retrieval systems, without permission in writing from Seven Paws Press, Inc.
Reviewers may quote brief passages.

ISBN 978-1-939510-02-0

Cover art by Diren Yardimli

Printed in the United States of America
LCCN 2018966507

ACKNOWLEDGMENTS

Deep gratitude to my friend, student, and benefactor, Jeff Parrett. As he recounts in his introduction, his financial support bought me the precious time I needed in order to write this book. Without his help, *The Book of Fire* would still be "something I would love to have time to do someday..."

Once again, my gratitude to my manager, web-wizard, and dear friend, Tony Howard. He has built the bridges that connect my work to the wider world. Without him, I would be singing in a canyon without any echoes. Thank you, Tony.

Thanks to Carol Czeczot for nearly four decades of friendship, not to mention another monumental editorial job.

Even though this book was truly written rather than transcribed from talks, it was an enormous help to be able to refer to a transcript of my original "Fire" program, offered back in 2015 at my bi-annual Apprenticeship Program meeting in Alpine, California. For the painstaking, tedious work of producing that transcript, I thank my student, JoAnn Anderson.

A profound *gracias* to the people who have run my various Apprenticeship Programs around the world over the years. The workload is enormous and I wouldn't have the patience to do it myself. Here are their names in lights, in no particular order. In southern California, Ingrid Coffin and her team at the Blue Sky Ranch Fellowship. In China, Felicia Jiang and David Railey, along with the amazing NoDoor team. In North Carolina, Kathy Hallen and her able assistants, Carol McLauren and Tricia Mickleberry. In Nelson Bay, Australia, and various places around Europe, the indomitable Mercurial Connections team, Lisa Jones and Christine Murfitt. Finally, in northern California, I thank Joyce Van Horn.

My Apprenticeship Programs have come and gone, as have the people who have made them possible. Thanks, emeritus, to Karen Davis, Vinessa Nevala, Barbara King, and the late David Friedman.

Finally, my gratitude to the following people who were actively engaged with me in various ways during the writing process: Scott Ainslie, Virginia Bell, Gail Boulton, Chip Conley, Cui "Chloe" Ying—my intrepid Chinese translator, Rona Elliot and Roger Brossy, Michael Faith, Hadley Fitzgerald, John and Suzanne Fouts of Mountain Home Ranch, Rishi Giovanni Gatti, Robert and Diana Griffin, the Grossenbacher clan: John, Tracy, and Ryan, Susie Latimer Hodge, Sylvia Hsiao, Bariş Īlhan, Kathy Jacobson, Bill Janis, Robert A. Johnson, Mark Jones, Trent Kleinkopf, Peter and Ingrid Kondos, Kate and Alex Laird, Jackie Larsen, Rick Levine, Elizabeth Long, Ralph MacIntyre, Barbara Matson, Mary Ann McGuire, Cristin McVey, Randy Meeks, Dominic Miller, Linnea Mirron and Ricky Williams, Billy Murfitt, Laura Nalbandian, Carey Nash, Rafael Nasser, Marie O'Neill, Carol Peebles, Claire and Dan Pleym, Steven Poster and Susan Williams, Aminah Raheem and Fritz Smith, Claire Rauwel, Dusty Recor and "Indian Joe" Stewart, Ray Ristorcelli, Evelyn Roberts, Vernon Robinson, Paige Ruane and Jack McDonald, Jonathan Sacks, Fran Slavich, Cristina Smith, Sting and Trudie Sumner-Styler, Tem Tarriktar and Nan Geary, Kay Taylor, Elaine and Mark Thomas, Lupe and Pati Torres, Julia Trawick, Dick and Artemisa Walker, Paula Wansley, Brittany Wymore, and Helen Zou.

And thanks to my life-partner Michelle Kondos for her sanity, courage and love, not to mention for filling our home with oil paintings worthy of the finest art museums in the world.

TABLE OF CONTENTS

PART THREE: MARS, THE SUN, AND JUPITER THROUGH THE TWELVE SIGNS AND HOUSES

PART FOUR: SEEING POSSIBLE FUTURES

In grateful memory of my first true spiritual teacher,
Marian Starnes, 1926–2016.
She believed in me before I believed in myself.

INTRODUCTION

Physicists say that matter and energy can neither be created nor destroyed, only change form. Yet we forget one of the predominant theories of cosmology, The Big Bang. It purports that in an instant shorter than we can conceive, all matter and energy burst into existence. So I wonder if those physicists really understand the full nature of the universe? And in fact what happened was the initial expression of the Fire Element.

On a personal level, we each have our own Big Bang experience; we call it birth, and with it comes this thing we call our birthchart! For me, with my Sun/Moon/Uranus grand trine in Sagittarius/Aries/Leo, the Fire Element is very alive in me. One might say it defines an energy that runs through much of my life.

In June of 2013, when transiting Uranus in Aries was trining my ninth house natal Uranus in Leo, I trekked across the country to North Carolina for my first astrology class with a man named Steven Forrest. I'd read a few of his books, had a curiosity about this thing called evolutionary astrology and had no idea of the mentorship, friendship and partnership that would be birthed from that day.

I've now done over ten apprenticeship programs (APs) with Steve and I'm struck by the clarity, humor and wisdom he brings into his teachings. He has dedicated his life to his work in Evolutionary Astrology and the students he teaches to carry on the tradition. He brings the practice alive through his personal stories and anecdotes which are often humorous and always deeply meaningful.

It has been my great fortune over those ten-plus programs to get to know Steve on a personal level and develop what I consider a treasured friendship. You know the kind—you can count them on one hand. These are the people with whom you can drop the facade of propriety and talk about our deeper nature and the challenges of life. It is a big part of what is possible with evolutionary astrology, and Steve is one of those people for me.

It wasn't long after that first AP when we were sitting together sipping a fine single-malt Scotch when I posed the question: "What's next for you?" He talked about his desire to write, sharing his astrological insights with more people, and the challenges of making the time in his life to do it.

Now, being an engineer, I figured this was an easy problem to solve, so I asked the obvious next question: "What would it take to make it happen?" In my years of knowing Steve, there have been few times when I've found him struggling for words—yet in that moment, I could see him reflect on what he was about to say... because the simple answer to my question was "money." Money is one of those things "proper" people don't talk about. It was one of those times when the facade of propriety was dropped and a deeper conversation ensued.

For me, my second house Sagittarius Sun/Saturn/Mercury have provided me a journey through the world of finance and a gratifying level of success. Over the next few weeks, Steve and I talked about dollars and timing. That was the inception of our partnership through which it was my privilege to provide the financial support that gave life to his 2016 volume, *The Book of Neptune*.

Our partnership continues as Steve develops the evolutionary perspective of astrology through the topics he teaches in his AP. It gets richer and deeper every time, as he boldly goes where few astrologers have gone before.

Sadly, I was unable to attend the programs where Steve delved deeply into the four elements, yet as a student, I was able to get recordings of the programs. As I listened, I appreciated the unique doorway through which he was viewing the astrological fundamentals—something I knew had to be shared with a broader audience. The next time I was with Steve at an AP in Northern California, we were once again sitting around the table sipping a fine single-malt Scotch... I bet you know the question I asked him and where the conversation took us.

Now, in the spirit of the life-giving energy of the Fire Element, it gives me great personal pleasure to introduce my mentor, friend and partner, Steven Forrest, as he takes us into an evolutionary perspective on the astrological "Life-Givers."

—Jeff Parrett
Pleasanton, California

1

FLYING OVER THE TERRITORY

Back in 1978, the late, great and very complicated M. Scott Peck opened his monumental bestseller, *The Road Less Traveled*, with a simple statement: "Life is difficult."

Who could argue with him? The "lessons of life" seem never to end. Astrology merely holds a mirror before them. It is not magical; it solves nothing. But maybe, by gazing long and hard and bravely into that mirror, we can better understand the point of those lessons and the patterns behind them. Maybe, with some wisdom added to the mix, life's difficulties are lessened.

But it is hard work. If we choose not to bother with it, the universe shrugs its eternal shoulders. We are always free to learn things the hard way.

Maybe we look at our transits and progressions for the next couple of years; that can be helpful. I often reflect on my own. Every day I try to help people understand theirs.

I hope that the people who come and sit with me leave with a deeper sense of direction and some spiritual encouragement.

I will admit it: they also often look kind of tired.

Facing life's lessons through the clear lens of astrology is not for the fainthearted; I respect my clients for their courage, and even more for their commitment to living examined lives. But if I wanted to be really mean, I might say: "How would you like a free peek at your transits and progressions for the next five years? How's about ten? How's about the next fifty years?"

By the time we got forty years down the road, the poor client would want to jump off a bridge. I would probably follow right behind.

Life is sweet. But life is also relentless, exhausting, and often haunted by tragedy. We have got to take it one day a time. Simply surviving can seem challenging at times. As we will soon see, that is where the Fire signs show their mettle.

In all my years as a counselor, I have heard any number of complaints, but I have never heard anyone complain that his or her life was too easy. That never seems to happen. We all face disappointments. Everyone has dreams that do not come true. We age; our bodies fail us. The unfairness and brutality of life appall us as we sit dumbfounded before the evening news. Dear friends die of terrible diseases. We all come to realize that the leading cause of divorce is marriage. Why do our beloved pets live such short lives? Why do friendships fail? Why does a child ever die before a parent?

But these difficult things are part of almost everyone's reality.

Let's not slip into negativity here; let's not forget about rainbows and kittens and precious, lasting friendships. Let's not forget about Beethoven's Ninth Symphony.

But M. Scott Peck was right: life is indeed often difficult. And treacherous. And dispiriting. We all have scars to prove it.

This element of suffering that is woven into the fabric of life can be expressed simply and humanly, without recourse to philosophy. But metaphysically, one way to say it is that each one of us is in a karmic predicament. That is where evolutionary astrology comes into the equation. Your birthchart reflects that predicament unerringly back to you, along with suggestions about the path for getting beyond it.

Earth can be understood as madhouse where crazy souls come to heal. And the healing works—or at least, it can work. But that healing process is almost never quick: it takes a lifetime—or lifetimes, plural.

That step-by-step journey to deeper wisdom and inner ease is reflected specifically, individually, and helpfully in your birthchart. To understand it is to understand with fierce clarity the exact nature of your evolutionary situation, warts and all. *And how to get beyond it…*

… which brings me right back to my ugly Scorpionic thought about driving my poor clients to the verge of suicide by offering them a "free lifetime transits and progressions reading." Who could stand it? "The work of a lifetime" is a familiar phrase, but when you start to think of it, step-by-step, lesson by lesson, year by year, it is nearly overwhelming.

A wise man once told me that while experience leads to wisdom, a lack of wisdom tends to lead to experience. And of course "experience" does not automatically equate with growth. Experience must be digested honestly and humbly before it can metamorphose into true wisdom. It is possible—common in fact—for a person to do dumb things and to learn nothing at all from them. True growth only happens through conscious, intentional processes. Furthermore, the soul-victory we call personal growth does not really diminish the pain of a difficult experience; what it does, however, is absolutely precious: *it gives meaning to the pain, and shows us a way to avoid it in the future.*

But how much growth can you take, even in principle, in a single day? We all have our limits. To say it more harshly, we all have a boundary of pain beyond which life would not be worth living. That boundary is hardwired into our mortal existence.

I am very aware as I write these words that there are undoubtedly some people who are wondering why they bought this bummer of an astrology book! Please bear with me—*The Book of Fire* is, emphatically, not a negative book. This book is a triumphant celebration of the human ability to bounce back from life's nightmares. More than that, it is a practical manual about exactly how to accomplish that.

Each one of us has something else hardwired into our souls: that is *a set of functions in the psyche which allow us to tap into our fundamental resilience.* The human spirit, in other words, can survive hell—and go dancing the next day. Is there anything more precious than that?

We all can do it—and astrology can help us all get better at doing it. Astrology offers each of us a unique set of custom-tailored methods for keeping life in our bones. That is the energizing, life-affirming promise of the "Fire Family."

By "Fire Family," I mean the three Fire signs: Aries, Leo, and Sagittarius. But I also mean their associated houses: the first, fifth, and ninth. And I include the three planets that rule those signs: Mars, Jupiter, and the Sun itself.

Together, they are the Life-Givers.

Without a healthy, active relationship with each of them, something inside us just gives up. With them on our side, we can eat the Devil for breakfast and spit him out before lunch.

Read on, and learn about how to make allies out of these nine inestimable Fire-friends, each one of them a vibrant gift from the sky—and each one of them as close to the core of what it means to thrive in this human world as the living marrow in your bones.

2

ASTROLOGY'S HOLY TRINITY: SIGNS, PLANETS, AND HOUSES

Back in the 1970s, before I wrote *The Inner Sky*, before my hair fell out and I got all round and soft in the middle, I was living in Chapel Hill, North Carolina, where I had gone to college. I was the local astrologer and, pretty much like everyone else in my generation, a guitar-player—and, of course, "on the spiritual path."

My community received a rich gift: the great Ram Dass visited our town to offer a talk. For me, that was a double-header: seeing a teacher of that level was good for my spiritual sustenance—but, lucky me, there was a second gift: my old band, Silkworm, had the privilege of opening for him.

Even better, Ram Dass showed up at our sound check and I was able to have a few quiet moments with him. In my youthful arrogance, I even offered him an astrological reading. In retrospect, that was like my offering the Dalai Lama a few meditation tips.

Ram Dass graciously declined, citing scheduling difficulties.

I guess there were about fifteen hundred of us in the audience that night. The great man was on the stage, sitting in a chair, doing his talk. All of a sudden he looked thunderstruck. He stopped speaking and just stared at the back of the hall for a few seconds. Most of (us) turned around, but there was nothing unexpected there.

After a while, Ram Dass pointed over our heads and said, "See that exit sign?" Then he deadpanned, "Don't believe it."

We all cracked up, of course. But it wasn't just a joke. It was a teaching. On the other side of that Exit, life continued for all of us.

There are people who use spirituality to inflate their egos, priding themselves on being "on the spiritual path." But really, do any of us have a single alternative? We are all on the spiritual path, and there is no exit. That was the point Ram Dass was making.

Notice something going on inside of you energetically as you read these words? I enjoyed delivering that Ram Dass story and I expect that you had fun reading it. "Don't believe it" was a funny line.

That is an example of a "Fire" moment. Laughter gives us strength. Getting ahead of myself, this particular illustration, with its element of humor, specifically has more of Jupiter's signature in it than that of Mars or the Sun—but it is still a Fire moment.

And Fire, as we have seen, is what gives you the spunk to go on living.

One more comment about Ram Dass. Many of you probably feel as I do: that he is a treasure. And of course many of my younger readers have probably never heard of him. What did he bring to the generations he touched? Obviously, spiritual teachings. But more than that: he brought us inspiration and faith, as well as an injection of devil-may-care enthusiasm for the spiritual path. Briefly, he was a professor of psychology at Harvard; he "blew it" by experimenting with psychedelics. He bounced back from getting fired by re-inventing himself as a spiritual teacher, and he did that by rolling the dice and traveling to India.

Ram Dass was born with a mission. The astrological symbolism behind that statement is that his Sun conjuncts rebel-Uranus in his tenth house, which is classically, the "house of career." Both bodies are in Aries, the Warrior—and there is the astrological signature for which we are looking: *his mission in the community was to bring us all a dose of pure, wild, damn-the-torpedoes Fire*. Sheer life-force. As he lived it, he demonstrated it to us all. By the way, a fiery Sagittarian Moon and a fiery Mars in Leo complete the Fire-sign trigon in Ram Dass's chart.

And again, what was his message? "See that exit sign? Don't believe it." Like Ram Dass, we have all signed up for the big ride. It is too late to stop now. Dive in. Everyone is on the spiritual path—and may God help us. And God will, so long as we are willing to help ourselves. How? Read on: we are entering the domain of the Life-Givers.

DEALING WITH IT ALL

How do we "deal with everything?" The Fire family can be summarized as astrology's answer to that pressing question. Fire keeps us strong enough to bounce back from defeat, disappointment, and the most grievous losses life can throw at us. By "strong enough," I do not just mean remaining grimly determined. Fire is not about Stoicism, it is about resilience. It is about how to be sincerely glad to be alive. With Fire, we are talking about your happy inner animal wagging its tail. We are talking about you actually *wanting* to get out of bed in the morning. We are talking about libido, appetite, and creativity.

How do we feed that inner Fire and keep it burning? Live the message of your birthchart as a whole—that means following the highest calling of that entire Great Symbol, with nothing left out. If you get your birthchart right... if you are brave and wise and tuned into yourself enough to live that life... you are going to be vital right down to the core. Even better, if you have lived your life guided by those stars, you will lie on your deathbed in a state of radiance. You will have lived the life you were born to live. There is no greater victory in the world than that one.

That alone is enough reason to call astrology a sacred art.

Astrology is, of course, more than simply a study of the Fire element. As this series of four books unfolds, we will explore the spiritual and evolutionary roles played by the other three elements: Earth, Air, and Water. Each one plays a critical role in maintaining our well-being. Trust them, and that famous Exit sign has a lot less appeal.

But the cycle begins with Fire.

We might immediately think of Aries and Leo and Sagittarius. Those three Fire signs are the foundation; in the following pages, we will study them deeply. But there's more: we need to include planets in our explorations—the rulers of those three signs. When a planet is said to "rule" a sign, that means that the two symbols share many energetic textures. As we think of Fire, we must also think of Mars, the Sun, and Jupiter, the planets locked in eternal resonance with Aries, Leo, and Sagittarius respectively.

For our third step in framing astrology's "Holy Trinity," we add the Fiery houses to the mix. Aries—the first sign of the zodiac—has a natural resonance with the first house, and so on around the circle: Leo resonates with the fifth house while Jupiter resonates with the ninth.

The skillful marriage of a planet, a sign, and house provides astrology's DNA. Individually, each one is like a gene—interesting, charged with data. But the life-giving magic only arrives when we are looking at the "double helix" of planet, sign, and house in interactive dialog, bound together by rulership. Later in the book, we will dive into the methodology for melding these three distinct symbols together. Rulership is the glue.

That is all true and accurate—but there is one phrase you will not encounter in these pages...

"IF YOUR SATURN IS IN ARIES OR THE FIRST HOUSE..."

In evolutionary astrology, we do not blur the meanings of the signs and the houses. While we recognize that Aries and the first house, for example, possess certain parallel structures, we also recognize that there are significant distinctions between them. In the proverbial nut shell, houses are correlated with *actions*—they are *behavioral expressions* of certain underlying agendas, attitudes or motivations.

The twelve signs, meanwhile, represent those inward psychological agendas, attitudes and motivations.

We are our signs and we do our houses.

Here's an illustration: the ninth house is classically "the house of long journeys over water." It has other meanings, but it refers concretely to the physical act of travel—or a little more broadly, to cross-cultural experiences.

Let's imagine someone is a "stay-at-home" type—astrologically, she has both the Sun and Moon in Cancer, plus a stellium in the fourth house. At some point in her life, she finds herself experiencing major *transits or progressions* to her ninth house. When that happens, she still might not *want t*o travel—but through synchronicity, circumstances arise that call her to travel. For example, she has always lived in Boston and expects to die there too, but her husband takes a two-year job in Dubai. Or maybe her best friend, who moved to New Mexico a few years ago, is going through a divorce and really needs her support.

So she reluctantly packs her bags for Dubai or Santa Fe.

That's how houses work: *they represent behaviors, not motivations.*

On the other hand, we might imagine a Sagittarian who dreams of adventure and the call of the open road—but who is bound to home-life by circumstances beyond his control. Maybe he has a sick wife. Maybe his aging parents are dependent on him. Maybe he has a big mortgage and five children, all of them college material. The motivation to expand his horizons, Sagittarian-fashion, is powerful in him; he feels it deeply. That is sign-energy. But a concentration of planets in, say, his fourth house *(domestic life)* or sixth house (*duties and responsibilities*) define the *behavioral shape of his biography.*

In writing these words, I am intentionally turning up the contrast between signs and houses in order to clarify their differences. I think that's a good initial practice. That is because the blurring of signs and houses has cost astrology some of its potential granularity and precision. I like to beat this drum as loudly as possible whenever the opportunity arises; internalizing it makes for better astrologers.

BEING AND DOING

Signs are "being" while houses are "doing." That's clear enough—but the harder we look at those two words, the more we recognize how much they interact. Some blur arises naturally. "Being" must always unveil itself through action, while "doing" ultimately reveals our inward motivations, values, and personal agenda—sign stuff.

The practical upshot of all this is that we will often find ourselves using some of the same language in describing Sagittarius as we use in describing the ninth house. It's the same for Aries in relation to the first house, along with Leo and the fifth house.

There is no problem with doing that—as long as you don't get so lazy that you are drawing an equal sign between the two symbols. Countless times in my practice, I've "cracked" a confusing configuration simply by thinking of a Sagittarian type "trapped" in a fourth house situation versus a Cancer type "condemned" to travel because of an emerging ninth house circumstance.

For similar reasons, in speaking of Mars, we will often find ourselves using the same language that comes up with Aries or the first house. No worry—just remember, planets are like little sub-personalities in your head. You give them flavor and distinction by matching them with signs and houses. Venus, for example, always wants love and connection. But what *kind* of love and connection? Tender? (Venus motivated by Cancer or Pisces) Hot? (Venus motivated by Aries). And where to look for that love? On the road? (Venus in the ninth house) Wait for grandma to introduce you? (Venus in the fourth house).

We will dive very deeply into this process of integrative synthesis as these pages unfold. Mastering the Holy Trinity of sign, house, and planet is the heart of our craft.

IN PRACTICE

Our practical bottom line is that when we think of the Fire Family, we are talking about nine pieces of archetypal astrological machinery. All are related, but all are distinct as well. This book is an attempt to define those nine basic words in the astrological vocabulary—and in some ways to redefine them by placing them in an evolutionary context.

Each one of the nine has its own unique qualities and its own unique gifts to offer us—but all nine share common ground: they are the fountainhead of our vitality, our animal sprightliness and verve, and our ability to fight back against anything that tries to rob us of life—literally or figuratively.

In the course of these pages, we'll explore these nine symbols as they operate in concert within the larger context of the birthchart. You may not personally have any planets in Fire signs or in the three Fire houses—but you surely have Mars, Jupiter and the Sun somewhere in your chart. In that case, much of your resilience and vitality pivots on your response to those three planets. That is true regardless of their sign or house positions. For you, these three planets must carry much of the entire load.

Going a little deeper, while maybe it's true that you have nothing in Leo, it is very likely that we would find Leo on the cusp of one of your houses (unless you have Leo intercepted in a house). Leo then sets the tone for that house—and eternally links that house to the Sun's position in your chart. That Leo-on-the-cusp configuration may not represent the same level of life-force as having your Sun, Moon or Ascendant in Leo, but it is still a significant manifestation of Leo energy—and one of the keys to your ability to bounce back in the face of life's difficulties.

In other words, this Fire material is relevant to all of us. We might even make the case that if your birthchart has a low Fire quotient, the material is even more important to you. Fiery people are naturally buoyant; those of us who are not so Fiery benefit from knowing how to intentionally boost it.

THE TERRAIN AHEAD

As we lay out the scheme of this volume, let's add that we will work with each of these nine symbols not only in terms of their relationship to the natal chart, but also in the context of transits, progressions and solar arcs. Again, even if your natal chart is not particularly Fiery, you will surely go through some very Fiery periods in your life. We will explore how to walk that tightrope across the volcanic caldera with as much grace and aplomb as possible.

How is progressed Mars different from transiting or solar arc Mars? We will explore those questions too—and ask the same ones for the Sun and Jupiter.

There's more: what happens when any of those nine Fiery points in your natal chart is itself stimulated by any transit, progression, or solar arc? That is a Fire event in your life for sure—even if the moving planet is a softy, such as the Moon, Venus, or Neptune.

Here is an Illustration:

Let's say your natal Mars lies in Cancer in the fourth house—even though that is a very "wet" Mars, it is still Mars; it is still a Fiery energy.

What happens when transiting Saturn conjuncts it? That is a complex event, with many Elements represented in the equation—but there is definitely a Fire-thread in the tapestry. Maybe you have to face some *difficult task* (Saturn) in order to *defend* (Mars) your *home or family* (Cancer and the fourth house).

If you accept that challenge and rise to it, you are also preserving and protecting your own life-force. You stood up to the bully. You faced down the bureaucrat who was trying to deprive your kid of his rights. Walking away from that victory, how do you feel?

Good!

If you wimp out, you are inviting depression, not to mention feelings of shame and failure. You may be a Watery person, but you will still face Fire-tests from time to time.

Each one of the nine words in our Fire vocabulary has a multifaceted definition, with many shades of meaning ranging from our loftiest aspirations down to the lowest swamps into which we are all capable of plunging. Throughout this book we will aim for "lofty"—but we will keep our aim true by being mindful and honest about the dark side of life, especially the kinds of darkness we create for ourselves when we fail to roar at the right time.

We begin our journey with a long, deep look at how the Aries Clan of the Fire Family operates in the context of the birthchart.

Later we will get to Leo and Sagittarius, and eventually to their associated transits and progressions.

Part One

THE THREE FIRE CLANS

The next four chapters are extended essays in which my aim is to explore in detail what I have learned about each of the nine words which constitute the vocabulary of Fire. We begin with a long look at the Aries clan. We move on from there to reflect on Leo's symbolic territory and wind up with Sagittarius.

These are big subjects with many dimensions; my initial intention in these first pages is to dive as deeply as I know how into the pure essence of each of these symbols, trying to define their core natures. We'll look at them as they exist outside the defining strictures of their interactions with the rest of the birthchart.

That interaction is, of course, the practical heart of the craft of astrological counsel. We will get there! In Part Two, we will take what we have learned about our nine words in their comfortable vacuums and begin to understand how to place them in dialogue with each other. How is Mars in Leo different from Mars in Cancer—and how might all that be affected by placing the configuration in any one of the twelve astrological houses?

In Part Three, still in the realm of the natal chart, we get very practical, laying out specific "cookbook" instructions for each possible configuration.

But first, let's build the foundation…

3

THE ARIES CLAN

Each of the three clans within the larger Fire Family has its own nature and purpose. All are connected via their basic DNA—which boils down to everything that keeps us vital, engaged and alive. As we will see, each clan fulfills that singular aim in its own way.

Let's begin our in-depth investigation of these Life-Givers with the Aries clan—and, as we saw earlier, that includes Mars and the first house.

YOU MUST BELIEVE IN SPRING

In the northern hemisphere, Spring begins when the Sun enters Aries. The Vernal Equinox is, in fact, the very definition of the sign. The two mean the same thing. Our Western zodiac—called the *tropical* zodiac—is based on the seasons, not the stars, unlike the constellation-based *sidereal* zodiac commonly used in India.

Aries Sun people born in the southern hemisphere are still 100 percent Arian, so the association is synchronistic, not causal. But the springtime symbolism is evocative.

Springtime! The flowers are blooming and liveliness returns to nature. Days are getting longer and warmer. How do we feel? Sap is rising. Let's dance! Let us praise the Lord for the pansies and the marigolds! Probably the squirrels and the sparrows feel something similar.

That's all true—but we need to penetrate the mysteries of Spring more courageously and honestly in order to get to the heart of the symbolism. Aries is a far edgier symbol than happy-face springtime greeting cards.

Maybe you step out your front door around the Vernal Equinox. You hear urgent chirping. You have startled and annoyed a bird hiding in a bush. It quickly flies away, but you notice a nest. You take a peek; there are five little bluish eggs. A few days later, you step out and again hear chirping. This time, there are five baby robins crowded into the nest, each one of them with its mouth wide open demanding breakfast.

Right away, with that simple springtime image, we learn something important about Aries, but the lesson is not for the faint of heart. That tiny newborn robin, unable to fly, not yet even fledged *is living in a world full of creatures that would eat it in a heartbeat.* The bird has no ability to defend itself; its only defense against this inimical, violent, antagonistic universe is another couple of birds.

And they are gone most of the time.

If this little robin had a brain in its head and some appreciation of the extremity of its circumstances, it would be hiding in a corner of the nest, hoping for invisibility. But that is not what we see. *What we actually see is that feisty little bird, its mouth wide open, demanding a right to live in this universe.*

That's the spirit of the Aries clan—the sign itself, along with Mars and the first house. If Aries could speak, here is what it would say: "I have a right to be here. If you value your life, stand back. Feed me—feed me, or I will eat you myself."

Or I will die trying.

Think of all the "he-man" movies, such as the old ones starring John Wayne, or a Tom Cruise flick, or any of the various incarnations of James Bond. They all truly convey some of that Aries archetype, at least as it is typically represented in the astrological literature. But I prefer the image of the baby robin. That little bird embodies the spirit of Aries far more accurately than does any testosterone-addled Hollywood star. That's because we fully appreciate the peril of the robin's circumstances. We appreciate its raw courage in the face of a truly scary universe.

Life choosing existence over surrender and extinction is the essence of the Aries clan.

Let's go back to our robin's nest. A few days later, you step out your door again to check on those five little robins. Only four of them are left. What happened to robin number five?

Nothing good.

The furthest thing from my mind is to sound cynical, but what we are looking at here is the actual Arian reality of springtime. It is a time of the *survival of the fittest*. We see that the robin's will to live—the robin's courage—will not necessarily be rewarded with survival. Of the initial five birds, it would not be too surprising if only a couple of them made it to adulthood. That is the way of nature. That is reality.

It is a hard world out there.

I feel a little awkward—almost apologetic—writing these words. Just like many of you, I was socially conditioned by positive thinking. I like to be encouraging. I like to drink out of the full half of the cup. But in truth, some aspects of life are very raw. The Arian branch of the Fire Family is attuned to those survival-truths.

It is the part of you that is very good at staying alive.

The larger Arian dharma cannot be reduced to the "law of the jungle," or even less to "eat or be eaten." Life is full of sweetness and healing too. We can exchange love with each other. We can be exhilarated and uplifted by beauty, both the beauty of nature and the beauty humans are capable of creating. We can feast at the table of life, as safe as house cats snoozing in a patch of sunlight.

But to face the parts of life that are not so kind, we need to have Aries on our side.

A ROMANCE

Our life-and-death story about our plucky robin sets the tone for these three archetypes, but our horizons are wider here. The competitive energy of the Aries clan manifests in many ways that are not directly connected to survival.

Here's a situation that you have surely witnessed. In fact, many of you have played a part in it. I know that I have.

(By the way, in what follows, please adjust my pronouns for whatever gender and sexual orientation you prefer.)

Two men are in love with the same woman. It is, of course, a mess. Even if everyone is trying to be of good will, there are no real compromises available in a situation like that. Somebody is going to win the woman's affections, and somebody is going to have his heart broken.

Here's the same story, told in a different way: there are two dogs and one bone. What happens? Only one of those dogs is going to run away happy.

Contending over a partner or a contending over a bone—neither situation is like a contested inheritance or a contested apple pie. In those kinds of situations, we might come to a harmonious agreement about the exact angles of the slices. Not so in a romantic triangle.

When the Aries clan is in the spotlight, it is about partners, not pies. That is simply the note Aries strikes on the synchronistic harpsichord—it resonates with situations in which compromise, however desirable it might be, is simply not a possibility.

Like all astrological symbols, Aries has a dark side. We will explore that Shadow dimension in detail before we are done. But for now, let's strive to emulate that little robin. Let us focus on an aim that is natural and legitimate for all beings: *survival.*

Maybe you have a right to that bone. Maybe the object of your affection is your soul-mate. More broadly, you have *a natural right to exist.* You have a natural right to take up some space. You have a natural right to win sometimes.

Here's the key: *sometimes you have to fight for those rights.* Sometimes you've got to fight to be free.

SHADOWS DARK AND BRIGHTER

The English Prime Minister Neville Chamberlain tried to appease Adolph Hitler so England could have "peace for our time." The phrase became ironic; about a year later, the United Kingdom was at war with the Nazis. Chamberlain's peaceful initiative had only given Hitler another year to prepare the *Wehrmacht.* His noble but mistaken commitment to peace only increased the intensity of the ultimate violence.

Again, I am not happy writing these words. I, like you, prefer peace. My discomfort is fitting: Mars, Aries, and the first house are not comfortable energies.

Let's bring it all down to earth. Perhaps you are in a relationship. Perhaps your partner has a habit that hurts you. Perhaps, like Neville Chamberlain, "in the name of peace" you always let the behavior slide, never mentioning it. And when it all finally explodes, it looks like a nuclear holocaust.

Congratulations. You are now the Neville Chamberlain of intimacy.

Forgiveness and forbearance are of course not negative things. That remains true, as we will see, even during Arian times and dealing with Arian issues. But when this clan takes center stage, you may have to "fight for peace."

And that is one of the most dangerous truths that can be uttered.

The Dalai Lama once said, "The world is drunk on anger." Those six words epitomize the dark side of Mars. Like being drunk on alcohol, anger can cloud the mind. Like alcohol, it can add such an overdose of passion to the mix that it can turn even a righteous position into something demonic.

The point I am making is that the Arian function has both a positive face and a negative one. Once we are in its grips, it is very difficult to sort out which side of the seesaw we are riding.

When we get to exploring the Leo and Sagittarius clans, we will see more subtle expressions of Fire. The Aries clan, however, is raw and primal. It is inextricably entwined with the *survival instinct* and its close cousin: the instinct to *protect those whom we love*. Think of Mama Bear when she thinks her cubs are threatened.

Personally, I would love to take the simple Buddhist vow to be nonviolent, but we are taught that breaking such a vow is far worse than not taking it—and I know in my heart that if I found a crazy teenager torturing my cat, I might kill him with my bare hands.

Maybe you would too. That's Mars. That's Aries.

What about someone hurting your partner—or your child? Is there anything you wouldn't do to save them? What primal, instinctual Fire might such a situation bring to the surface of your consciousness?

A step further: notice how difficult it is, despite the disquieting violence of the metaphors I am invoking here, to simply label these protective reactions as "bad?" To understand this branch of the Fire family, we need to avoid making that reflexive judgment. Until this world is ruled by angels and peace prevails on Earth, Arian energy is deeply linked to our animal dignity and self-respect, along with any full-spectrum sense of adult responsibility.

The trouble is, these feelings can also excite us in dangerous ways. To illustrate that notion, here's the outline of half the action movies you have ever seen: in the first two minutes, bad guys do something terrible to the hero's child, partner, or comrade. With such a situation established, the audience feels justified in enjoying another 118 minutes of gleeful bloodshed in the spirit of righteous vengeance.

Much of the tragedy of the human race lies in how easily we are seduced by this ancient Arian storyline.

EVERY STORY HAS TWO SIDES

In questions of violence, whether in emotional or physical form, there are typically many complicating questions of perspective. Imagine you're watching one of those masterful David Attenborough nature programs—*Planet Earth*, for example. There's a pack of wolves in pursuit of a herd of caribou. The wolves separate a newborn caribou from its mother and bring it down. They've got their dinner now and you know the chase is over. Mama caribou is off in the mournful distance, helplessly watching. Our hearts go out to the mother who has just witnessed the violent murder of her child.

But now switch channels: imagine starving baby wolves. That is the alternative.

Can we call the wolves' action evil? Evil seems like too strong a word, doesn't it? But who can feel comfortable thinking about that young caribou and its poor mother?

This is hard territory. Welcome to the Aries clan. Killing and living are linked forever. That truth is primal and inescapable. It is also fraught with overwhelming emotions which come welling up like gushers out of our reptile brains, placing us temporarily on autopilot. The legal plea of "temporary insanity" has doubtless been a hiding place for scoundrels countless times over the years. But it endures because we all know it also represents a fundamental fact of human existence. There is perhaps no truer test of our evolutionary states than how we react in the heat of the moment when the Aries clan comes to call.

MURDERED TOMATOES

I have personally murdered countless tomatoes. You may laugh, but I do think about it. Am I cruelly ignoring the miserable plight of innocent tomatoes merely so I can enjoy a *caprese* salad?

When I was a lad, I read a book called *The Secret Life of Plants* by Peter Tompkins and Christopher Bird. They wrote about how, if you love a plant, it grows faster and bigger. Being a rational Capricorn lad, I had my doubts, but I gave it a try anyway. I got myself a bag of potting soil, a packet of seeds and a couple of pots. I divided everything up and planted the seeds and treated both pots the same way—except that I would come out and serenade one of the plants with my guitar, sending it love-vibes as best I could. As for the other plant, I just took care of it in typical farmer-fashion.

Sure enough, the plant I loved got markedly bigger. It really worked.

I only tried the experiment once, but that was my experience. In a way, it isn't surprising. We know that people respond to love. Animals too. We understand that. But plants? Exactly how "alive" are they? As I said, I've murdered a lot of tomatoes. The phrase seems like a joke—but is it?

So, all you vegans and vegetarians—wipe that self-righteous smirk off your faces! Like the rest of us, you too must kill in order to live.

For the record, I eat fish and birds, but I have not eaten a mammal in over four decades. That is arbitrary and personal, not a prescription for anyone else. When I look into the eyes of a cow, the idea of killing it feels way more appalling than the idea of killing a fish—those fish eyes do not look back at me in quite the same way. But murdering a fish is harder than murdering a tomato.

Living with the Aries clan is all about moral relativism. And the essential point is that all beings must kill in order to live. We accept that fact or we die of starvation—and we must all thread a path through that philosophical labyrinth and somehow emerge from it with our spiritual dignity and self-respect intact.

HUNTER OR PREY?

Sitting with a client, talking about Mars, there is a metaphor I often weave. I tell them that, at the end of the cosmic diving board, God posed them a dilemma with the following words: "We're going to restage a popular play.

We need you to play a role. In fact, we insist. The play is called *Hunter and Prey*. Which role would you prefer?"

If we are in the Spiritually Gifted and Talented program, we might ask the Lord if there might possibly be a vegetarian course. But there is not. You must choose from a very short menu: hunter or prey.

God goes a little further and adds, "Don't worry if you can't decide. We will choose for you—no problem".

You know the rest. When "God chooses for you," you are going to be that night's dinner.

To concretize that metaphor, let's picture a person with natal Mars in the tenth house. (Note that we might equally use any other astrological expression of that Mars nature, such as an Aries midheaven or tenth house planets in the sign Aries.) From the evolutionary point of view, wherever you find your Aries-energy, *you need to learn courage*. You need to *develop initiative*. You must cultivate the ability to claim what is rightfully yours. That is how you become "the Hunter, " which is the correct evolutionary response. And if you don't get "Hunter" right, you automatically turn into "the Prey."

By the way, one modern translation of Prey could be "the designated victim." Another could be "the sacrificial lamb" or "the scapegoat."

In the case of a person with Mars on the Midheaven, the focus for this entire evolutionary drama lies in the arena of *career* or *reputation*—tenth house terrain. In this case, that's the specific school for the Mars lessons.

What might it look like if this person responded well and positively to this configuration? One possibility is that she takes the frightening risk of starting an independent business. In this context, Mars can be *entrepreneurial.* Entering the territory, we must accept the fact that ninety-nine times out of one hundred, starting a business is going to place you in competitive circumstances. You may take no particular delight in defeating other people. Maybe you are just not wired that way. But there are a certain number of dollars out there and everybody wants them. Throw that "one bone" between two dogs and you know what's going to happen.

When we think of spirituality, we free-associate to meditation, acts of charity, and sitting at the feet of masters. But with Mars conjunct the midheaven, starting a business can be understood as a spiritual path.

One beautiful thing about the practice of astrology is that it helps us learn to honor the enormous diversity of evolutionary possibilities. What are the metaphysical implications of this woman starting a business of her own? We can easily imagine that what she learns endures in her consciousness beyond death and forward into future incarnations. That's just the larger, evolutionary perspective.

Let's emphasize that to succeed in an entrepreneurial situation, she does not need to become bloody-minded. She does not need a dorsal fin. She can operate within a moral framework. Mars does not require any compromise in those areas—in fact, the highest expression of Arian energy retains a certain nobility of spirit, and is capable of grace and good humor even in defeat.

But it plays to win.

Let's consider the consequences of this woman, born with Mars conjunct her midheaven, choosing to be Prey rather than Hunter. No one, of course, would ever frame it that way, but it boils down to the error of letting fear make her decisions. Let's say she decides not to start that business after all. Let's say she considers the idea, then abandons it, preferring the steady paycheck that goes along with keeping her boring, soul-sapping job.

Naturally, if she makes these sorts of mistakes, she's likely to rationalize them as practicality or the exercise of reasonable caution. Perhaps she decides her job really isn't so bad after all. Here's a line fit to break the hearts of angels: perhaps she says to herself, "in seventeen years I can retire."

As if she could count on seventeen more years in this world.

As if seventeen more years of cowardice and spiritual compromise would not take such a bite out of her soul that she would spend those retirement years wasting away in front of a television.

Strong language! Immediately, it is important that we recognize that the decision to acquiesce to a dull career might very well be the wise choice for many of us. From the evolutionary perspective, not everyone's life is about career or mission in the world. We would only raise these questions if Mars or other significant Arian symbolism is connected with the tenth house.

We are not yet done with our imaginary woman. There is one more dire consequence of her turning away from her own evolutionary path. In the happy version of our story, her being "Hunter" translates into her claiming her appropriately independent career path: starting her own business. What if she refuses to take that brave step and thus becomes "Prey?"

Well, no one is likely to actually eat her.

But here's a further possible scenario: her beloved boss retires and is replaced by a new one. The new boss is the reincarnation of Attila the Hun. He abuses her and shames her. In the immortal phrase of Carlos Castaneda, the new boss is a *petty tyrant*—and incidentally, that suggests that he himself is probably making a bad response to his own Mars energy.

His arrival in our woman's life is a synchronistic out-picturing of her own inner spiritual failure, mirroring it back to her.

That last line is worth reading twice. It would be "common sense" to understand the arrival of the new boss as simple bad luck—a random event in a chaotic universe, in other words. But it is not. That outer event is linked directly to the inner event of our hero chickening out and not starting her own business. Inwardly, she was afraid of the world. So her world manifested in a literally fearful way, echoing right back to her. This is synchronicity in action; this, contrary to most of what we learn in school, is how the universe actually operates, down to details. Even the new boss is a reflection of her own misguided Aries energy.

What does this woman now experience on the job? Here's a simple answer, straight from the Aries clan lexicon: *stress.*

Nothing in this miserable scenario would surprise an old-school astrologer. Seeing Mars—the so-called "lesser Malefic"—in the woman's house of career, such an astrologer would likely frame this kind of misfortune as "fate." The idea that it is "inescapable" is the error. Becoming Prey is only one item on the menu. The deeper truth is that anyone can rise to the higher call of Fiery energy. The woman in our story could have been a hero; she could have quit her job and started that business.

But if she—or you—fails in that, she will certainly attract stress into her life. And she might very well find herself overwhelmed by the dark Aries Fire of another person. Petty tyrants will flock to her like ants at a picnic flock to the *crème brulée.*

THE HEART OF THE MATTER

Here is a line you wrote down in your notebook back in high school science class: *Energy can be neither created or destroyed, only changed in form.* Those words underlie all the laws of physics. There is no principle more basic to science. It is also the most basic principle in astrology—and it should be, because astrology is just another one of the laws of the universe.

The energy of the chart—as expressed by the signs and planets and so on—has already been created. It's there. You're living it. So it cannot be destroyed. It cannot go away. Thus, inevitably—and with no possible exceptions—it will manifest. But it can be changed in form...

...and the entire founding principle of evolutionary astrology is that consciousness is the critical variable in determining that form.

It is your inescapable fate that these archetypes will express themselves somehow in the biographical realities of your life. There's no way around that. It is your fate to spend your life dancing with these questions.

But they're questions, not answers.

The astrological symbols are quantum fields of possibility and probability. With your consciousness, you can influence how these energies manifest—but there is one choice that is forbidden to you: you cannot choose to have the energy disappear and become irrelevant. You cannot make it go poof.

There is an ancient technical term for all of this—a term for how human consciousness might be potentially trained to influence the actual positions of the atoms and molecules in the world. That term is *magic.*

In this rigorous, deeply precise sense of the word, evolutionary astrology is a form of magic.

Mars on the Midheaven? How do you want to employ your magic? Which would you prefer, to be Hunter or to be Prey?

If you have that configuration and choose to be the Hunter, you might go back and reread the last few pages.

There's your first textbook at our astrological *Hogwarts Academy.* Learn the Transforming Spell, and miracles start to happen.

THE POSITIVE SIDE OF COMPETITIVENESS

Maybe you would like to make your living as an astrologer. It's a good life; I recommend it. And it is doable. But if you attend an astrology conference and you ask around about the professional and financial climate, you will probably hear that it is very hard to make a living as an astrologer.

So what's going on? How can we be successful in the field?

I can speak with some experience. I haven't had what many would call "a real job" since my first lunar return, when I was twenty-seven. That was seven years before my first book, *The Inner Sky*, came out. Being good at what you do helps. Word gets around. If you help people, if you do quality analysis and a professional presentation of it, people tell their friends.

"Being good at what you do"—how do people judge that? Inescapably, your reputation entails some comparison to other astrologers, whether or not it is spoken. We are all "graded on the curve." The drive toward excellence simply does not happen in a vacuum. Inevitably, naturally, and pretty much without exception, we humans compare ourselves to each other.

And thus, whether or not we think of it that way, we compete with them.

There are, praise God, other planets and other perspectives on life. A world defined only by the energy of the Aries clan would be brutal. There are many good things we can affirm and celebrate about community and teamwork and win-win situations. There are astrological symbols which represent all of those things. Noncompetitive ways of relating have a sweetly spiritual quality. In the course of these four volumes, we will explore them deeply—and gratefully.

But now we are exploring the Aries clan of the Fire family. We're talking about survival, and that includes acknowledging and embracing the reality of competition. It is part of life; denying it only turns it into an autonomous psychic function. Other than choosing to be drunk on simple berserk bloodlust, I can think of no more dangerous path to follow with these volatile and inescapable energies than unconsciously letting them grab the steering wheel.

Maybe you are not the only person in your community who would like to make it as a professional astrologer. Maybe, in other words, there are two dogs and one bone. Maybe each dog—or each astrologer—is motivated to excel. Each one studies hard. Each one polishes his or her craft until it gleams. Still, sometimes there remains only one bone. Maybe there will be a loser as well as a winner. Let's not gloat about that—there lies dark Mars—but let's recognize that it is not only one astrologer who wins. Assuming that the winner is the best astrologer, the entire community wins.

Some perspective on all this, as an aside: for what it's worth, I believe that the astrological pie is potentially huge. I believe that there is a terrible dearth of truly competent astrologers and that every community has room for ten times more of them. "If you build it, they will come."

Still, the point is that the urge to excel—the simple, primal urge to *be the best*—is pure Arian energy, and it is far from being an entirely negative quality.

MARS AND DEPRESSION

Here's another major clue in understanding the Aries clan. Sigmund Freud once observed that depression is anger internalized. Those are just four words, but they say so much. Astrologers have always related Mars to anger, but not so much to depression. Yet the link is very real. It plays a critical role in our understanding of this branch of the Fire family.

Let's explore it.

When people are really peeved, they might say, "I want to kill something." Hopefully those words are metaphorical, but at the primal animal level they convey the bloody-minded face of Aries energy quite authentically. A milder illustration of the same principle: an angry person might slam a door or slam down a telephone—a symbolic expression of violence.

Here's an illustration, this one from real life. In October 1984, the late and much-lamented rock star Tom Petty got angry during a recording session and punched a wall. In doing that, he broke his hand—not the best move for a professional musician. It took four hours of surgery to put him back together again. I couldn't find an exact date for the event, but transiting Mars was exactly opposite his natal Uranus on the eighteenth of that month. Was his anger directed outwardly? Well, yes... but he hurt himself badly. For a while, there was talk of him never playing the guitar again.

It is in the nature of Aries, Mars, and the first house that if, for any reason, the "offending object" cannot be directly attacked or addressed, the Martial force tends to turn inward. But it still remains Mars energy—it still "wants to kill something." And so, instead of hurting something in the visible world, that murderous energy is internalized. Somehow or in some way, we take life away from ourselves.

Tom Petty might have never played the guitar again.

"Taking life away from ourselves"—right there is a fair characterization of the mental state we call depression. It is a *lifeless* condition. A person is flat. Nothing matters. Everything appears to be impossible. And there is no energy anyway.

The most radical expression of depression is of course suicide. But the lifeless, sighing person, seemingly bored by everything, whose reflex is always to say "No" or "Whatever," and whose face and body show no sign of any emotion—such a person illustrates what Aries clan energy looks like when it's been starved for too many years.

MARS AND SEXUALITY

Want purple passion? Some body heat? Want to make like James Brown and "get on up, like a sex machine?"

Don't ask Venus! Pure, unabashed erotic enthusiasm is in the domain of Mars. Venus "makes love," but Mars... well, how shall we put it in a book the kids might read?

The Mars clan of the Fire Family is fundamentally connected to our sexuality. Any fourteen-year-old philosopher quickly comes to realize that being "pretty" and being "sexy" are not quite the same. Somebody can be physically beautiful, but not "hot"—while another person is maybe a little funny-looking, but somehow he or she just radiates that ancient *juju.*

"Pretty," by the way, is a word that often gets feminized; I don't mean it that narrowly—males can be "pretty" too, and many very Venusian males are.

But *sexy* energy—that is purely a Mars signature.

The entire theoretical foundation of this book is that the Fire Family of symbols are the Life-Givers. Unless we are very prim, when we think of what stokes those furnaces of our primal hunger for life, the mind rather quickly adds sexuality to the short list. With Mars, perhaps only survival itself is the more fundamental drive, taking priority over everything else. If something is intending to kill you or to eat you, you're not thinking of sex. First things first. It's the same, really, if you're starving. Food is survival, and dire hunger erases sexuality.

But once you've escaped the tiger's jaws and had a decent meal...

A short look at most of the traditional "Holy Writs" quickly reveals much that would teach us to be ashamed of our sexual desires and our bodies. In appreciating the Aries clan as one of the fundamental Life-Givers, we stop looking at sex through the stained glass of shame. Instead, we look at it through the bright, feral eyes of the innocent animal inside us. And we recognize that our sexual energy, if we relate to it clearly enough, can ally its ancient Fire-power with the highest potentials of our consciousnesses. It can bring us life.

SEX AND THE INTIMATE ENEMY

I picture a loving couple, long committed to each other. They are both sane adults. They have been together for a decade. They have a child. And given the monkey-business of actual human reality, over the years they have naturally internalized some frustration with each other.

That is the nature of that pressure cooker we call intimacy.

Adult partnering is famously difficult sometimes. Resentments build. No human being is ever going to meet another person's needs perfectly. Because of this accumulation of unresolved Mars energy, couples tend to have spats—little border wars.

And there ain't no cure for it, other than dating for the rest of your life.

Back to our couple. They are both dealing with the day-to-day yoga of committed love. Enter the erotic face of Mars: they have sex. They're both "in the mood," not because they are feeling romantic, but rather because there's that primal fire between their legs. There is an itch that wants to be scratched. And the itch is in fact not just in their genitals—that's just how a pornographer would say it. That itch has as much to do with their souls as it does with their flesh.

Another way to put it is that Fire-energy has built up inside both of them. As we learned earlier, that energy can be "neither created nor destroyed." It is going to express itself somehow.

How? In a fight? Possibly; accumulated sexual tension indeed makes people edgy. Might that energy become internalized and manifest as depression? Certainly—there's no shortage of depressing, sexless relationships in the world. Maybe they can resolve these tensions through a constructive argument—but, hey, maybe we have a better suggestion...

They make love. Their accumulated Fire is released that way. Animal joy!

But the result is even better than that—picture them *après le sexe.* They are lying in each other's arms.

Tenderness has woven them together again.

Sex heals. Sex bridges distance. Sex melts ice. Happy couples have known this since the Lower Paleolithic. There is good evidence that chimpanzees know it too. This healing energy that weaves love together again in the face of the frustrations of intimacy is a blessed gift from the cosmos to us all—and it comes, not from Venus, but rather from Mars.

THE FIRST HOUSE

We have looked at Mars and Aries in some detail, but we have not yet really contemplated the first house. As always, signs and planets—Mars and Aries in this case—represent energies, or motivations, or agendas. But an astrological house always symbolizes something active, something behavioral, something we can see with our eyes. It represents how—and where—we apply those sign and planetary agendas in actual practice.

With the first house, we are considering the reality of *positive, decisive action*. We make choices there, and if we get it right, we don't look back.

A strong concentration of first house planets correlates with *leadership*. Let's begin our meditation there.

Every leader is familiar with the following situation: a hard choice must be made in an imperfect world. The leader might realize that in order to be fair to seventeen people, he or she has to treat three people unfairly. The leader may feel terrible about it—but perhaps that unfairness is simply the best choice among choices that are actually available.

A good leader makes the call.

And of those three people who were treated unfairly, probably two of them think the leader is being selfish or insensitive. The accusation in this case is not fair or accurate—but it's understandable that such judgments would arise in the minds of people who felt they had been ill-used.

The word "selfishness" is complex. It is also inseparable from our understanding of the first house. There are situations where selfishness is simply bad behavior—what we might call "garden-variety" selfishness. That is the usual use of the term. But to truly grasp the first house, we need to recognize that each one of us has a natural right to be selfish, at least sometimes. You have a right, in other words, *to live your own life and to make decisions that are healthy for you.* When you do that, you may not please everyone around you. Very probably, they will take a darker view of your "selfish" action. And yet you are only exercising a natural right—a right that is centered in first house evolutionary logic.

In a nutshell, with planets in the first house, you must take your own part. You need to behave in ways that reflect the Aries-clan wisdom of personal autonomy and your natural right to live the life that is right for you. As the old saying goes, you can't make an omelette without breaking a few eggs.

People with a strong concentration of planets in the first house often display genuine leadership qualities. The laws of synchronicity often place them in actual roles of authority or influence over others. At the very least, they tend to be influential people—style-setters and role models. Memorable people. When I sit with a client with a strong first house concentration, one of my favorite remarks is, "you would make a terrible spy." Those words always raise their eyebrows a bit. Then I add that the ambition of every spy is not to be remembered—to be forgotten, to be invisible.

Even with one of the milder planets, such as Neptune, in the first house, these principles remain true. If you have Neptune in the first house, to pursue your spiritual path, you will sometimes need to be selfish. That sounds contradictory—we think of spirituality and "selflessness" as a matched set. But it's not always true.

I vividly remember a session with a client who had become a Roman Catholic nun. She told the story of how she had broken the news of her intention to enter the convent to her parents. They were appalled and saddened. They wanted grandchildren. And my client basically had to say to her parents, "Mom and Dad, your sweet dream of holding your grandchildren on your knees—forget about it. I'm going to become a nun. Deal with it."

She didn't express it that way, of course. She was a very Neptunian person—sweet, compassionate, sensitive, and warm. But the bottom line was that in order to serve her spirituality, she had to make a decision that her parents perceived as selfish.

CONCLUSION

That merry idea about our natural right to some degree of selfishness completes our exploration of the Aries clan of the life-giving Fire Family. Many of you are probably wondering, what if Mars is in Aquarius or

Cancer? What if Saturn or Uranus is in Aries? What about Venus in the first house?

Later we will explore how to go beyond these foundation principles and answer those kinds of questions. What I hope I've accomplished so far is to give you a rather complete introduction to the underlying principles of this first clan of the Fire Family.

We have two more Fire signs to go—Leo and Sagittarius. As we'll see, they are not as raw as Aries. Advancing through the Fire triad, the energies express themselves with increasing sophistication and subtlety.

But the core purpose remains the same throughout all three: how we recover from the slings and arrows of outrageous fortune; how we regenerate; how we sustain ourselves; and how we return ourselves to life—and stave off the forces that would rob us of it.

4

THE LEO CLAN

Exit the Ram and enter the Lion. We leave the realm of raw survival and enter more subtle territory—more subtle, but not necessarily "more evolved." That's not how it works. Leo does not inherently represent higher ground than Aries. But it is true to say the questions now become more paradoxical, less obvious, more slippery. The black hats and white hats of the Arian realm now turn to shades of beige. Cans of beer turn into martinis.

We have left the jungle behind; bright city lights loom before us.

Technically, as we approach the Leo clan, we also face the literal linchpin of our solar system: the Sun itself, Leo's ruling planet. And, as Leo is the fifth sign of the Zodiac, we also confront the arena of human behavior called the fifth house.

As with the Aries clan, these are all vast subjects. How vast? Imagine taking the entire universe and all the possibilities in it—everything that's ever happened, everything that could have ever happened, everything that might possibly happen—and dividing it all into twelve boxes.

These astrological archetypes are really big boxes.

A BRIEF SERMON BEFORE WE FACE THE LION

Maybe Mercury transits through a square aspect to your Sun. As that's happening, you drop a filing cabinet on your big toe. "Hey, I could have told you that would happen—Mercury represents filing cabinets."

Well, it does. Mercury is connected with information and so are filing cabinets. But so are encyclopedias, radios, billboards, road signs, DVDs, televisions, universities, communications satellites, and carrier pigeons. I'll spare you the rest of the list. With Mercury transiting through a square to your Sun, you might've had an unpleasant experience with any of those things. As easily, you might have received an unpleasant letter from the tax people. Maybe you had a difficult conversation with a friend. Maybe you drank too much coffee and felt jittery all day.

These are all Mercurial realities.

Remember: if we divide the universe into twelve boxes, they are all really big. That line may be droll, but as astrologers, it is critical that we remember it—from it, we get a fundamental understanding of how astrology actually operates, not to mention of its limits.

Astrology always works, which means these symbols correlate reliably with the manifestation of archetypal fields of possibility. When Mercury squares your Sun by transit, it is your inescapable fate to deal with a certain form of energy. But the fields of possibility it represents are so vast that guessing what will actually happen is virtually impossible.

Bottom line, we never really know what is going to happen—only what the questions will be. A good astrologer will not put you in the passive role by "foretelling your future." Rather, he or she will counsel and advise, trying to help you aim your free will in the most constructive direction.

Astrologers often say, "I could have told you that!" But they really couldn't have. No one could have foreseen that filing cabinet landing on your big toe. In retrospect, whatever happens is consistent with the symbolism—but may God help any astrologer who is trying to "make predictions."

All of that applies to everything in the realm of astrology. This is why psychological and spiritual astrologers generally achieve more accurate results than the ones who claim to have a crystal ball. Let's see how all this applies to the realm of Leo, the Sun, and the fifth house.

SET THE CONTROLS FOR THE HEART OF THE SUN

The almighty Sun rules Leo and is the natural ruler of the fifth house. We will concentrate initially on our central star. In fact, for a while, you might think that I have forgotten all about Leo and the fifth house. Don't worry—we'll dive deeply into them in a few pages. But in letting our inner poets contemplate the Sun and its meaning, we will have built a foundation for understanding its sign and house expressions.

With its massive gravitational field, the Sun holds the planets in their courses. If it were to disappear, one of the many unpleasant effects of its sudden absence would be that the planets—and we along with them—would simply fly off into space.

This is our first hint about the astrological meaning of the Sun: as with the solar system, so with your head—the Sun's task is to hold you together too.

Everything revolves around the Sun. If your college astronomy professor says that line, you write it down and you pass the test. But maybe an hour later your political science professor says, "In politics, everything revolves around money." Again, you write down and have no trouble understanding the professor's intent. Obviously, the usage here is different from the astronomical one. We know what our political science professor meant—in politics, money is always a pivotal concept.

In understanding anyone astrologically, the Sun is the single most pivotal concept. The core Hermetic principle of our craft is famously, "As Above, So Below." Nowhere do we see that notion demonstrated so vividly as with the Sun. Again, it is the gravitational center of your head. It is what holds you together.

And "holding you together" is often a formidable task.

SANITY

Jean Houston, asked to define "normal," once famously said, "A normal person is someone that you don't know very well." I suspect she successfully danced out the door before anyone could catch her. She is, of course, correct. We say it lightly, but we all know it's true: we are all a little crazy, at least the broad sense of the term..

Are you going to take the job in South Dakota? The stakes are high; the outcomes are uncertain. You tell your friends that struggling to decide is making you "feel crazy." They all know what you mean; they have all been "crazy" that way at times themselves.

After deep, honest reflection, after taking council with everyone you trust, here is what you have realized: 51 percent of you wants to move to South Dakota and 49 percent of you thinks you would be nuts to do that.

Hey, it's cold up there! But, on the other hand, the job is great. But, on the third hand, it's a thousand miles from all your friends. But on the fourth hand, it would double your income... but, but, but.

Feeling crazy yet?

So there you are: 51 percent yes, and 49 percent no. *In that moment, the Sun is the part of you that says: "Okay, that's settled then. We're moving to South Dakota."*

And then other 49 percent of you roars in protest: "Wait a minute! What about us?"

And the Sun says: "Hush. It is settled. I have spoken. Deal with it."

What follows that brutal act of the repression of dissident voices in your head is a feeling of sanity. At least you know what you are doing. At least you have made a stand.

SHOULD A PERSON BE MARRIED?

What a dumb question! *Who are we talking about?* Life is complicated. We are torn between courses a lot of the time. Life is not always as simple as choosing between good and evil. And what's good for you might not be good for me.

Marriage—or not—is a very individual question. What follows is a gross oversimplification, so please don't take it literally. Should you get married? If your Sun is in Libra, yes. If your Sun is in Sagittarius, then no.

Once again, this is just a talking point. It's only a way of cartoonishly illustrating an absolutely central solar idea. The Sun represents the basic values to which you must be true if your life is going to make sense to you. It is the common denominator in all your wise decisions.

If you are a solar Libran, then your core values—the ones that will most consistently give you a feeling of sanity—are very much connected with partnership.

So: get married.

If you are a solar Sagittarian, then your core values—again, the ones that will most consistently give you a feeling of sanity—are very much connected with the freedom to have wide experience.

So: think twice before you sacrifice your freedom in a marriage.

I will probably have nightmares thinking I just talked a poor Libran into a rotten marriage or talked a loving Sagittarian out of a good one! These are terrible oversimplifications, but they do make the core point: *the values that best suit your evolutionary journey are solar in nature.*

If you are true to your natal Sun, you'll be glad you're alive. As much as it is available in this madhouse of the world, you will experience a subjective feeling of sanity. You will know who you are.

THE TWELVE SUN SIGNS

In each person's birthchart, the Sun takes on a unique flavor based on its sign and house and the array of aspects it makes. The analysis can become very detailed. Later on, we will lay this all out more deeply and systematically. But as starting point, let's quickly think of the Sun in the twelve signs.

Here's the whole theory in a nutshell: *each sign represents a set of core values or evolutionary aims. When the Sun lies in a sign, those particular values will never fail you.*

If you trust them, you will live a meaningful life, guaranteed.

If the Sun is in ARIES, let your guiding star be the development of courage, directness and the right use of force.

If the Sun is in TAURUS, let your guiding star be the development of calm, simplicity and an acceptance of that which arises naturally.

If the Sun is in GEMINI, let your guiding star be the development of curiosity, open-mindedness, conversation, and a willingness to listen.

If the Sun is in CANCER, let your guiding star be the development of gentleness, nurturance, and an acceptance of human frailty.

If the Sun is in LEO, let your guiding star be the development of forthrightness, creativity, spontaneous self-expression, and a sense of Theater.

If the Sun is in VIRGO, let your guiding star be the development of service, groundedness, and skill.

If the Sun is in LIBRA, let your guiding star be the development of negotiation, teamwork, and love.

If the Sun is in SCORPIO, let your guiding star be the development of honesty, Shadow-work, and courageous emotional investigation.

If the Sun is in SAGITTARIUS, let your guiding star be the development of faith, belief, commitment and mind-stretching experience.

If the Sun is in CAPRICORN, let your guiding star be the development of self-discipline, integrity and objective accomplishment.

If the Sun is in AQUARIUS, let your guiding star be the development of individuation, unusual experiences, and escape from social constraint.

If the Sun is in PISCES, let your guiding star be the development of meditation, surrender and mystical experience.

And remember: the Sun is the basis of your sanity and your vitality. In general, everything in the Fire Family helps you bounce back from life's hardships. It's what puts the sparkle in your eyes. And the Sun is its very heart of the matter.

So, no matter what your Sun sign is, be lionhearted about orienting your life around these core values. They're what keeps your heart beating.

THE CENTER OF THE UNIVERSE

The Sun is literally the center of the solar system. As above, so below: it therefore reflects the natural human urge to feel like the center of everything. This observation brings us face to face with the psychoanalytic term "Ego."

We have to be careful here. Ego, in this psychoanalytic sense, is not a negative thing. It is not to be confused with "ego" in the street sense of inflated self-importance or arrogance.

Fear not; we will explore those solar disorders too! They're also in the domain of the Leo clan. But let's not throw the baby out with the bathwater quite yet.

To know who you are; to know your core values and to act on them, thus shaping a meaningful existence for yourself: these are self-evidently healthy behaviors. And they are also a textbook description of a strong response to the Sun, at least in the context of evolutionary astrology.

It is natural and inescapable that we look at the world through our own eyes.

It is natural and inescapable that we are the central characters in our own narratives. From these very human perspectives, feeling "like the center of the universe" arises naturally and is not fundamentally a problem. If you meditate in a Himalayan cave for a few decades, you might get past that ego-identification. But for many of us, such an ascetic path would entail our missing out on the life we actually need to live. Your birthchart, in other words, might be an active one—and your birthchart is never a mistake.

What about actual egoism? What about arrogance and self-importance? That's Sun energy too, running amok. That is a reference to solar dysfunction—but solar dysfunction is simply a bizarre exaggeration of something that is actually inborn and necessary to us all.

As we saw with the Aries clan in the previous chapter, a healthy, necessary kind of fierceness resides in us all—but it can potentially overflow its banks and turn into something destructive. Similarly with the Leo clan, there's a healthy kind of ego in us—and yet, it too can overflow its banks and become dangerous or damaging.

An over-functioning solar ego creates distortions—but, as we will soon see, so does an under-functioning one.

OUR STORYLINE

Long ago, I opened my first book, *The Inner Sky*, with a very solar quote from Rodney Collin's masterpiece, *The Theory of Celestial Influence*:

"Now the fundamental madness or abnormality of men lies in the divergence between essence and personality. The more nearly a man knows himself for what he is, the nearer he approaches wisdom. The more his imagination about himself diverges from what he actually is, the madder he becomes."

I have a version of *The Steven Forrest Story* in my head, just like you have a version of your own story. When I say "story," I don't mean to overemphasize the idea that it is false or intentionally self-flattering, only that all of our stories about ourselves are always somewhat fictional.

How could it be otherwise? If I asked my mother for her version of my story, I am sure that she would tell a different one. And she has known me all my life.

This is delicate territory. As we think about sanity, we can only see it through the lens of its opposite: craziness. A standard joke about craziness revolves around grossly mistaken identity: "He thinks he is Napoleon" or "He thinks he is Jesus." Not to make fun of people with serious mental illness, but we all recognize these profoundly flawed cases of "mistaken identity" as the earmark of madness. This is pure Rodney Collin: such a person's "imagination about himself has seriously diverged from what he actually is."

But we all do that.

This form of madness represents a fundamental vulnerability in the solar ego. Who are you, really? Figuring out the answer is an ongoing process. For starters, here is Exhibit A: the Sun actually *believes* that it is "the center of the universe." Much subsequent error stems from that initial mistake.

Ask anyone: they will point out that they, not you, are the actual center of the universe.

Beyond that egregious error of judgment, we enter the ego-driven psychological realms of denial, repression, compartmentalization, and selective memory. The list of distortions goes on: the lies we tell ourselves, the lies we have been told and believed, inappropriate shame, the static in your head created by sexism, racism, homophobia, and the rest of the sad litany.

As Bob Dylan sang in *Idiot Wind*, "it's a wonder we can even feed ourselves."

So who is right about my solar story, my mom or me? If she is right—and I am sure that in some ways she must be—then I guess I need a straitjacket.

Strangely, it is often easier to sort all this out if we do it backwards. By that, I mean to look back on our own history. Deep truth—perhaps deeper than the truth you think you know—is revealed in the actual biographical reality of the life you have actually lived. To add the X-rays to the mix, do that analysis through the lens of a full technical analysis of the place of the Sun in your birthchart. It represents a path. It represents a set of values and evolutionary intentions that are the truest moral compass you will ever have. All through our lives, via synchronicity, those core solar values arise as challenges and forks in the road, whether or not we like it. We have signed up to face those questions. We signed a contract with the universe to learn certain things. *Sometimes we have succeeded and sometimes we have failed.* Sanity is helped by our successes, of course—but our failures are not strictly madness.

Our madness only lies in our denial of those failures.

THE MOMENT OF TRUTH

So, in the light of all that we just explored, let's go back and review our simple Sun Sign list from a few pages ago...

If you are a solar Aries, can you be honest enough to recognize when you have succumbed to the temptations of anger, aggression, and fear?

If you are a solar Taurus, can you be honest enough to recognize when you have succumbed to the temptations of denial, stubbornness, lassitude, and materialism?

If you are a solar Gemini, can you be honest enough to recognize when you have succumbed to the temptations of mind games, attachment to intellect, defensiveness, dithering, and distraction?

If you are a solar Cancer, can you be honest enough to recognize when you have succumbed to the temptations of self-indulgence, hiding from life, whining, and the compulsion to rescue malingerers?

If you are a solar Leo, can you be honest enough to recognize when you have succumbed to the temptations of role-playing, superficiality and the compulsive need for approval?

If you are a solar Virgo, can you be honest enough to recognize when you have succumbed to the temptations of self-doubt, endless preparation, fussiness, insecurity and loss of perspective?

If you are a solar Libra, can you be honest enough to recognize when you have succumbed to the temptations of codependency, dithering indecision, the need for people to like you, and too much compromise?

If you are a solar Scorpio, can you be honest enough to recognize when you have succumbed to the temptations of generating unnecessary complexity and psychodrama, vengeance, and mistrust?

If you are a solar Sagittarius, can you be honest enough to recognize when you have succumbed to the temptations of rigid opinions, illusory certainty, and self-righteousness?

If you are a solar Capricorn, can you be honest enough to recognize when you have succumbed to the temptations of control issues, repressed depression, and stoic long-suffering?

If you are a solar Aquarius, can you be honest enough to recognize when you have succumbed to the temptations of going along with the herd, dissociation, alienation, and overidentification with the intellect?

If you are a solar Pisces, can you be honest enough to recognize when you have succumbed to the temptations of absent-mindedness, being a ghost in your own life, ungrounded idealism, and a vulnerability to escapism?

THE SUN AND SELF-JUSTIFICATION

Going through that list of "temptations to which we have succumbed" is not everyone's favorite sport. The human ego hates any such process, feeling as if it does not behoove "the center of the universe" ever to be anything less than right about everything. Right or wrong, the Sun excels at justifying itself.

A man with a serious Mars dysfunction beats his wife. She has to be hospitalized. Maybe there's a police officer on the scene, skillful and experienced in the area of domestic violence. The cop wants the perp to confess, even though it is quite obvious what happened.

Here is a technique that police officer probably knows how to use. He establishes a "man-to-man" appearance of empathy with the wife-beater. Then he says, "So how did your wife provoke you? Why did you need to beat her?"

And the beater falls for it. He talks about "why she deserved what she got," thus confessing his sins, all the while imagining them to be virtues or necessities—and himself, God's avenging angel.

Obviously, this man did a terrible thing. Anybody looking at the situation would see that he was wrong. But in his own solar ego-mind he has a reason. He has justification: She deserved it, she needed it, she had to be punished, boundaries had to be set.

The ego loves to justify itself; it always does—and being "the center of the universe" helps. Bottom line, the Sun can be extremely defensive, reflecting its *need to be right.*

Mars can punch—but the Sun is what *justifies* the punch. Earlier we connected the Sun with the idea of our core values. Here we're looking at how the entire concept of values can be distorted and pulled into the service of ego-centered defensiveness.

The story I just told illustrates the absolutely awful side of the Sun—"I am the god-almighty center of the universe, and I am right about everything and everything I do is in accord with certain values that the Lord has appointed me to uphold in the universe." There's that ego energy.

The only cures are honesty, humility, and self-knowledge. That is where our list of those twelve temptations can save your soul.

JEHOVAH'S WITNESSES

A couple of weeks ago a pair of Jehovah's Witnesses knocked on my door. Their agenda boiled down to this: they were there to tell me how I should live and what I should believe. They were pressing their values on me. Astrologically, it was as if two Suns had knocked on my door and tried to exert their gravitational fields to change the course of my life.

Their faith was powerful; they believed in everything they were telling me. In some ways, I suspect their beliefs had worked well for them.

But they would not have worked for me. Their values were not mine. Had I let them convince me to join them, I would have "gone crazy"—which means that "my imagination about myself would have diverged from what I actually am," paraphrasing Rodney Collin from a few moments ago.

Even though, in talking about the egocentric dysfunctions of the Sun, we are peering directly into the heart of darkness, there is still light. Sometimes, in order to be true to our own paths, situations arise where we genuinely need to *shield ourselves* behind our solar capacity for self-justification and self-defense. Sometimes we need some of this selfishness—although in this case I would prefer to use a term I introduced in the previous chapter in the context of talking about the first house: *enlightened selfishness.*

LIVING IN A GALAXY OF SUNS

For most of you readers, I suspect that keeping your values distinct from those proffered by the Jehovah's Witnesses doesn't present an insurmountable problem. But let's take this broad issue in a more subtle direction: what about the influence of your parents on you? If you have a partner, what about his or her gravitational field?

Because we humans are social beings, we are constantly blasted by these kinds of distorting influences. In a way, the more we love someone, the more vulnerable we become to getting pulled into their narrative. There is no way to avoid any of this other than living as a hermit on a mountaintop.

Years ago, I was involved in an astrological music project that never got off the ground. I wrote a tune about the Sun in which I tried to wrestle lyrically with this question of the solar ego's need to sort out dangerous compromises from necessary ones. Here are the words I wrote:

When I yield to the field of your gravity
my center fails, you're pulling me.
My planets cannot orbit your Sun.
No one can give that to anyone.

You are the Sun in your universe
I am the Sun in mine.
What stuns and separates us
is the Sun that makes us shine, shine, shine.

In calendars and clocks,
we live this ancient paradox:
Will you warm me or burn me
in our circling journey?

You are the Sun in your universe
I am the Sun in mine.
What stuns and separates us
is the Sun that makes us shine, shine, shine.

Pretty good lyrics, I think. I wrote the song—but I still haven't sorted out all the questions it raises.

Stars in a galaxy interact gravitationally. That's why galaxies hold together. No one would ever call that gravity a negative thing. Similarly, everyone you love is like a star; together you are a galaxy—or at least a double star. Each one of those loved ones has a gravitational field. It pulls on you. That's not a bad thing either. But each ego—each person's narrative and value system—inevitably sometimes exerts a distorting impact on everyone else. The nearer they are, the stronger that impact. If you are in bed with a Jehovah's Witness, your beloved's beliefs are going to seep into your dreams.

So we are all in the same boat—or galaxy. My ego-gravity is pulling yours; yours is pulling back on me. Each one of us wants to be the center of the universe, and each of us denies it. We are all "selfish" like that to some extent. Selfish is the right word—but let's be careful not to make it entirely dreadful. My life revolves around my narrative; your life naturally revolves around your narrative. That is the way of our existences. That is the labyrinth we must thread in living with the Sun.

As we saw earlier, taking care of the Sun is the secret of sanity and vitality. We cannot fail, not if there is to be any hope for our living a meaningful life. All you have is that compass needle pointing true North—and that compass needle is the position of the Sun in your birthchart.

How much easier it would be if each star had its own universe! But who would want to live in that lonely condition?

LEO THE LION

Imagine a ten-year-old child in a playground with her family. She is swinging on the swing set with daredevil vigor. Daring the fates, she swings higher than she has ever swung before. Pretty soon, what do we hear? You already know the answer. It is absolutely archetypal—and 100 percent Leo:

"Mommy! Daddy! Look at me! Look at me! Look at me!"

You saw that one coming, right? It is universal and archetypal. The child—and your own inner child—wants her glorious victory to be *acknowledged.* For it to be real, it must be witnessed. That is a sentence worth reading twice. It is the distilled essence of the Leo clan. The child on the swings is expressing a classic Leo sentiment in a primal way: *Behold me.*

And of course what are mom and dad going to do? Because they love her, they will squeal in delight, acting a lot more impressed and amazed at her Herculean feat than they probably truly are. "Oh yes! Oh, you're amazing! It looks like you're flying. Be careful you don't go into orbit! Wow!"

Any decent parent would react the same way, by instinct. Good people pay attention to children. They celebrate them. They "behold" them. Kids need it—and adults do too, but we will soon get to that.

With children, we understand that they will not grow up right unless we pay attention to them. This urge to be seen, celebrated, and simply acknowledged carries us straight to the Holy Grail of the Leo clan. It boils down to this: *the happy synthesis of sincere self-expression and the right appreciative audience.*

A Sun-in-Pisces kid runs into the house. He is beaming. There is a beatific look of wonder on his face, as if he has just seen an apparition of the Virgin of Guadalupe.

He catches his breath and says, "Mommy, a tree talked to me!"

How does mommy react? Let's hope she looks that sensitive child right in the eye, enraptured and patient enough to ask for the whole story. Let us hope she shows every sign of honoring her child's mystical experience, thus "beholding and acknowledging" his Piscean nature.

But of course many parents, even good ones, would react dismissively, probably without realizing that was what they were doing. Maybe mommy smirks and says, "That's nice. What did the tree have to say? Business is nuts, right?"

And the child gets the message. His experience has been discounted. Something vital—and very much part of the Leo clan—goes out of him in that moment.

Attention is a life-giver. Being taken seriously is a life-giver.

THE BIG PICTURE

The study of the evolutionary role of the Fire Family comes down to the question of how we stay truly alive in this world "despite everything." The three faces of Fire each play a critical role in that life-sustaining process.

With the Aries family, we encountered some primal—even primeval—dimensions of this life-giving function: our ability to defend ourselves and to protect those we love. We looked at our ability to satisfy our necessary appetites, to claim territory, to defend boundaries, and to make a space for ourselves in a universe that might sometimes stand against us. We tried to make peace with the fundamentally competitive, eat-or-be-eaten aspects of human existence.

With the Aries clan, we are, in other words, talking about raw life force.

What are we now looking at with Leo? What sustains our vitality here?

In a nutshell, it is authentic self-expression. We can get all the attention in the world, but if it's not a reaction to who we really are, then it is only as nutritious to the soul as cotton candy is to the body.

With Leo, you've got to take an emotional risk or it won't work.

THE COURAGE TO BE VULNERABLE

When I was in college, I played in rock bands. It was fun and it paid the rent too. One Saturday morning, a friend who was a drummer in another band knocked on my door. He was in a difficult spot: his band had a gig, but their bass player had wound up in jail the previous night. My friend wanted me to fill in for him. I knew the material, more or less, so I loaded up my amplifier and my bass guitar and off we drove in his car.

On the way, I asked him where we would be performing. He said, "Duke Stadium. We're opening for a football game."

I gulped. Duke Stadium holds forty thousand people!

Actually, it wasn't too bad. There might have been forty thousand people there—but none of them gave a damn about a bunch of hippies playing Chuck Berry tunes. They were there for the game. They probably didn't even notice me. I knew that; and the knowledge that they were ignoring me was a great comfort.

A month or two later, I wrote my first song. In a state of absolute terror, I offered to play it in front of my own band. I loved these three guys, Jim, Tommy, and Ty; they were like brothers. But to play a song I had written in front of them was like marching stark-naked down Main Street playing a kazoo. That song came from my heart; it revealed my heart. I couldn't hide behind phony rock-star swagger the way I could playing those Chuck Berry tunes.

That vulnerability is pure Leo. That is the kind of attention on which this sign thrives. If there is no emotional risk, it's just you making noise. Without that sense of your heart being exposed, you are only creating a theatrical illusion that has nothing to do with you. Even if the theatrical illusion is applauded, your soul was not fed at all—and it is your own fault because you didn't risk your soul in the first place.

In a word, if you don't have butterflies in your tummy, it ain't the Leo road. That's the whole thing in a nutshell. You have got to stand naked.

For the applause to matter, it would also have to matter if there were no applause.

NEGLECT AND THE SUN

Maybe you are a stranger somewhere. Maybe you are in an airline terminal or a bus station. Nobody knows you. You might as well be a potted plant, for all they care. We all know this feeling. It is part of modern life. It's not a big deal.

But what if that feeling lasted, lasted and lasted...

Some people would prefer to be actively hated than to be invisible. Kids "acting out" illustrate the principle. So do adults acting out. Chronic anonymity breeds dragons in the psyche—and their breeding ground is the Leo clan.

What happens to the child on the swing when the parents are too busy to notice her? What happens to the author whose books are never published? What happens to the partner who feels unseen and unappreciated, taken for granted? What happens to the human soul when nobody sees you, nobody acknowledges you, and nobody holds the mirror before you? What happens when you never see yourself reflected in the attention of other people?

Since these are all archetypal Leo questions, we all know the answers—we all have some Leo in us. It is part of being human. Treated that way, any one of us would feel their elemental vitality leaching out. That's a "life-giver" standing on its head. That's a death-giver.

Think of that child on the swing to whom nobody paid any attention. Think of her face one minute after her parents ignored her. She gives up swinging. Why bother anymore? *But what does she look like?*

The answer is painful: she is without affect. Dull. Desperate—or more likely, just broken-spirited.

When the elements of the Leo clan in our charts are starved this way, there may be other behavioral distortions, depending on the nature of the rest of the chart. But that sad child's face conveys the fundamental wound. It comes down to the fact that, as human beings, our vitality derives partly from the attention of others. We see it so clearly with children. The myth is that as adults we "need to get over it."

But we do not get over it. We are not supposed to get over it.

This *voluntary vulnerability* to each other is fundamental to any positive understanding of the Leo clan.

Note how elegantly this all links back to what we learned about the Sun a few pages ago. The Sun represents those core values to which we must be true if our lives are going to be worth living—and it's these same core values which must be bravely expressed if we are going to be true to the Lion's evolutionary path.

Otherwise, no matter how much money we make or how star-studded our guest list is, we're just playing Chuck Berry tunes for a bunch of football fans who aren't even listening.

A MOMENT OF SCARY VULNERABILITY

Thanks for reading this book! Thanks for coming to my classes and tuning in to my webinars! Thanks, in other words, for paying attention to me. I appreciate it!

Here is a terrifying personal fantasy: what if nobody was interested in astrology anymore? What if no one bought my books? What if I got an email from one of my organizers that said, "Steve, class is cancelled. Nobody signed up. Seems like you are yesterday's news."

It's horrifying!

Obviously, all that would be hard on my ego. But my intention is a little deeper here.

Faced with that disaster and loss of face, someone might tell me to take heart and think of it as a spiritual lesson. They might point out that I would still be myself, that my truth is my truth regardless of the reviews, and that I should stand tall for my truth even if nobody salutes the flag.

That's a compelling philosophical argument. And God bless all the brave souls who have stood up for their truth even with no applause coming from anywhere. That is in fact true *Aquarian* wisdom—and it's no accident that Aquarius is the sign opposite Leo. (We will get to Aquarius eventually, when I write the third volume in this series: *The Book of Air*.)

Leo represents a different path entirely than Aquarius—one that involves a different kind of risk: baring our souls and being brave enough to let it matter if they are received and appreciated—or not. That evolutionary pathway implies a lot more vulnerability than does Aquarius—and a much more interactive, symbiotic, and interdependent relationship with other human beings.

None of this makes Leo "good" and Aquarius "bad," or vice versa. They are just different evolutionary tracks. It just happens that here in these pages we are talking about Leo.

TELLING A JOKE

You're a Leo. You find yourself at a professional meeting in Pittsburgh, Pennsylvania—and this story will work better if we assume you don't have close personal friends in Pittsburgh.

Since it's a professional meeting, to some extent everyone is wearing his or her formal social mask. There is a certain stiffness, in other words—everything is happening on that narrow bandwidth of emotional interaction called "professionalism." Maybe the meeting is worth attending, but you are not there for the fun of it. You're there to network and to learn. Your soul is basically invisible, and that's fine with you and completely appropriate under the circumstances.

As the afternoon winds down, you fall in with a group of attendees. One of them is extroverted and starts organizing a dinner. You don't particularly want to go, but it would be awkward to bow out. Eleven of you head out for enchiladas and maybe a margarita or two.

Drinks are served. As you await the meal, somebody tells a joke. It is actually funny. Everyone laughs—and loosens up. The person who told the joke had a Leo moment; he took a chance performing in front of everyone, and it worked.

Feel how the energy around the table changes?

It's just someone telling a joke—a trivial thing—but the shared laughter warms the atmosphere. Jokes are contagious; pretty soon someone else tells one. Ten minutes later, everyone is having a better time than they'd anticipated, including you.

Watch this next sequence carefully; this is the microsecond-by-microsecond evolutionary process we call Leo…

Just before you left your hometown, you heard a joke. You're thinking of maybe telling it… but then you look at all those strangers.

Nah…

Unless you are absolutely extroverted, you probably know what I am talking about here. It's frightening to put yourself out there in front of these people. What if you blow the joke? What if no one thinks it is funny?

No force in the universe is going to make you take that risk. Why? *Because you don't have to.* You can sit there politely and just laugh at other people's jokes; no one will think the worse of you for it.

Why take the risk of rejection?

But before you can stop yourself, you hear yourself saying, "I heard one." Suddenly all eyes are on you. You tell your joke and you get the loudest laughs of the evening. These strangers are now all beaming at you. It's as if they can actually see you now, three-dimensionally, humanly. And they like what they see.

If I'd asked you two hours earlier what you thought of these people, perhaps you would have said they were okay. But now, after they all loved your joke, you like them a lot better—and not just for the silly reason that they laughed at your joke, but for the deep reason that you took the risk to be vulnerable with them. It worked.

The establishment of that warm, easy, spontaneous relationship with the human family is the evolutionary North Star of the Leo clan.

What I describe here is seemingly the most forgettable of human interactions—just some people relaxing after a hard day at a conference, telling jokes. But the honest description is that such self-expressive performance is absolutely terrifying for almost everybody.

I am intentionally using the simplest of illustrations here; there are of course far greater voluntary acts of vulnerability available to us. I am talking about being the first one in a relationship to say "I love you." Or writing a serious poem—and being brave enough to show it to someone. Or stepping out on a stage to perform your own work.

The greater the risk and the deeper the sincerity, the more life-energy is fed into the Leo clan.

THE FIFTH HOUSE

If Leo, when healthy, represents to *urge* to express one's self and to thus to be noticed, appreciated, or applauded, then the fifth house represents the *actual behaviors* those urges produce. If Leo and the Sun represent life-giving vitality, then the fifth house represents literally jumping up and down with it—smiling, laughing, and bursting with joy.

Concretely, the fifth house correlates with *recreation*—all the things we might do in order to "re-create" vital force in ourselves. In conventional astrology, the list of behaviors related to the fifth house reads like a hedonist's shopping list: love affairs, sports, the arts and creativity, games, shopping, feasting.

In other words, if it sounds like fun, put it on the list.

In our Leo example a moment ago, our hero told a joke. Humor is fun—but it's also a kind of performance that reveals a lot about us. Every joke we think is funny maps—and publicly illustrates—our defenses, wounds, and the profiles of our unconscious minds. Therefore, perhaps more than we know, we embody the active, behavioral dimensions of the fifth house whenever we dare to say those fateful words, "I heard one..."

The act of sharing a poem or stepping out on a stage to perform takes us into edgier terrain than telling jokes. The stakes are escalated—so the evolutionary paycheck for taking the risk is that much fatter.

What about falling in love? That is a joy too. Remember: the fifth house is traditionally the house of love affairs. Little reveals more about the actual reality of our psychic and spiritual condition than a meditation on the natures of the people to whom we are attracted. Double that for our actual behavior in intimate situations. It may be fun—but falling in love also reflects those two strands of Leo clan DNA: risk and vulnerability.

There's one human situation that is even more revealing than falling in love: *having children.* And of course, the fifth house in all the astrological traditions is the "house of children." Genetically, our kids reveal us by carrying forward so much of what we are. More tellingly, their social behavior reveals much about how we raised them and trained them to function in the world, for good or for ill.

These notions taken all together—love affairs, children, creativity and performance—constitute the essential profile of the fifth house, at least as it's dished up in mainstream astrology books. In all this, they are accurate. But the heart of the matter lies in acts of intentional vulnerability—acts in which we risk revealing the actual and unvarnished condition of our souls.

And underlying it all, right in the archetypal marrow of the fifth house: the healing, life-giving *mystery of joy.*

HAVE A REALLY GOOD TIME, THUS SAITH THE LORD

If you have a planet or two in the fifth house, God marched you out to the end of the cosmological diving board and said, "Just go on down there and have yourself some fun."

Immediately, note how it's almost impossible to read those words without dismissing them as lightweight—"just a joke."

But they are not a joke. They are as serious as the proverbial heart attack.

Why might anyone need more joy? Why might the hunger for the ecstatic be an evolutionary need so profound that it played a central role in your birthchart?

We start off with an arbitrary assumption. It's something I cannot prove, but something with which I suspect you will agree; otherwise, you would not have your nose in this book. My assumption is that life is inherently meaningful. That we have been born for a purpose. That there is nothing random about anything.

Translation: you have your birthchart for a reason.

Add one more rather obvious link to the logical chain: you have had your birthchart ever since the moment of your birth—therefore, anything that caused you to have the chart that you have must've happened before you were born.

Welcome to the evolutionary essence of the fifth house. *What might have happened to you before you were born that makes it so pressingly important that you now "have a good time?"*

Obviously the answer is that something hurt you. Something took away your joy. And it happened before your birth. What might it have been? There are many, many possibilities. Here I use the language of past lives and reincarnation. The astrological techniques for focusing our understanding of our unresolved karma are complex; I covered them in great detail in my book *Yesterday's Sky: the Astrology of Reincarnation*. For our present purposes, it is enough to affirm that if you have a significant concentration of either Leo or fifth house planets, you were harmed somehow in a prior life. Something squashed your joy.

And you have come back into this world to reclaim your right to be enchanted with life, to trust it, and to celebrate it.

Leo refers to that underlying drive itself, while the fifth house refers to the behaviors and actions that can help you accomplish it.

BACK TO THE MEXICAN RESTAURANT

A few pages back, we had you telling a joke at a Mexican restaurant. At the time, we presented the situation in literal terms. Now let's go back and understand it metaphorically. The strangers at that table represent the world—a world that presumably hurt you in a prior life. As you entered that restaurant—or as you entered this present life—you were suspicious and inclined to be guarded. You had "learned your lesson" long ago: trust no one, take no chances.

But there was good news: in our story, you got over yourself enough to tell a joke. You took the risk of self-revelation. And they laughed at your joke; they loved you in Pittsburgh, Pennsylvania. Your attitude toward them quickly changed: you liked these people better. You felt more comfortable with them. You had warmed to the world and taken a step toward forgiving it. That statement applies concretely to the joke in the restaurant—but it applies metaphorically to a kind of soul-healing that can happen to you over the course of a lifetime, provided that you continue to take those kinds of risks with people.

This alchemy is the evolutionary heart of both Leo and the fifth house.

To dramatize all this, when I sit with a client who's working with these Leo clan energy-paths, I often say, "You were once burned at the stake as a witch." I quickly affirm I have no idea if that is literally true, and that in fact it most probably is not. But that dramatic imagery gets us thinking in the right way: in another life, people somehow hurt you. Humanity showed you its dark side. For understandable reasons, you came into this world scared—and profoundly motivated not to get "burned at the stake" again. The last time you took the risk of revealing what you thought was beautiful and holy, it didn't go very well.

You are in recovery from that.

LEO, THE FIFTH HOUSE, AND PAIN

What's the most misunderstood symbol in astrology? The Leo clan is right at the top of my personal list. Often in popular astrology, Leo is characterized as histrionic, egocentric, and comically self-important, as if it represented a bad case of self-appointed royalty, needing to be taken down a notch or two.

Meanwhile, the fifth house is trivialized as merely the "fun-house"—harmless enough if we don't go overboard, but not anything that would long engage the attention of anyone who is serious about the spiritual path.

The truth is so much more profound than that. Here are some classic Fire Family questions that come to a sharp evolutionary focus in the Leo clan:

**How do we recover from monumental pain?*
**How does the soul heal from unthinkable wounding?*
**How do we become whole again when evil and darkness have triumphed over us?*

These are the underlying issues that surface behaviorally in the context of the fifth house. How do we do it? How do we heal? The path of recovery lies in exploring everything that is a source of joy for us. Joy is the cure for pain; where there is an excess of pain, there must be a pagan affirmation of our appetite for life and its pleasures, both those of the flesh and those of the spirit. We are talking about celebration and creativity, along with the joys and comforts of intimacy.

And that line of thinking leads us directly into the path of a major shadow-expression of the fifth house...

THE FIFTH HOUSE AND ADDICTION

Maybe you have a friend who's destroying her relationships and her career with cocaine or alcohol. Why is she doing that? The map that leads to that world of pain is no secret. In frustration with your friend's self-destructive behavior, you perhaps wonder how she could possibly be that stupid.

But your friend has an IQ of 145. Stupid is not her problem. So why is she destroying her life?

Very probably the answer is some kind of existential, psycho-spiritual pain. In almost any drug and alcohol rehabilitation program—at least, one that has a chance of succeeding—there is an underlying working assumption: *people who get into trouble with addictions are practicing a form of self-administered anesthesia.* They hurt badly and they've found a way to make the hurt stop.

The trouble is that the more they use addiction to make that hurt stop, the worse the pain grows.

A busy fifth house was historically correlated with "debauchery." (I've seen that association much less with Leo, for some reason.) But any astrologer working daily with clients can easily corroborate the basic principle that planets in the fifth house and escapist, self-destructive behavior are a common pairing.

Perhaps you tell your friend that she simply "needs to stop" the drinking or the cocaine. That advice is understandable, but famously futile. The problem, in a nutshell, is not that she's having too much fun. The problem is that she's not having enough fun.

Pleasure balances pain. As we've seen, planets in the fifth house suggest a person who has incarnated in a state of hurt. He or she also has the evolutionary intention—and the capability—to address that pain.

The central insight here is that one who goes down the road of addiction wins the famous "close but no banana" award. Such a person does indeed need some fun! He or she is just going about it in the wrong way.

A glass of wine enjoyed with your friends is one of life's joys, but drinking the entire bottle of wine all by yourself is simply not a very joyful experience.

Loudly and clearly: part of a strong, healthy response to a fifth house planet lies in a *right relationship with the appetites of the flesh.* Abstemiousness is simply not indicated here. However, the pleasures of the flesh *alone* are not sufficient to address the magnitude of this karmic wound. To the mixture, we must add pleasures of mind, spirit, and soul—for example, the pleasures of creativity. The pleasures of human intimacy in the broad sense. The pleasures of sports and games and celebration. The comforts of the garden. The ecstasy of the glorious sunset. The joy of learning. The joy of traveling.

To cure the fifth house pain-dilemma, we need the entire package of life's pleasures. Meanwhile, the royal road to getting in trouble with the fifth house is to *ask too much of any one single joy*. We shame none of them; we simply keep balance among them.

Typically when a person falls into that addiction trap, he or she is asking too much of the pleasures of the physical body. That might refer to cocaine or alcohol, as in our example. But the list is long: one can get into trouble with sexual pleasures. Or food. One can get into trouble with spending money we don't have—or spending our lives playing video games.

Basically anything that is pleasurable and repeatable can be used in an escapist way. These are all the soul cages built into fifth house astrological structures. That is what the fifth house looks like when a person gets it wrong.

FIFTH HOUSE "LOVE AFFAIRS"

The fifth house, as we mentioned earlier, is the house of love affairs. While the term is useful and accurate, let's expand its meaning. Immediately we need to recognize that these fifth house "love affairs" are not necessarily sexual. Instead, they embrace a wide range of possibilities, even including our relationship with our own children.

Essentially, a fifth house "love affair" is a relationship that meets the following three criteria.

Number one: there is an inexplicable and instantaneous sense of recognition between two people. If we are the sorts of people who are open to reincarnation, we probably actually say the words, "I feel like I've known you before." If we do not believe in reincarnation, the sentiment remains about the same, just not so easily explicable.

Number two: There is a compelling sense of urgency about these relationships. It feels important that we have met, although we may not be sure exactly why that is so.

Number three: These relationships tend to not take very long to work out. There's a quality of brevity to them. When they do end, the finale may not be bitter, awkward, or painful, although sometimes of course it might be. We all have a little box in our heads labeled, "I wonder whatever happened to..." The people in that box represent your fifth house connections.

Criterion number one—that weird sense of familiarity—is really the key. I take reincarnation literally myself. To me, that's what the fifth house is all about. It literally represents people with whom you have unfinished business from prior lifetimes.

We can understand this most easily by thinking in simple, non-metaphysical, present- tense terms. Almost all of us, as we look back on our lives, can remember relationships of various sorts that did not end well. Perhaps you're breaking up with someone. Maybe you have a friend who's versed in metaphysics. She suggests that you should "work things out with your partner or you will just have to meet again in a future lifetime." In a sense, what she's saying is correct, because in this universe there is ultimately no such thing as unfinished business. We don't get away with anything. What your friend is missing is that you and your partner are actually working as hard as you can to straighten things out—but the harder you work, the more you hurt each other.

We're only human, and we all have our limits. Sometimes the kindest and wisest thing we can do in a difficult relationship is simply to end it before we do further damage.

All we need to do in order to complete our deeper picture of fifth house "love affairs" is to apply exactly that same common sense to prior lifetimes. We can assume that in past lives you also had unfinished business with certain people and that you couldn't work it out at the time.

Ultimately, you do in fact need to work it out—just maybe not in that lifetime. Maybe you weren't ready then. Maybe you both are ready now.

Broadly, this situation would of course be relevant to all of us regardless of whether we have any planets in the fifth house: we all have unfinished business with other souls. But for many of us, the unresolved interpersonal karma has not yet ripened. We will not meet those people until we are ready.

With planets in the fifth house, the time has come to reconnect, and hopefully to resolve things and release each other in a spirit of blessing.

WHAT ABOUT KIDS?

The idea that the fifth house represents children is ancient and accurate. The connection between love affairs and pregnancy was perhaps more vivid in the past than it is today, and that was certainly part of the connection. But the archetypal linkage here is deeper.

Warning: our first step in understanding it will feel strange and unnatural.

We just observed that the purpose of these love affairs is to end them. That means to exit the relationship with the other soul in a state of release and resolution.

Here's how we connect that idea to kids: the purpose of our relationships with our children is also to end them.

That's the "strange and unnatural" statement I warned you about a couple of lines ago. Clearly, most people who have children anticipate a long and fulfilling connection with them as the kids move into adulthood.

So how can we make sense of this?

The heart of the matter is actually very simple: all healthy parents aspire to end the part of their relationship with their kids that takes the form of a parent-child relationship. You want your children to eventually move out. The aim is not alienation or distance, but rather the transformation of the relationship into a friendly connection between two adults who respect and support each other. The relationship itself has not ended, but it has died, been released and resolved—and reborn in a new form.

Let's add an obvious point: to be somebody's child or to be somebody's parent could be characterized as serious karma—it is most unlikely, in other words, that we would give birth to a child whose soul was a complete stranger to our own. The contract may be as simple as "you changed my diapers last time, now it is my turn to change yours." If we ever have kids and are open to metaphysics, this is a rather starkly evident principle. (It also helps explain why many psychotherapists drive expensive, late-model automobiles.) Simply said, the parent-child bond is often fraught with complications. As in any other kind of relationship, the two have come together for a reason. Thus, the parenting relationship can often be understood as a fifth house "love affair," which always means two souls doing their ever-changing, centuries-old dance, and hopefully on the road to life-giving healing, release, and resolution.

5

THE SAGITTARIAN CLAN

Let's flip our cosmic dial one more notch. We now arrive at the last phase of the Fire trigon: Sagittarius, Jupiter, and the ninth house. This trio of symbols represents the third set of Life-Givers. In some ways, it is the most sophisticated and complex of them all.

As with Aries and Leo, it would be wrong to pronounce Sagittarians "more evolved" than Leo, meanwhile telling the Leos that they can safely look down their spiritual noses at all the lowly Arians. That's not how it works at all. In the human world, each astrological sign represents a spectrum of possibilities, from low to lofty. One can make a highly sophisticated response to Aries, or a destructive response to Sagittarius.

Still, at the purely archetypal level, as we contemplate the mandala of the Zodiac, we can detect increasing levels of complexity, subtlety, and high potential as we move through the Fire signs. In that sense, and only in that sense, Sagittarius is the most sophisticated and complex of them all.

With the Aries clan, we looked at *raw survival*—I have a right to exist and I have the skills to fight for it. And if you don't like that, "make my day."

With the Leo clan, we contemplated the *celebration of personality*—I am somebody in particular, with something to express. Please notice me. Please nourish me with the energy of your attention.

What about the Sagittarian clan? Here, with Arian survival secured and Leo individuality established, we begin to wrestle with broader questions. What is the meaning of my life? Why am I here? What's it all about?

The Quest begins.

We launch our fragile vessel into the ocean of life. We surf the waves of experience. Endlessly, we are searching for something, not even knowing exactly what it is, yet having perfect faith in its existence. A great restlessness arises here. There is a hunger that is hard to name. Somehow, deep inside, there's an unquestioning sense that just over the horizon lies a realm of pure magic.

So we search, we stretch our boundaries—and whether we know it or not, that Holy Grail we are seeking is nothing less than the meaning of life.

DEATH BY TEDIUM

Let's get down to the Sagittarian bones:

We all have a certain number of seconds left in this world. A clock is ticking and we don't know when it will wind down.

We have an intuition that we were born into these brief bodies for a reason. We don't know what the reason is. Just possibly, if we hurl ourselves wholeheartedly into experience, we can perhaps figure out the answer before the final bell rings.

Complicating the situation, we are all surrounded by people who claim to already know the answer—but we often see desperation and insecurity in their eyes. Yet, some of what they say might be useful. But which parts? How can we know? Only by testing what they've preached at us against the realities of our own experience. And the more experience we're open to having, the clearer our thinking and reality-testing becomes.

All this is Sagittarius.

We must always remember that in this third clan of Fire symbols, *experience itself*—not adherence to belief systems—is the engine that drives the evolution of consciousness.

When I'm counseling people with these symbols prominent in their makeup, one of my favorite lines is, "In this lifetime, you have been wired to make a lot of interesting mistakes." The words always generate laughter and recognition—but they also represent a serious point. To be afraid of life and thus never to take any risks or chances is likely to leave us no wiser at the end of it all than we were at the beginning.

The Sagittarian path depends upon our remaining wide open to a vast range of experience, willing and eager to feast at the table of human existence. That includes digesting our "interesting mistakes." And of course it includes other possibilities as well: travel, education, cross-cultural experience—everything that stretches our horizons, along with everything that challenges our tendency toward dogmatism and blinding opinions.

Let's now supply the dark background—mindfulness of the Shadow always allows us to better see the light. Imagine yourself listening to a fundamentalist (of any sort) droning on and on, as predictable as a puppy at dinnertime. How do you feel as you sit through the endless sermon?

We all know the answer: as we listen, we feel the life-force being drained from us.

Now let's go deeper with the same point. How do you feel *listening to yourself* drone on and on with your own predictable, memorized position papers? Down that road, you too become as predictable as that puppy. Once again, life-force drains from your body, mind, and spirit.

Ask Sagittarius, Jupiter, or the ninth house: is that any way to live?

THE SAGITTARIAN TOTEM POLE

When I was a young astrologer, still in my teens and just beginning to internalize the symbols, I learned somewhere that there were "three kinds of Sagittarians."

At the top of the totem pole was the *Philosopher.*

One notch below the philosopher was the *Scholar.*

And at the bottom of the totem pole was the *Voyager*—the actual word that I learned was "Gypsy," but I don't want to confuse or offend my European readers. This is the romantic American vision of the Gypsy, not the actual reality of the *Roma* people. In this context, the term reflects an openness to traveling—but more broadly, an eagerness to live life passionately—to "dance with a rose between your teeth."

Our first move here is to kick that totem pole over. Let's make it a horizontal system rather than a vertical one. The Voyager is as central to Sagittarius as is the Philosopher. As we will see, all three principles are essential to the healthy functioning of this archetype.

These expressions share one underlying principle: *stretching our boundaries*. In all three, we move beyond the *tyranny of the familiar*. The Voyager expresses this principle of stretching through the means of the physical body, along with an openness to embracing fleshly, in-the-body experience.

The Scholar reflects the same principle, but here the stretching is centered on the *intellect*. The Scholar is eager to move beyond the familiar, limiting horizons of her or his present state of knowledge.

The Philosopher—the third expression of the Sagittarian principle—refers to *intuition* reaching out to embrace the far horizons of life and experience, attempting to figure out "what it all means."

By the way, in thinking of the Philosopher in this context, it is important not to confuse it with any university philosophy courses. The Sagittarian Philosopher is not about the neutral abstractions of the intellect. Those are legitimate expressions of the energy, but they are manifestations of the Scholar, not the Philosopher. With the Philosopher, we are talking about the human heart stretching outward, trying to wrap its consciousness around some sense of the meaning or ultimate purpose in life.

None of that can ever be deduced through purely intellectual means.

BEANS AGAIN

I love heirloom beans. Often when I am starting my day, I put some in my slow cooker with some vegetables and some spices. By dinner time, they are ready. Usually that turns out a whole lot of beans. No problem—by the second day, they're even better.

But by the third day? Beans again? They still taste good, but by then my palate is jaded. I want something different.

In a very minor way, that "beans again" feeling reflects the quintessential Sagittarian misery. We all have a natural desire for some variety in life—but if this clan of symbols figures prominently in your birthchart, that desire for "something new" is not only more driving, but also inseparable from your evolutionary intentions. This questing spirit can express itself through the *body* (the Voyager), the *intellect* (the Scholar), or the questing *heart* (the Philosopher)—but it is all Sagittarius.

THE TEACHINGS OF DON JUAN

Like many people of my generation, I was profoundly impacted by the books of Carlos Castaneda. Quickly, for those of you who have never heard of him, Castaneda was a University of California graduate student who allegedly apprenticed himself to a Yaqui Indian shaman named Don Juan back in the early 1960s. The shaman's home ground was described as being situated on the western coast of mainland Mexico, on the Sea of Cortez, opposite the Baja California peninsula.

Castaneda's books are mystical and fantastical. To put it mildly, they are not universally accepted as factual. I understand that they are, however, based fairly authentically on anthropological sources and traditions. Here's the most cogent comment I ever heard about them: "I don't know if they are true, but they should be."

Already we have hit upon a Sagittarian insight: truth is more important than facts. To me, Castaneda's books are full of genuine wisdom. I want to share a couple of them with you here as we pursue our understanding of this third clan in the Fire family. By the way, Castaneda was a solar Capricorn, but his Sun was in the ninth house and his Mercury was in Sagittarius. He embodied many of the principles we are exploring here both biographically and astrologically.

Castanada writes that Don Juan taught him that there were "four enemies of a man of knowledge." It is the fourth one that helps us understand Sagittarius. Let's quickly get there by going through the first three.

The first enemy of a "Man of Knowledge" is *Fear*—Don Juan's mystical world is scary. If you let fear paralyze you, game over.

The second enemy is *Power*. If you conquer Fear, you become incredibly powerful. And maybe you get hooked on power. It is famously addictive—just have a look at a typical politician. In power lie the soul-cages of the Oppressor or the Tyrant.

If you defeat that second enemy, your vision becomes very clear. You are no longer seeing everything through the dualistic, competitive lens of power-games. You are free of vanity and self-importance. And thus arises the third enemy of a Man of Knowledge: *Clarity*. You can get hooked on that too. Being "right"—who doesn't love that? The hook of Clarity really gets in your mouth. Even worse, at this high evolutionary stage, you really *are* right most of the time.

Clarity can be very addictive. Astrologers have to be very wary of this third enemy.

Conquer your addiction to Clarity, and the fourth enemy arises. Don Juan called it *Old Age.* Carlos Castaneda wrote the words down, but I do not think he understood them. I do not think Don Juan was talking about old age in the literal sense. I believe that what he was referring to was an attitude of being threatened by anything new or different—and perhaps it's fair to observe that older people are more susceptible to this trap than are younger ones. If we become attached to it, the price we pay to maintain this deadening stability is terribly high. This living death is, I think, what Don Juan meant by "old age."

In that sense, I've met people who were dying of old age in their twenties.

The moral of the tale: if you carry the mark of the Sagittarian clan, you are here to pack the experience of several lifetimes into one body—so don't go and voluntarily "die of old age." The deepest betrayal of your own soul imaginable is *willingly to surrender to boredom.* Even when you're old, you can resolve to dance like a gypsy, endlessly feed the hungry intellect of the inner scholar, and, above all, maintain the questing heart of a true philosopher.

AVOIDING THE TRAP OF CLARITY

Let's say you want to be "right about everything"—or at least to *believe* that you're right about everything. Here's a method that will do the trick: just arrange to be born in a little farming county in Mississippi *and stay there.* Everyone there is a Southern Baptist—and everybody agrees that God is a Southern Baptist too.

That will work. All you have to do is to insure that this culturally defined model of reality never encounters any disagreement, challenge, resistance, or any alternatives to its own version of things.

Now, before I get any nasty letters from people living in little counties in Mississippi, let me add that I could say exactly the same thing about almost any other cultural framework. There is, for example, no world quite as conservative—that is, as narrow, predictable, and punitive toward dissent—as the so-called *avant-garde* in the world of art. You can almost see the trendsetters glancing at each other to make sure that they are marching in lockstep with the latest trend.

And, to me, there are few groups of people as tedious as those who are attempting to be cool or hip. May God protect us from the tedium of the company of *fashionistas.*

Voyagers travel—in other words, if you are Sagittarian, maybe it's time to "get out of Mississippi."

RELIGION AS CLARITY

Napoleon is alleged to have once said, "History is a lie agreed upon." Any questions? Just ask a Navajo—or a woman.

We can go further: we can say that *reality itself* is a lie agreed upon. The only trouble with putting it in those terms is that it makes it seem like a conspiracy theory. It isn't—at least not in any conscious sense. The point is only that "reality" is very much a cultural phenomenon. We all look at life through the window of our culture's explanation of things.

Illustrations: every society has its own definitions of gender. What does it mean to be a man or woman? Each culture defines success in its own way. Each one has different interpretations of the meaning of death, or the nature of childhood, or the meaning and purpose of sex.

Sagittarius has always been seen as the sign of "religion." Normally, when we use that word, we're thinking about churches, mosques, and temples. We are thinking about theology. But here, as we attempt to understand this third clan in the Fire Family, we must expand our definition. In this sense, religion refers to a culturally-determined, collective understanding of the way things are. We are talking about belief-systems. In this sense, we would have to recognize *materialism* as a major world religion. We would have to recognize *cynicism* as a religious perspective. There's ultimately no concrete evidence that life is pointless and empty—but some people choose to "take it on faith" that our existence has no meaning at all.

Normally, when we use the word "religion," we're thinking of Catholicism, Buddhism and so on. But to understand the "religious" corollary of Sagittarius, we need to think more psychologically. The bottom line is that humans have always felt a need to try to make some sense of their lives.

And every religion is potentially a soul-cage. It can trap us in "clarity"—which quickly degenerates into "old age," at least if you are a Sagittarian. I know that sounds harsh—and we can surely say good things about religion too. But the key here is to recognize that the healthy heart of Sagittarius lies in the idea of eternal stretching. It represents the endless quest.

When we take cheap comfort in mere clarity, we have missed the entire point of this sign of the zodiac.

THE INTERDEPENDENCY OF THE DISEASE AND THE MEDICINE

Maybe you were born in that conservative county in Mississippi; it's all you've ever known. It's understandable that these cultural forces would profoundly condition your thinking. They started working on you when you were still in the cradle.

But let's say you're also Sagittarian. Your cultural training might be very limited, but your instincts are sound. What is the cure for your spiritual dilemma? Easy! As we saw a moment ago, *all you need to do is to get out of town*. Remember: one correlate of Sagittarius is the Voyager or the Gypsy. This is an astrological sign whose evolutionary potential is eternally linked to the desire to travel, eternally linked to curiosity about the larger world, and to a fascination with cross-cultural experience.

Perhaps our Sagittarian friend from Mississippi visits Europe. There, he or she encounters Catholics or Muslims—or French existentialists—who practically glow in the dark with the power of their faith. For anyone carrying the mark of the third Fire clan, that *culture shock* is evolutionary rocket fuel.

Here's the underlying principle: experience is the cure for rigidity. Or, to use the language of Don Juan, experience cures Clarity.

There's something truly elegant about this particular combination of Sagittarian insights. The questing desire for meaning has an enormous potential for getting us into trouble. Simply said, we can settle on "a meaning" too quickly. Paradoxically, this noble desire for understanding can freeze the evolutionary journey in its tracks.

Countering that liability, in our Sagittarian trio, there is a restless, compelling curiosity to see what lies over the far horizon. *If we act on those feelings, inevitably we encounter information and perspectives that shock us into freshened awareness.* These adventurous impulses, if we heed them and feed them, are the remedy for the dark side of the Sagittarian "religious" impulse.

Similarly, under the banner of the Scholar, we recognize the compelling desire to learn. Learning is another way to stretch your horizons—with the added benefit that education can be a good medicine against rigidity or simplistic views of the world. It's the same mutually-correcting pattern, in other words.

As ever, life presents us with choices. If you are navigating by the stars of the third Fire clan, you can aim for the wild ride that takes you to the higher ground—or you can rot in front of a television, in the pews of a boring church, or spend your life in that "little county in Mississippi," never leaving it.

SAGITTARIUS VERSUS THE NINTH HOUSE

Always, to keep our astrological craft as crisp as it can be, we need to be aware of the distinction between signs and houses. I beat this drum quite a lot—you've heard its rhythms a few times already. You probably have some books on your bookshelf with chapter headings such as "If Your Moon Is in Sagittarius or the Ninth House…" That wording of course implies that the sign and the house are interchangeable. The truth is that they're only *partly* interchangeable. That's why this pervasive sign-house confusion is the most insidious sort of mistake—even though it is a mistake, you are still right a lot of the time.

We've seen it before, but here it is again:

A sign represents a psychological impulse. It represents a need, or a drive, or a value. It sets the agenda for whatever planet it contains.

A house represents the behaviors that arise naturally as we act upon the agenda or impulse.

Sagittarius represents the need, drive or value to stretch one's horizons. It's the part of you that hates to be bored. For this sign, boredom—at least, willingly accepting boredom in the name of practicality—means we have turned our back on our spiritual path. We are lost, and we feel that way.

The ninth house, on the other hand, represents the actions we might undertake—or recommend, in the counseling room—that express or embody those Sagittarian impulses. Here we encounter a list of familiar ninth house key words: travel, education, the act of making philosophical inquiries.

Those are accurate and helpful references, but we can go a lot deeper into the soul of the ninth house.

Let's listen to the Yaqui shaman, Don Juan, again...

HUNTING RABBITS

Don Juan and a young Carlos Castaneda are in the desert hunting rabbits. The older man explains their strategy, which is to rise early and sit quietly, just observing the paths the rabbits take. The rabbits could be anywhere in the wide desert, but it soon becomes apparent that they always follow the same pathways. As Don Juan explains, once you've got their routes figured out, you can make snares and set them on those established paths.

The way Don Juan put it was that, to snare a rabbit, you just need to *learn their routines*.

Some hours later, Don Juan and Carlos are in the middle of the tedious and complex process of actually making the snares and setting them. Suddenly Don Juan jumps up on a rock and begins to howl, "Woo! Woo"! And he won't stop. Carlos starts to feel a little tense.

Finally, Don Juan stops howling. He breaks the tension by announcing that he is "the lunch whistle." It's time to eat. Carlos looks at his watch and sure enough, it's around noon. He starts putting out the food.

Don Juan interrupts, "Are you hungry?"

Carlos says "Not really, but it's lunch time." And Don Juan reminds him of how they're snaring these rabbits—by learning their routines.

And, hungry or not, Carlos reliably dines at noon.

The point is that he—and maybe you and I as well—have a routine of eating a meal at midday. We're more like those rabbits than we like to admit.

In a classic melodramatic moment, Don Juan says to his young apprentice, "Death is stalking you, just like we are stalking these rabbits."

If death learns your routines, you are doomed.

So break up your routines.

Strong imagery! And it hits the bullseye right in the heart of the ninth house. What can you do to shatter your own routines? What can you do to become less predictable ?

Those routines aren't just about when you eat your meals. We must understand this idea much more deeply: they include your attachment to your blinding, limiting routines of thought—your "position papers," so to speak.

Again, we go back to our familiar list of ninth house key words: travel, education, philosophical inquiry. We can now understand that each one is potentially a way of shattering your routines, both mental and existential.

THE PHILOSOPHER

If you are carrying strong Sagittarian signatures in your chart, you have the nature of a philosopher. That quality is hardwired into you. Another way to say it is that you think in *moral categories.* Rephrasing the same point yet again, you are motivated to align yourself with cosmic principles—along with possessing a strong desire to live in accord with those cosmic principles.

Note that here I am speaking of Sagittarian configurations—it is sign material, in other words, since we are looking at values, motivations, and agendas.

With the ninth house, we move into the realm of behavior. As we think of positive ninth house moral actions, we are talking about living in a way that is oriented to constant stretching and learning in an effort to figure out what life is about.

When we think of ninth house behavior in dark terms, it almost always refers to a need to defend an existing belief system against any threat of growth or evolution.

In both cases, we are talking about the human predilection for *connecting the dots.* That's how we make sense of things. The ninth house is about the behavior of making those kinds of connections and drawing conclusions from the patterns of our experience.

Illustration: *a person might affirm that if you are loving and kind in your disposition toward other people, you will attract loving, kind people into your own life.* Exactly how true that is will probably vary from person to person and situation to situation. But, in my own experience, I think those words are worth saying—and the point is that they would represent the distillation of many individual experiences, along with the detection of the underlying pattern which unifies them.

We can do this well or we can do it badly. In both cases, it represents ninth house behavior.

Passionate engagement with a philosophical orientation is basic to these kinds of configurations. When it is lively and healthy, the quest is ever-deepening. When the ninth house goes dull, it correlates with a mental disorder we might call fundamentalism—and in using that term I am not pointing the finger at Christian fundamentalism in particular; I would as easily include the kinds of scientific fundamentalists who will not open their minds or hearts for a moment to the truth of astrology. There are fundamentalist cynics, and fundamentalist materialists, and fundamentalist existentialists.

The list goes on. Ninth house disorders are certainly not limited to religious fundamentalism.

Everyone has a ninth house and so everyone "connects the dots." If you have planets in your ninth house, you are simply more engaged and passionate about that universal human process.

JONATHAN KELLERMAN

I like murder mysteries. One of my favorite authors in that genre is a former child psychologist, Jonathan Kellerman. One night, while reading one of his books, I realized that in the midst of the mayhem of the good guys chasing the bad guys, he had said something absolutely brilliant. I can't remember in which book this line occurred, but I do remember the exact words: *Religion makes good people better and bad people worse.*

I am humbled by Jonathan Kellerman; here he takes only nine words to embrace the high and the low ends of both Sagittarius and the ninth house.

Zealously avoiding all dogmatism in this highly-charged matter, what can we honestly say about religion? What has it meant in the history of the world? I cannot improve on the fairness of Kellerman's straightforward insight.

Certainly, it would be rigid to claim that religion has always been a force for good—obviously an awful lot of blood has been shed in its holy name.

But religion has also often been a true moral beacon in this crazy, blood-soaked world; it has been the repository of our moral sensibilities and our loftier spiritual aspirations.

It has always, in other words, "made good people better and bad people worse."

If you have a strong ninth house, you are destined to be involved with religion—at least in the very broad sense that we've been using that word. How do you wind up on the right side of Kellerman's line? In a nutshell, here is the critical nutrient for your ninth house planets: *questions*. A constant openness to questioning our existing beliefs is the key to getting the ninth house right. Without questions, the higher religious impulse is quickly corrupted into dogmatism, certainty, and that terrible dead-end that Don Juan called "Clarity."

When opinion stands between us and the possibility of growth, we have collapsed into the lowest form of ninth house behavioral expression.

BACK TO BASICS FOR A MOMENT

There are simple truths about life. Deep down, everyone knows them. We all need to remember them or we wind up lost in the woods.

Examples: Love is better than hate. Practice kindness as much as you can in your everyday affairs. Try not to hurt other beings. When it comes to money and power, keep perspective: you can't take them with you when you go.

Simple ideas, but they are the lighthouses that can guide us across the stormy seas of life. We might call them "natural law." All along, we have been emphasizing that in order for this family of symbols to remain healthy, they must constantly question themselves. This is the only way they can counter their vulnerability to "being right all the time."

And yet there is another point we need to make, and in many ways it is even deeper: Sagittarius is in fact the sign of natural law. Sagittarius is an astrological reference to the part of us that is attuned to these fundamental moral truths about how to live.

The trouble is, the same Bible that tells us not to kill or steal also tells us that it's a sin to eat shellfish. Really—see Leviticus 11:9-12, if you're interested. Here are the verses, straight out of the King James version:

> 9 These shall ye eat of all that are in the waters: whatsoever hath fins and scales in the waters, in the seas, and in the rivers, them shall ye eat.
> 10 And all that have not fins and scales in the seas, and in the rivers, of all that move in the waters, and of any living thing which is in the waters, they shall be an abomination unto you:

> 11 They shall be even an abomination unto you; ye shall not eat of their flesh, but ye shall have their carcases in abomination.
> 12 Whatsoever hath no fins nor scales in the waters, that shall be an abomination unto you

I do not kill or steal, but I guess I have eaten enough oysters in New Orleans to guarantee me a place in hell.

There is a natural law, and there is arbitrary cultural custom masquerading as natural law. The distinction is critical, and it leads us directly to a contemplation of the Sagittarian clan and its relationship to...

MORALITY

You have the misfortune of finding yourself serving on a budget committee. Worse, the committee is locked in a heated disagreement. Everyone has an opinion. Finally it is your turn to speak—or, more precisely, it is time for your Sagittarian ninth house Moon conjunct Jupiter to speak.

"We're arguing about this as if it were a practical problem, but I think that what we are actually facing is a question of what we stand for as an organization."

Those are your words—and immediately everyone agrees that we are indeed facing a question of principle. And then they begin to fight about that instead.

At least it's the right question.

The point of that little anecdote is that *you were the first person at the table to recognize that what was actually at stake was a question of principle*—a question of values, a question of right and wrong. A Sagittarian perspective. You were the first one to place the question in the category of *morality*. With your Sagittarian ninth house Moon conjunct Jupiter, you are psychologically optimized to connect the philosophical dots and thus to be a voice of conscience.

When a child of the Sagittarian clan is in an ethically-charged situation, his or her behavior becomes nearly 100 percent predictable. In general, the behavior of such people is not predictable—they thrive, as we've seen, on the unexpected and the exotic. But in circumstances of moral decision, they will reliably take the action that reflects their values rather than the one that makes them money or affords them some practical advantage.

Underlying all of this, we see two core principles in this third family of Fire symbols: *a fascination with fathoming cosmic principles, and the desire to align one's actions with them.*

To keep it all healthy, every moral principle must be tested against the realities of experience, endlessly. An acute sense of discrimination must arise as well, focused on distinguishing what is truly natural law from that which is simply arbitrary cultural custom. Oysters, anyone?

A splendid way to accomplish that is to open the heart and the mind to people and ideas from different cultures, letting them duke it out with everything we were taught to believe when we were still in the cradle.

JUPITER

The Roman "King of the Gods" rules Sagittarius and the ninth house. That is to say, its energy suffuses them both, and *vice versa.* Classically, Jupiter is "lucky." Among conventional astrologers, one might get a chuckle by wishing aloud for a permanent transit of Jupiter. The idea is that such a transit means that you will always get exactly what you want.

But if your wish came true, just think what you might weigh...

Oscar Wilde once quipped, "I can resist anything except temptation." That's Jupiter too—and his insight brings us to more cautionary perspectives on the "greater Benefic."

We can get into enormous trouble with Jupiter. But let's not throw the baby out with the bathwater just yet. It's complicated. Jupiter represents the impulse to look at life and say Yes. We can make a plausible philosophical case that saying Yes to life beats saying No—but before we dive into life's shark-infested waters, we'd better develop some skill at *aiming* our Yes.

A woman I know confronted her teenage son about some infraction of the household rules. The boy, who was perhaps a little bit too smart for his own good, riposted with the following question: "Mom, at the end of your life, would you rather regret the things that you did or the things that you did not do?"

I believe he was able to dance out of the room before his befuddled mother could stop him.

Lord Jupiter has no doubt about the answer: he would vastly prefer regretting the things he did over living with the feeling that life had slipped through his fingers. Jupiter is the part of you that wants to join the feast of life and to eat heartily. It wants you to live with no regrets. It wants you to say yes.

"All that glitters is not gold." That's solid cautionary Jupiter wisdom. But let's add another fact: *gold glitters.* In that simple juxtaposition of notions, we have an elegant summary of the basic human dilemma with Jupiter.

Bottom line, we need to learn how to sort mere glitter from life's genuine gold.

WINNING A CONTEST

Someone told me about a psychological study. Researchers had allegedly followed up on people who had won gigantic contests and gone from rags to riches overnight. Five years later, 80 percent of them said they wished it had never happened.

A zillion dollars represents a lot of gold, and it certainly glitters brightly. But the family problems, psychological problems, and social problems such an influx of cash generates can be sufficiently catastrophic to outweigh any joy the money would bring.

The mere fact that you're reading this book assures me that I really don't need to explain this to you.

Let's go a little bit further. When I refer to this study while sitting with a client, everybody nods their heads sagaciously. They understand. And then probably 80 percent of them look at me conspiratorially and assure me that even though they understand, they themselves could handle a zillion dollars with no problem.

And in all honesty, dear reader, I feel that I would be just fine with all that money as well.

Glitter is very seductive.

So what's actually good for you? What will actually increase your happiness? The subtle problem with Jupiter is that everyone immediately believes they are perfectly cognizant of the answer. And yet, are we? To what extent have we been bamboozled by the glitter of this world? I suspect the people who say they haven't been bamboozled at all are actually the ones most susceptible to Jupiter's dark seductions.

I once sat with an older woman whose last name was synonymous with fabulous wealth. The subject of her fortune had come up in the context of a reading I was doing for her. With the glint of hard-earned wisdom in her eyes, she said to me, "Steve, money does not buy happiness." Then, after a moment, she added, "It buys pleasure."

Her point was profound, and implicit in her eyes and her words was the fact that she had learned this one the hard way. Simply said, if you don't have happiness, it is very tempting to fill the vacuum with pleasure. And money can buy a lot of it. But pleasure and happiness, even though they resemble each other, are far from being the same thing. It is a pleasure, for example, to buy a fine pair of expensive shoes. But how much pleasure do you derive from buying your fiftieth pair of shoes?

JINGLE BELLS

The gods never die, we just give them different names every few centuries. One form in which the ancient god Jupiter is worshiped in modern Western society is Santa Claus. The correlation is really quite precise. Santa Claus brings us stuff. Santa Claus eats well—and judging by the redness of his nose, I might speculate that he drinks pretty well too.

These are all Jupiter qualities.

What is the most famous quote from Santa Claus? The answer has to be, "Ho, ho, ho." And Jupiter is the part of you that laughs from your belly, radiating celebration, generosity of spirit, and a sense of being at home in your kingdom.

So Jupiter is Santa Claus. But to make the metaphor perfect, we have to add a tweak: this particular Santa Claus has no brains at all. It's just a blind force of nature, designed to give you what you want. The trick in working consciously with Jupiter is to supply the brains yourself. In other words, the trick is that you have to actually know what's good for you.

Everyone thinks they already do. That's the illusion we must penetrate. Just think about a kid on Christmas morning about three hours after he opened the package that he'd been hoping Santa would bring him. His ecstasy at possessing the desired object might have lasted half an hour.

Now he's sitting in the corner, grumpy and out of sorts, for reasons he doesn't quite comprehend.

That's a Jupiter story too.

HOW HAVE YOU SETTLED FOR TOO LITTLE?

That simple, penetrating question really goes to the heart of Jupiter, at least from an evolutionary perspective. We often settle for too little in life. Jupiter is about correcting that error.

Let us add another similar inquiry: how have you underestimated yourself?

These two questions lift us above fortune-telling; they lift us above the idea that during times of Jupiter stimulation, some mechanical law of the universe is going to magically produce your lucky day. These two questions turn our mind inward, reflectively—which is where it truly needs to be under any kind of astrological stimulus.

Your seventeen-year-old daughter announces that even though she loves her boyfriend, she doesn't feel ready to marry him. Is she underestimating herself? Not likely. She's still in her teens. You applaud her wisdom.

But is that "estimation" still true for her ten years down the road? That humble, accurate self-appraisal has served her well for a decade. Jupiter comes along and raises the question of whether she might perhaps have become too attached to it. Maybe she now begins to realize that what had formerly been an accurate estimation of herself has now become inaccurate and limiting. She's moved on, as we all do.

The critical point here is that, while it is of course possible that we might underestimate ourselves because of wounding or shaming psychological experiences, we can also find ourselves at some point simply outgrowing what was previously a grounded sense of our own actual limitations. You might, in other words, have to "grow into" your Jupiter. But wherever it lies in your birthchart, you need to have faith in yourself. That faith is the heart of the matter. Jupiter is the Roman King of the gods. Where it lies, you need to walk like a King, think like a King, and act like one.

Are we talking about arrogance? That is always a risk with Jupiter—but the far greater risk lies in not believing in the far limits of your own potentials and thus coming to the end of life with the feeling that you let something precious slip through your fingers.

A QUICK PERSONAL TALE

I was born with a Sun-Jupiter conjunction in the middle of Capricorn in my second house. All my life, the insecurities and the self-doubt correlated with Capricorn and the second house have had to do battle with Jupiter's big plans.

When I was in college, an understanding came to me in the form of an image. The image was of a ladder that I had to climb in order to achieve any "meaningful success" in my life. The trouble with this ladder was that it had no rungs below about eight feet up. I was not sure if I could reach that first rung, hoist myself up, and thus actually ascend it.

Mysteriously, I also understood the exact nature of that first rung: it was a book that I would write, and which would be widely read.

At the time I had two roommates. One of them eventually became a Christian minister. The other one became a rabbi. I grew up in the Christian tradition, but my inner guides wisely decided this was a question for the rabbi. I shared my vision with him. He didn't like it. He pointed out that getting a book published, let alone having it be widely read, was very difficult. He said that he could easily see me writing a book and that he didn't want to discourage me—but he had a real problem with me defining my life as a failure if I did not successfully get a book into print.

He suggested that my ladder needed some lower rungs, such as contentment in life, meaningful work, maybe a spiritually healthy family.

His words were wise and I took them in appreciatively at the time—but he was wrong. My vision, even though it was demanding, was accurate. It also reflected unerringly the expansive, ambitious nature of Jupiter.

Capricorn requires some kind of great work. The second house brings up issues of self-doubt and the corresponding need to "prove one's self to one's self." Right there is where Jupiter entered the equations: *I had to be careful not to settle for too little.* Simply living a good life—being kind to animals, eating my vegetables, and paying my taxes on time—would be laudable, but insufficient. Jupiter declared that in order for me to feel that I had lived successfully, I had to do something bigger than that.

Twelve strange years later—which is, not coincidentally, one Jupiter cycle—I got the contract to write my first book, *The Inner Sky*, for Bantam Books.

My vision, though demanding, proved accurate.

HEALING OUR ABILITY TO HOPE

Hope, when we really think about it, is a truly frightening thing. We hear, "Don't get your hopes up, you'll just set yourself up for disappointment." That sounds cynical, but it is not always bad advice. *Where Jupiter lies, here's what you're up against: every disappointment that has ever come to you, every time you've ever hoped for something and have not gotten it, every time reality has fallen short of your expectations.* In all those situations, something hardened inside of you—something in you learned to accept the fact that you are going to be served lentils without salt sometimes, and that's just the way it is.

Those are legitimate lessons of Saturn, and we will learn a lot more about them when we get to *The Book of Earth* later in this series. But now we are on a different wavelength. In this branch of the life-giving Fire family, we must never, never give up hope.

And that is a tall order sometimes.

In Aesop's fables, the famous fox cannot leap high enough to get to the grapes, so he decides those grapes were sour anyway. After a while, we become adjusted to disappointment. We start to "like" our lentils without salt.

Every one of us has been battered in various ways. A certain defense against the pain of hope arises in us.

Not to whine bitterly about it, but life does not always conform to the shape of our dreams. How do we recover from disappointment? Here, in *The Book of Fire*, we are looking at the Life-Givers. We are looking at the family of astrological symbols that give us resilience, the ability to bounce back, the courage to hope again. Jupiter is one of them. Classically, Jupiter rules the mystical symbols: Pisces and the twelfth house. A deeper look at those connections is a subject for *The Book of Water*, but let's point to them right now: when it comes to healing our capacity for hope, without some kind of spiritual faith—or better said, without some direct spiritual experience—life is too tough for most of us.

But that's a daunting subject. For now it's enough to honestly acknowledge everything that wounds our ability to hope—and to celebrate the glorious, healing power of the planet Jupiter, that ancient Santa Claus, which can potentially bring its gift and place it under our Christmas tree.

That gift is the restoration of our faith in life.

To claim it, you have to bet on yourself. Where Jupiter lies in your chart, you are capable of extraordinary—and meaningful—accomplishments.

Trust that statement, act as if you believe in yourself, and roll the dice.

6

THE HANDOUT

I first developed the material upon which this book is based for a four-day seminar I offered in one of my astrological apprenticeship programs. That particular meeting happened in Alpine, California, back in 2015. Those programs consist mostly of me talking. After a while, we cut to the chase and draw the names of class members out of a hat in order to test and apply the principles I've been teaching.

Four days is a long time to listen to anyone. Miraculously, to my knowledge, no one has yet fallen asleep in class—or at least snored loudly. To me, the most delicious part of the apprenticeship program lies in what I learn myself as class members respond, telling the stories of their lives and their experiences as reflected in the astrological symbols.

To supplement the oral material, I always offer a short handout. Usually it's just a single page aimed at summarizing in a few words the essential points underlying what I'm teaching. Naturally, there is no way to squeeze the entire contents of a four-day class onto a sheet of paper. The handout is intended only as an aid to memory, nothing more. I hope that in later reviewing it, my students will remember some of the deeper things we explored in class—deeper things very much along the lines of what I am writing about in this book.

I am including that Fire Family handout here, along with some expanded explanations, in hopes that it will aid your memory as well.

THE LIFE-GIVERS: EXPLORING THE FIRE FAMILY

Life's a bitch and then you die. Those words might not constitute a complete cosmology, but we all know what they mean and why people might say them. Who hasn't wondered from time to time if life was actually worth the effort? Given the blows of loss and misfortune, given the disappointments, given the endless holocaust of the daily news, how do we find the strength to go on?

Being true to one's natural path—that is, living the life prescribed by our birthchart—is the ultimate astrological answer. Taking care of the Moon, with its regenerative, healing powers, is a necessary piece of the puzzle too.

Perhaps above all, we must heed the impulses of the life-giving Fire Family of symbols in the chart—Aries, Leo, and Sagittarius, along with their associated houses, plus the planets that rule them. These symbols correlate with everything that directly supports our basic animal vitality—and have you ever heard of an orangutan contemplating suicide?

To Survive...
Aries and Mars:
Antagonist: Fear. That which wants to eat you.
Key Concepts: The raw fire of life. Competitiveness. Assertiveness. Territoriality. The law of the jungle. Self-defense. Protection. Claiming territory. Passion. Punch. Rivalry. Sexual hunger. A rush of adrenaline. Thrills. Clearing the Air. Risk. Blowing out the cobwebs. Defense of boundaries. Being dangerous enough to discourage attack. Having something in your life for which you would willingly die.

To Thrive...
Leo and the Sun
Antagonist: Ghost-life. That which wants to erase you.
Key Concepts: Play. Celebration. Creativity. Vulnerable self-expression. Claiming your right to take up some space. Drawing life-force from others' attention. Meaningful roles. Performance and applause. Attracting appreciation. Visibility. Honest nakedness. Leaving your mark on the world. Stepping into the spotlight. Confident self-ex-

pression. "Pretty clothes." Moving with dignity and elegance. Sparkle; drama; color.

To Expand...
Sagittarius and Jupiter
Antagonist: Boredom. That which wants to numb and mechanize you.
Key Concepts: Belief and faith. Hope. The eternal Quest. Keeping perspective. Staying engaged with life. The need for novelty. Expansion beyond known boundaries. Optimism. The long view. Imputing meaningfulness to events. Happy indulgence. Appetite. Learning and curiosity. Rolling the dice. Improvisation in the face of emergent circumstances. Avoiding death-by-boredom. Adaptation to the unexpected. Standing up for something.

ONE HUNDRED TWENTY-FIVE WORDS TO SAY IT ALL

In a quick summary of what we have explored so far, we have the three Fire families:

* *Aries and Mars,* whose core motive is survival. Before all else, in order to truly shine, we must claim our right to exist. Assertiveness is fundamental to existence. Sometimes you've got to fight to be free.
* *Leo and the Sun,* which aim to take us beyond survival and into actually thriving, expanding, and celebrating our existence. To do that, we need to be seen—and beyond that, to be appreciated and applauded. You have a right to take up some space.
* *Sagittarius and Jupiter,* where we wrestle with transcendent questions of meaning and purpose, questions whose answers give us a broader reason to live. We can only pursue them by boldly stepping into experience and being willing to make mistakes—and being willing to learn from them.

THE ANTAGONISTS

Antagonists arise for each of these energies. These are the catabolic and entropic energies of the mind. They are the Shadow. They are the ancient enemy. In extreme form, they are what medieval monks cringing in their monastic cells called demons.

* The Antagonist that arises to battle our healthy response to Aries and Mars is *fear*. We are all naturally afraid of anything that wants to eat us. In creating the handout, I wondered about my use of that exact phrasing—that which "wants to eat you" is not intended narrowly as a literal reference to a mountain lion dining on your flesh, but rather to all the things that would destroy you and bar you from any meaningful manifestation in the world.
* The Antagonist to Leo and the Sun is what I call *ghost life*. Down that sad road, you are physically here in this world, but you're not really here. Your soul is not manifesting in your life, in other words. You haven't been willing to risk that kind of nakedness or vulnerability. You may be rich. You may be beautiful. But you are generic; it's as if your entire existence is designed around a plan to disguise yourself as someone no one would want to hurt or insult. You may shine—but your soul remains hidden, despite whatever seductive appearances you might generate. The Antagonist is that which wants to erase you.
* For Sagittarius and Jupiter, the Antagonist is *boredom*—a self-imposed tedium that slowly leaches the life out of a human being. Life thrives on experience and requires it. The Antagonist we call boredom usually approaches the gates of our soul hidden inside a Trojan horse—one that almost always goes by respectable names: practicality, maturity, common sense, respectability, financial realism. None of those are dirty words, but we must consider the price we pay in order to claim them. For Sagittarius and Jupiter, that which wants to numb and mechanize you is the ancient Antagonist. And in some of its many forms, that Antagonist would be mis-read as a set of moral virtues.

THE QUOTATIONS

To try to illuminate Aries and Mars, I quoted Anaïs Nin, a wonderful writer who's sadly often unrecognized today. She was born on February 21, 1903, in Neuilly-sur-Seine, France. Some of you may know her as a paramour and patroness of the long-banned American author Henry Miller.

"Life shrinks or expands in proportion to one's courage."

Nin had a Libran Mars in her first house, so I suspect she had lived these words before she wrote them.

For Leo and the Sun, I choose a hilarious line from none other than Oscar Wilde, who is probably quoted more widely than anyone outside the Bible, William Shakespeare, or possibly Mark Twain.

"Be yourself; everyone else is already taken."

I love how Wilde's words here underscore the centrality of honesty, emotional nakedness, sincerity, and vulnerability to any healthy response to this branch of the Fire family. Appropriately, Oscar Wilde had the Moon in Leo.

When I was looking for good quotations to illustrate Aries and Mars, I started by searching through the words of Gen. George S. Patton, one of the more colorful heroes in World War II. I liked the one by Anais Nin a little bit better, but Patton came through for Sagittarius and Jupiter.

"Live for something rather than die for nothing."

How sad it would be to have nothing loom larger in your own mind than yourself! At the risk of being melodramatic here, can we imagine the arid emptiness of a life in which a person had nothing for which he or she would willingly die? The aim is not to die; the point has more to do with having something in our life for which we are willing to live, something that gives meaning even to the more difficult moments of our existence. Patton, by the way, had Mercury in Sagittarius, ruling his Gemini Ascendant—thus a major Sagittarian influence played a central role in his chart.

PART TWO

MASTERING THE ALCHEMICAL MARRIAGE OF SIGN, HOUSE, AND PLANET

The word Archetype has a lofty, transcendental ring to it, and well it should: the astrological archetypes are the basic DNA of the universe and of our consciousness within it.

Still, it helps us to keep perspective if we remember that no human being is ever truly an archetype. Each one of us is in fact vastly more complex than that. This is because every one of us is composed of an ironical, ambiguous synthesis of all the archetypes at once. What varies—and what makes us vary from each other—is simply the mixture.

Learning to mix the members of the Fire Family with each other and with the rest of the astrological symbols is the essence of the following chapters. Here we learn how to put it all together.

Master what we have explored in these pages so far and you are a philosopher; master what follows, and you are well on your way to becoming a working astrologer.

7

SYNTHESIS I: PUTTING A PLANET IN A SIGN

As astrologers, we speak glibly of Mars and Jupiter and the Sun, but in a very real way none of them exist except as abstractions. There really is no such thing as Mars—only Mars in a specific astrological context. Ditto for the Sun and Jupiter and the rest of the planets, not to mention the lunar nodes and the angles and everything else.

All that I have written about these three Fire clans presumably has some relevance to your experience. But we each experience them in different ways. Some of those differences can be attributed to karma and individuality. An understanding of much of it, however, can be derived from technical astrological analysis.

Maybe your Mars lies in Gemini in the eleventh house. That's quite distinct from having Mars in Cancer in the fifth house. The context of sign and house condition the archetypal energy that we blithely call "Mars"—and the modifying impact of that conditioning is so extraordinarily powerful that the actions of these two expressions of Mars bear very little resemblance to each other.

Mars can be in any one of the twelve signs; each one is a different beast. And any of those twelve different expressions of Mars can manifest behaviorally via any one of the twelve houses. Twelve times twelve is 144. In a very real sense, there are that many distinct versions of Mars. We need to learn to understand each one and to describe them fluently and helpfully.

Even that "144" is an oversimplification—we haven't even mentioned the aspects other planets make to Mars. What if it's squared by Neptune or opposed by Jupiter? Aspects such as those flavor the archetype too.

Ultimately, the real craft at the heart of astrology lies in global, integrative synthesis of everything in the chart.

SIGNS AS MOTIVATIONS OR AGENDAS

Astrological mastery begins with one fundamental skill: synthesizing a planet, its house and its sign. When you do that, you have truly become an astrologer. Before you fully embody that skill, you are essentially a parrot repeating lists of keywords. Learning those keywords is helpful and necessary; they are the foundation. But it is in artful synthesis that the astrologer's consciousness soars above the details and the chart really begins to sing.

Adrenaline hits your bloodstream; welcome to Mars energy. We're all familiar with it. To some degree, we all have that fire in our bellies. But what triggers it? What do we have to say to you in order to see fire in your eyes? And what purpose does that fire serve? What are its interests or its particular fears? What are its motivations? What values animate it? What goals excite it? What are its deepest fears—or the natures of its particular demons?

It's the sign in which Mars lies that answers those questions for us. Let's demonstrate how to put planet and sign together with an example.

EXAMPLE #1: MARS IN CANCER

I choose that configuration because if I started with Mars in a Fire sign, it would be too simple; the energies would harmonize in far more obvious ways since they are members of the same family. But I can readily imagine somebody who is just beginning to learn astrology feeling stumped by Mars in Cancer, thinking that Mars is so fierce, while Cancer is vulnerable and quiet, so how could they possibly work together?

Such a student might even be forgiven for imagining that this is a "bad" placement for Mars—in fact, our astrological ancestors came to pretty much that same conclusion: they described Cancer as the "Fall" of Mars, opposite Capricorn, which was called its "Exaltation."

In evolutionary astrology, there's no room for that kind of language. For one thing, it conveys discouragement to our hapless astrological clients. Even if you know nothing of astrology, how would you feel if you heard that your Mars was "in its Fall?" More fundamentally, it is imperative that we remember that every astrological configuration can potentially serve a positive purpose. The ones that were historically viewed as unfortunate—planets in their Fall or in their Detriment—are, in actuality, simply more complex, more fraught with paradox, and therefore more tolerant of life's ambiguity.

Mars-fashion, let me add that the kinds of people who assume that anything complex is bad are also generally people who breathe through their mouths.

Mars in Cancer? At the most primal level, we recognize that this is telling us that the sign Cancer simply supplies the *underlying agenda of values* for that Mars. The question becomes, what is important to Cancer? That's a complex subject with many dimensions—remember, with the twelve signs of the zodiac, we are dividing the entire universe into twelve boxes.

As we unpack this combination of sign and planet, let's start with something absolutely fundamental: Cancer represents the drive to *nurture, to heal and to protect*. It is ruled by the Moon, and thus it has the nature of the Great Mother.

Imagine a family on a picnic. Their new baby, ten weeks old, is lying on a blanket while Mom prepares the deviled eggs. Meanwhile, Dad is off exploring some rocky crags with his son. Baby makes a sound; Mother turns around to check—and immediately adrenaline floods her bloodstream. Three coyotes are beginning to drag the blanket with the baby on it off into the brush.

What's a mother to do? She attacks those coyotes with her bare hands, screaming. Seeing this fierce and terrible embodiment of Mars-in-Cancer energy, the coyotes wisely and rapidly retreat, seeking their lunch elsewhere.

Is there anywhere in nature a more terrifying apparition of warrior energy than a mother who feels her young are threatened?

This vivid image illustrates our key principle: the sign supplies the agenda for the planet. The motivation to nurture and protect is what animates the warrior function. Mars in Cancer, in and of itself, has no desire to climb mountains. It holds no fascination for skydiving or spelunking. All that Fire is directed toward protecting the home and loved ones.

There's much more that might be said about Mars in Cancer. We've also completely ignored the potentially negative side of it, which must always be part of the global picture with any astrological configuration. But in our simple illustration of Mom versus the coyotes, we zero in on the heart of the matter: signs give purpose and direction to the basic planetary energy. That's the fundamental principle.

EXAMPLE #2: MARS IN CAPRICORN

Let's shuffle the deck. Mars can be in any one of the twelve signs. In each case, it's almost as if switching signs turns Mars into an entirely different planet. Simply observing human behavior, you might have no idea that there was any unifying archetype underlying all of these possible expressions.

Let's expand our horizons by contemplating Mars in Capricorn, the sign of its (alleged) Exaltation.

There's a keyword for Capricorn that you almost inevitably read in the first paragraph of any Sun Sign astrology book: *practicality*. And it's true—if you want to know the sum of two plus two, go find yourself a Capricorn and ask. You will get the right answer—and probably some explanation as well.

Capricorn likes to get things done. Mars agrees—hence the notion of "exaltation." These two symbols get along like peanut butter and jelly. That metaphor actually says something quite precise: peanut butter and jelly are of course very different substances, but many of us feel that each one brings out the best qualities in the other.

And that's how it works with Exaltation—and specifically with Mars in Capricorn. Mars supplies the courage, the initiative, and the assertiveness, while Capricorn supplies sober, clear strategy and long-term self discipline. Together, these two can really keep their eye on the prize. They can face down any obstacle, or at least figure out a way around it.

One might immediately imagine this to be a "good" combination. Here's the fine print: much depends upon the nature of the prize they are chasing.

Let's think more deeply about Capricorn, for starters. Capricorn has a natural correlation with winter. If you're living close to nature, winter is a fierce and formidable enemy. How do you survive it? You don't pick a fight with it, even though fights are often the predilection of Mars. Winter is a time of the survival of fittest—but the fittest are not always the biggest or the meanest. The fittest are the ones who see reality most clearly, accept it as it is, and adapt to it rationally. That's the soul of Capricorn. Mars can be seduced into a fight; Capricorn cannot.

Speaking of cold, clear rationality, here's another Capricorn perspective: terrible things can happen at any moment. As negative as that sounds, it remains true. Some terrible things are predictable and you can therefore prepare for them. Some terrible things are not predictable—or perhaps they're so overwhelming that no form of preparation could allow you to survive them. One result is that fundamental to the mood of Capricorn is a chronic, low level of worry. The possibility of doom is always on the back burner. It is commonly and correctly said that 90 percent of the things we spend our time worrying about never actually happen. Capricorn's response to that? Ten percent of those things actually *do* happen. So, from the perspective of Capricorn's value system, rationally, the smart thing to do is to always be prepared for the worst.

There are obvious psychological pitfalls connected with that line of reasoning—and they constitute much of the Shadow side of this sign of the zodiac. We'll explore it much more deeply when we get to *The Book of Earth*. Suffice it here to say that Capricorn understands that winter is very hard on romantics. Just getting through it is a Great Work. And that term—a Great Work—is the essence of the highest expression of Capricorn.

So what energies and values animate Mars when it finds itself in this sign of the zodiac? All of that martial courage and intensity are focused on a distant, noble horizon. The Inner Warrior is in search of a Great Work worthy of his or her great heart.

Literally climbing a mountain is a fine example. I like the image because it represents *difficulty* (Capricorn) and is also something that requires *courage* (Mars.) So let's go with that metaphor.

How long does it take to climb Mount Everest? A literal-minded person might answer, "two or three weeks door to door, provided the weather cooperates."

The wise old mountaineer has a deeper and more Mars-in-Capricorn answer: *Years.*

The point is that if you want to get to the top of Mount Everest, you will need to start with some less formidable peaks. Capricorn-fashion, you commit to the great work for the long term. And if you are wise, you will spend many nights worrying about everything that could possibly go wrong. That's because Capricorn reminds Mars that 10 percent of your fears will actually come true, and you'd better be prepared.

Climbing a mountain is obviously only one illustration of this sign/planet synthesis. We might as easily speak of writing a novel. That's a more intellectual Great Work, but it too is a long-term commitment that requires the combination of Capricornian discipline and Martial courage.

Similarly, we could speak of staying married. Or meditating in the Himalayan cave for three years, three months, and three days.

Any expression of courage that requires sustained discipline, cautious but undaunted realism, and a compelling fascination with difficulty illustrates the synthesis of Mars and Capricorn.

As always, there's a tremendous diversity of expression with any sign/planet combination. These are archetypes, after all—those giant boxes we've been talking about .

By knowing the houses and aspects involved, we can make giant steps towards focusing all of this more precisely. But there's always an individual, creative dimension in our response to these energies as well. When I meet with a client for the first time—especially one who turns out to be fully engaged in the process of living—one of the delights of the work lies in simply seeing "how they are doing it." I never know in advance, any more than I know in advance the plot of the next book of my favorite novelist.

Let's work with one more example of Mars in a sign.

EXAMPLE #3: MARS IN SAGITTARIUS

When Mars lies in Sagittarius, we've brought together two branches of the Fire Family. There is a natural affinity between these two symbols. They support each other and easily share common agendas, assumptions and desires. Unlike what we explored a little while ago with Mars in Cancer, this magnetic attraction can make for a tremendously *efficient* expression of energy.

The cautionary note is that it can also make for shared blind spots.

Sagittarius, as we have seen, desires a broad experience of life. Its darkest antagonists are boredom and tedium. Adventure is a useful Sagittarian word—and that statement becomes even more reliable when daring Mars is added to the mix. We aren't talking about "Adventures in Shopping" here, either—a Sagittarian Mars is going to find that particular notion a bit tepid. Any meaningful use of the word "adventure" implies an element of risk, along with some voluntary exposure to the uncertainties of life.

The scuba tank is strapped to your back. The grizzled old dive master intones, "I believe them sharks have cleared out. It's been, what? Ten minutes? I believe it's safe to go get wet now."

And you shrug your shoulders and you dive in. "Hey, everybody knows there are sharks in the sea—seeing a few doesn't change that anymore than not seeing them does."

This image embodies a Sagittarian Mars at its best. It represents a willingness to dive, not only into shark-infested waters, but into life itself. The underlying Sagittarian agenda is to bravely pack as much experience into our minutes and hours on this earth as we possibly can. In so doing, whether we know it or not, we are seeking the meaning of life. And we are wise enough to understand that our enemies on that path lie in succumbing to the tempting traps of certainty, predictabillty, and self-satisfied lassitude in the face of the brevity of life.

Mars adds a physicality to the mix. To think of Mars as only relating to the physical body would be far too narrow, but it's also accurate to recognize that this planet really likes to keep your body in it. That's one reason why I often use physical metaphors when I'm illustrating Mars energy. A moment ago, I referred to scuba diving. A few paragraphs back, I had us climbing Mount Everest. That kind of imagery sets the right tone, putting us in the right mood for understanding martial energy.

But of course Mars also has mental and spiritual harmonics. Those are critically important too, perhaps even more important, and we must not forget them.

Pursuant of that idea, let's imagine that you've been studying evolutionary astrology. Synchronicity begins to work with your Sagittarian Mars, attracting experience of a foreign nature. You befriend a person from India. She asks you about your birthday. You tell her, "I'm a Scorpio, I was born on Halloween."

And she says, "No, you're a Libra."

The next thing you know, you're learning Vedic astrology, which uses an entirely different zodiac. And your Indian friend, using her "Jyotish" style of astrology, is giving you helpful, relevant advice and producing compelling results.

What you do think? How can your wrap your head around the idea of two different zodiacs? Perhaps your first thought is, "Steven Forrest will kill me."

(I wouldn't!—Hey, light is a particle and light is a wave and if one is true, the other cannot be. That's the way it is. I have no trouble accepting that the intelligence of the universe can express itself simultaneously through two different zodiacs.)

The Sagittarian mind wants answers. It would like them to be clear. With Mars in the mix, we add some "fight" to the stew. But would you kill anyone to defend one zodiac over another?

With Mars in Sagittarius, you attract this kind of disjunctive data into your life. Can you digest it and thus become more transparently attuned to the actual realities of the universe—or will your inner warrior make an unholy alliance with your inner fundamentalist as you set out to make your Indian friend wrong?

HERE COMES THE SUN

Let's move on to the second fire family, symbolized by the Sun, Leo and the fifth house. The underlying principles of synthesis are exactly the same here as the ones we just explored with Mars. Once we understand the basic solar function—the formation of a coherent identity—we will see how the Sun is given direction and an overriding agenda by the sign it occupies.

Earlier in the book we learned that taking care of the Sun is the secret of sanity and vitality. Being true to the Sun is the path to authenticity, integrity, and a meaningful life. The Sun is the *ego*—but we have to be careful with that word. Here, it doesn't imply inflated self-importance, only a clear sense of one's identity and one's values.

Bottom line, if we fail to take care of the Sun, we are as crazy as loons and, on top of that, so soul-tired and unmotivated that we cannot even make interesting mistakes and learn things that way.

SHOULD PEOPLE MOVE TO ECUADOR?

...and have you ever heard a more boneheaded question? There's no way to answer it. A critical piece of the puzzle is missing: *who are we talking about?*

Earlier in the book, in the chapter introducing the Leo clan, we asked a similarly stupid question: should a person be married? Everyone's natural values are different; those differences have to be respected—and they can be understood with some precision by knowing what sign the natal Sun occupies. For one individual, moving to Ecuador—or being married—might be a terrific choice. For another, it could be a psychological disaster. I will grossly oversimplify here to make a core point about the Sun: if your Sun is in Sagittarius, moving to Ecuador is a brilliant idea. If your Sun is in Cancer, it's a dumb idea.

Again, it comes down to values. And the word "values," while sounding a bit dry, is perhaps the single most central concept in understanding the healthy function of the astrological Sun. As we just saw with Mars, a planet is really nothing but an abstraction. It only takes on humanly recognizable meaning when we place it in the context of the birthchart. Otherwise, it is simply an archetype—a lofty sounding term, but actually something far more skeletal than a living, breathing human being.

The Sun might represent life-force. By putting it in a sign, we give that life-force something to live for. That is the heart of the matter.

EXAMPLE #4: THE SUN IN LEO

Let's dive into the meaning of the Sun in the sign Leo, the sign it rules. That means their natures are very similar. For that reason, this is a particularly strong position for the Sun. Everything else being equal, Leo people *shine*—but of course, "everything else being equal" is an essential clause here. Leo people, just like the other eleven signs, are a diverse group.

Leo is usually dished up in popular astrology as self-important, endlessly auto-referential, and obsessed with its hair. The reality is typically quite different. Leo is the lion, and the lion is famously the King of the Beasts. Now, if we met a king, we would probably be surprised if he displayed the kind of noisy "notice me, notice me" insecurity that is typically attributed to representatives of this sign. We would imagine the King instead to radiate a quality of *quiet dignity*. We would anticipate an aura of *presence* around such a person—and no further need for him to underscore it.

It works for queens too. If the Queen walks into the room, we all naturally stand up. She doesn't have to ask for that. That's Leo.

There are things that are invisible because they are so faint, like a candle burning fifteen miles away. And there are things that are invisible because they are so bright, such as the face of the Sun. To call the Sun "invisible" seems a bit strange; of course since we can see it perfectly well. But the point is that we cannot really *look* at it. We'd be blinded by the light.

Similarly, the outward appearance of people with the Sun in Leo often exists in sharp tension to their inner experience of themselves. Outwardly, like kings or queens, they often seem to radiate well-being and self-possession. Inwardly, the story can be very different. The exact nature of that story derives from the rest of the chart, but the core point remains: the shine of Leo conceals deeper waters.

In evolutionary terms, the purpose of having the Sun in Leo is the restoration of a feeling of trust relative to life, comfort relative to human society, and a simple, unambiguous joy at being alive. Underlying these ideas we find a metaphysical mystery: in a prior lifetime, there was some betrayal. Something dark happened—something that damaged trust, comfort, and joy.

To heal from that damage, anyone with the Sun in Leo must take the risk of genuine, vulnerable self-expression—and you're probably recognizing that these are the same principles we introduced earlier in the book as we began to understand the Leo clan as a whole. Here, with the Sun in Leo, we are linking the pursuit of these values to the elemental solar stakes of sanity, authenticity, and vitality.

We can fairly say that such a person "needs attention." But that attention swings us right back to the notion of genuine, vulnerable self-expression—without that risk, Leo is all noise and posturing. No soul-healing happens at all.

EXAMPLE #5: JUPITER IN AQUARIUS

Jupiter represents hope and expansion and possibility. It correlates with our ability to dream big and to live large. There are obvious potential pitfalls connected with those exuberant attitudes, but let's not dismiss them out-of-hand. Jupiter can indeed be "lucky." Jupiter suggests that we should doubt everything except our own limits.

As we saw earlier, the key questions with Jupiter are: how have I been underestimating myself? And: how have I settled for too little?

The right answers to those questions can carry us to the stars

But which stars? We must choose wisely. As the saying goes, all that glitters is not gold. The sign in which we find Jupiter supports us in making that critical discrimination. An ungrounded Jupiter—that is to say, one lacking roots in the guiding wisdom of the sign it occupies—can almost always be found chasing mere glitter, and probably catching it too. Reflecting approximately the same scope of imagination as a pornographer, such a loose-cannon expression of Jupiter goes after money, fame, and the applauding approval of similarly empty souls.

It's like a diet of cotton candy.

As ever, the zodiacal sign of Jupiter gives it a worthy agenda and a set of potentially healthy motivations and interests. It aims Jupiter in a direction that actually benefits the soul.

To illustrate this notion, let's contemplate Jupiter in Aquarius. This is the sign of the rebel or the genius—or the criminal, for that matter. Outsiders all. Aquarius represents the part of us that hears a different drummer, follows the road less traveled. *When the integration of Jupiter and Aquarius is healthy, a certain questioning of authority and a critique of "received wisdom" animate Jupiter's definitions of any truly meaningful success.*

We might, for example, imagine a successful attorney. Last year, she made a million dollars. She lives in a McMansion in a gated community. Her walls are beige and her suits are gray. Topping it off, she is conventionally married to a conventional man.

And when she looks in the mirror, she fears she is beginning to look like a character in a television ad for an overpriced automobile.

She realizes that this conventional tableau of success only embarrasses her. It has nothing to do with her real nature—only with how she has been misled by the world into believing that having all that "stuff" will make her happy. It is an Aquarian moment.

Grown tired of her diet of cotton candy, she quits her job, leaves the husband, cashes in her chips, and focuses on what she has always wanted to do: she moves to Paris and begins work on her novel. Just as easily, I could say that she begins to play the bagpipes—and that ten years later, she is a sought-after piper.

She has taken a 99-percent cut in pay—and she's happier than she has ever been in her life. Bottom line: *unconventional Aquarian values have now reshaped her definition of success.* She realizes that in becoming a successful attorney, she'd underestimated herself.

Being an attorney—what a waste of a good bagpipe player!

Naturally I had fun writing those words. They have a nice Aquarian rebel-ring to them. Bless our attorney for providing us with a fine example of how the Aquarian process of individuation can liberate Jupiter from a gold-plated, air-conditioned, first-class cabin—in a nightmare.

AND A FEW MORE JUPITERS FOR THE ROAD...

But what if we instead imagine Jupiter in Virgo? Here the agenda underlying a healthy expression of that energy is to have some craft at which we are skilled and which is of service to other beings. Unlike our previous example, a person with Jupiter in Virgo might thrive as an attorney—especially the kind of attorney who viewed the work as a service rather than as a path to wealth.

Jupiter in Gemini? Here is someone for whom any truly meaningful form of success entails the Geminian process of finding her own voice and having it heard.

Jupiter in Cancer? Let's honor the estimable success of raising a healthy family—a simple thing to say, but we should celebrate the soul victory it entails and the warm feelings that go along with it. With Jupiter in Cancer, we might also imagine a person who blossoms as a healer in some sense of the word.

You get the idea: once you understand the nature of a planet, you need to give it an authentic, compelling reason to live. You need to give it goals and values that are sufficiently meaningful to animate it for life.

That's where the zodiacal sign enters the equations.

8

SYNTHESIS II: PUTTING A PLANET IN A HOUSE

Life is complicated. The crown jewel of astrology lies in its ability to mirror that complexity back to us in a somewhat more schematic fashion than the tangled realities we experience directly. Hopefully, that mirroring allows us to make wiser decisions, better aligning ourselves with the cosmic principles that can guide us through life's apparent chaos and randomness.

If, out of mental laziness, we try to make astrology easy, we can succeed. And "easy" astrology can still be helpful. As we saw in the previous chapter, just knowing that you are "a Gemini" or "a Leo" can help you make the right decision about "moving to Ecuador"—or not.

But as we welcome astrology's full complexity, the mirror into which we are gazing becomes crystal-clear and brilliantly illuminated. Albert Einstein's famous quote immediately leaps to mind: "Everything should be made as simple as possible, but not simpler."

Let's actively welcome astrology's complexity by adding the twelve houses to the mix. Watch our mirror become twelve times clearer.

As we move from the realm of signs into the realm of houses, we're no longer talking about psychological motivations and emotional agendas. We are talking about action. We are talking about behavior—the things that we do. Houses add the active ingredient to the astrological formula. They reflect our biographies more than they reflect the inner life of the soul. In a material sense, houses simply "work." If signs are about Being, then the houses reflect Doing. They are like *yin* and *yang*—interdependent. In the ancient alchemy of consciousness, what we do—what we experience—flows into our consciousness and becomes our Being. And Being (sign energy) manifests as behavior, with Being underlying all of our active, outward choices.

In the last chapter, we explored how to integrate a planet with the sign it occupies. We thus established an evolutionary intention, filling it out with an agenda of values, needs, and attitudes. But in practical terms, how do we go about fulfilling that intention? What are our actual methods? What means for achieving that end will prove the most efficient and the most skillful? How do we roll up our sleeves and *actually do it,* in other words?

These are house questions.

Sometimes we hurl ourselves into a situation and we learn by improvising. We "make it up as we go along." We learn by immersion. That's another perspective on how the astrological houses work.

Here's an illustration: Once I was down in Mexico City teaching a class. I've got high school Spanish, polished by a couple of summers many years ago hoeing the fields with Puerto Rican laborers. When people ask me if I speak Spanish, I merrily say, *"Sí, como un niño de cuatro años."* ("Yes - like a four-year-old child.")

There I was in a restaurant in Mexico, in conversation with my Mexican friends, barely following the thread of what they were saying. I lamented out loud that my Spanish was so crude that it was embarrassing, and how much I wished it could improve. There followed some rapid-fire conversation and some shy giggles. In response to my quizzical look, they admitted that they'd all decided that what I needed was a Mexican lover. Alas, there were no volunteers and it went no further than that.

It's a fun story to recap, but there is serious strategy behind it. The point is that my Mexican friends' suggestion would have worked. If you dive into an intimate relationship with a foreigner, your language skills are going to improve like crazy. Nothing works so well—in language studies and everywhere else—as *immersion.* "Doing" quickly folds back into "being," in other words. Understanding the eternal conversation between these two poles of our experience—the inward and the outward—is the key to mastering what's probably the single most essential practical skill in the craft of astrology: the synthesis of planet, sign, and house.

As we saw in the previous chapter, each planet, each sign, and each house is simply an abstraction. Merely an archetype. In a very real sense, they do not exist at all in the human world. They are fictional fabrications—intellectual constructs designed to represent reality in simplified, graphic fashion.

What actually exists in your consciousness—and what probably keeps you awake at four o'clock in the morning—is never Gemini or Venus, but rather the ancient, living triads formed among these three families of symbols.

These are the actual strands of DNA that animate human life.

As we did in the previous chapter, let's now immerse ourselves in some practical experience. Let's put the three Fire planets into the context of the twelve houses. For a change, we'll work through them backwards this time, starting with Jupiter. And, as before, we will go deeply into a few examples rather than attempting to create a tweet for every possible planet-house combination.

Fear not: those tweets come later in the book.

EXAMPLE #1: JUPITER IN THE SIXTH HOUSE

So, what's the King of the gods doing in the house of servants? At first, this seems like an awkward combination, reflecting the idea that Jupiter is "in detriment" in Virgo, the sixth sign.

No worry: there is nothing wrong with this configuration, and much potential for joy in it.

The sixth house correlates with behaviors that reveal our skills and our competence. While the sign Virgo reflects the *emotional need* to be good at something, in the sixth house the rubber meets the road: we practice our skills in the real world and are appreciated for our competence.

In practice, the critical concept with the sixth house is *finding right work.* We just have to let that term "right work" breathe a bit in order to be perfectly accurate here. "Work" implies employment—something we are paid to do. And often the sixth house really does boil down to "Monday morning." But we can have meaningful responsibilities and areas of competence which do not come with a paycheck. Let's make sure that we include them in our understanding of the scope of the sixth house as well.

As we learned previously, the most critical question with Jupiter is always "how have I been underestimating myself?" Where Jupiter lies, you really need to bet big on yourself. You need to believe in yourself, and act that way. Right away, with Jupiter in the sixth house, we recognize that such a person needs to think grandly in terms of his or her innate potential to make a difference in the lives of other people. To find your right work, you need to "think big." The word "ambition" has relevance here—but we need to emphasize that true sixth house ambition is oriented towards effectiveness in addressing human needs. There's a fundamental caring—and a fundamental humility—underlying all healthy sixth house behaviors. It has nothing to do with any desire to see your face in *People* magazine.

In this chapter, I am focusing on the fine art of putting a planet in a house. The sign the planet is in naturally plays a critical role in our understanding as well, but I want to avoid muddying the water at this point. So let me just bow briefly here in the direction of Jupiter's sign without being totally distracted by it. As you might imagine, the sign in which we find that sixth house Jupiter gives important guidance about the nature of the right work. If, for example, Jupiter is in Cancer, then we might consider some form of nurturing or healing—those are the underlying motivations with the sign Cancer. If Jupiter lies in Aquarius, then we'd be looking at a service that had some unusual quality to it—something of an "alternative" nature, so to speak. Were Jupiter in Gemini, language skills would play a critical role. And so on.

The sixth house, as the house of servants, refers to *all human relationships characterized by a fundamental inequality between two people.* At the low end of the spectrum we find the tyrannical boss or the slave master—and of course the poor souls who have to deal with that oppressive situation. But the high end of the sixth house is very beautiful: it refers to the *mutually beneficial relationship between the mentor and the student.* Historically, the sixth house was a reference to aunts and uncles and their relationships with their nieces and nephews. We might equally think of the guru and the disciple, or the master craftsperson and the apprentice.

When you have a planet—any planet—in the sixth house, you're on this earth in part to seek your teachers. And, because of the way synchronicity works, those teachers are also looking for you.

How do you find them? When the planet in the sixth house is Jupiter, the first step in finding those who will be your evolutionary catalysts lies in simply not underestimating yourself. "Ask, and ye shall receive" is always a critical element with Jupiter. We might, as an illustration, imagine a yoga teacher here in the United States. She has always dreamed of traveling to India to study with a master yogi who offers year-long training sessions. But of course moving to India for a year presents many obstacles and difficulties. Her guardian angels—or we might say the great god Jupiter—are praying that she says "roll the dice" and makes the trip anyway. That's the behavior we would see if she were no longer "underestimating herself" or "settling for too little."

The catalytic impact of that master yogi upon her consciousness would be the trigger that allowed her to develop into the spiritual teacher she came to this earth to become.

This chain of sixth house cause-and-effect has one more truly elegant link: after a while, our yoga teacher becomes a master yogi herself. Eventually, her teacher in India passes away. But the flame burns on; only now she is the one who is carrying it. The sense of continuity and *lineage* is the bright diamond in the heart of the sixth house.

And what if she does not go to India? She still has Jupiter in the sixth house, but its avenue of positive expression has been blocked. That leaves only lower expressions available. Jupiter expands what it touches, and the sixth house is about work. And so even though her heart is with the practice of yoga, she finds herself working longer hours as a waitress in a restaurant, just trying to get by. She probably also, via synchronicity, encounters the out-picturing of dark Jupiter: the owner of the restaurant is a petty tyrant.

EXAMPLE #2: SUN IN THE THIRD HOUSE

Taking care of the Sun, as we saw earlier, is the secret of sanity and authenticity. Along with the sign it occupies, the Sun represents the core set of values that animate any life worth living. The Sun is our vitality and animal energy. Traveling down that good road, we experience an abundance of life-force, heightened recuperative powers, and strengthened immune response.

Topping it off, if we heed the Sun's message, we will have a "sunny" disposition.

I have always found that last phrase entertaining. Educated people understand the astrological origins of words such as "martial," "jovial," "saturnine," or "mercurial." But "sunny?" That connection seems to have been forgotten. And the reason behind that lapse is revealing: few astrology books today reference the relationship of a healthy response to the Sun to the simple idea of vitality. Typically, the astrological Sun is described as "ego" or "identity"—terms which are helpful and accurate, but which ignore the equally important dimension of the Sun's role in our maintaining a spirited response to existence. In a nutshell, the Sun is the universe's own natural antidepressant.

What happens when we find the Sun in the third house?

Classically, the third house is related to communication. And that's a good place to start: with the Sun in the third house, your path through life is intimately bound to language. You were probably born with considerable skills there, at least potentially. Developing and honoring those skills is the path of fire for you. The twin archetypes of *teacher* and *storyteller* are likely to make themselves visible in your biography. When healthy, your solar ego will naturally constellate around those kinds of themes.

Going deeper into the third house, we realize that language must rest upon the foundation of *though*t. And thought, in turn, must rest upon the foundation of *perception*. If we perceive nothing, we have nothing to think about and nothing much to say. This triad of notions—language, thought, and perception—lies right in the center of our understanding of any third house configuration.

And it all starts with perception.

With the Sun in the third house, if you're true to your essence, you will experience a compelling hunger for fresh perception. There's a simple word for that drive: *curiosity*. All meaningful paths forward for you in life reflect an open-minded hunger to learn that which you do not already know.

A writer might be criticized for sitting in a bar at four o'clock one afternoon, nursing a martini. His defense might well be that he's actually there "to gather material." And he actually might be doing just that: he might be listening to conversations around him, soaking up the ambience of life in that particular bar, watching the other patrons for those tiny little gestures and expressions that encapsulate their personalities. He might hit upon a catchy phrase coming from the mouth of a stranger, and that phrase might appear later in the novel our writer is creating.

Or he might just finish his martini and go home, none the wiser.

The point is, our writer doesn't know. He opens up to experience. He does not succumb to the neurotic drive to control the future by predicting it or limiting its capacity to surprise him—or to fail him. In good third house Sun fashion, he is *seeking fresh perceptions.*

If you're born with the Sun in the third house, you too are "gathering material" in this lifetime. Those perceptions, driven by curiosity, trigger the thoughts that later blossom as your speech. That "speech" can take many forms: literal conversation, teaching the class, or even writing a book.

Here's a piece of the puzzle I learned the hard way. I am a word guy, with Mercury in my third house. That particular dimension of my own nature blinded my own third house perceptions for a while. Then I began to see a pattern: *I knew a lot of fine photographers with planets in the third house.* And I realized that photographs can tell a story.

Going further, over the years I've developed client relationships with several figures in Hollywood in the film industry. These are "behind the camera" people, not the pretty faces. Many of them have strong third house concentrations too—they are the storytellers in the modern world.

The words "language" and "communication" are always helpful to roll out when you're talking to a client with the Sun in the third house. Here in the twenty-first century, I've found it helpful to add a third word: *media.*

Born with the Sun in the third house? If you were to remember one pivotal insight, this is it: *you have come into this world to find your voice.* To accomplish that aim, you must first immerse yourself in rich experience. You must feed your hunger for perceptions. You must, like our writer sitting in the bar, "gather material." You benefit enormously from travel and educational opportunities. You thrive on interesting conversations with people, especially ones who are capable of surprising you and stretching your mental horizons. Never let a month go by without having good reason to say, "Wow, I never thought of that before!" Trust your curiosity.

And never forget: whatever you've figured out, an even more amazing, mind-boggling truth is right around the corner hiding behind the next question.

Note the underlying solar point in all of this: we are talking about *values* that animate a meaningful life for you. We are talking about the principles to which you must be true if your life is going to be worth living. We are talking about your *authenticity.* With the astrological Sun, no matter in which sign or house you find it, those simple points are always the marrow in the bones of the interpretation.

EXAMPLE #3: MARS IN THE TWELFTH HOUSE

Moving on to the Aries branch of the Fire family, we come to the planet Mars. Everything quickly turns raw and primal—will you be the Hunter or will you be the Prey? It's your own choice—but if you don't want to wind up on the dinner plate, you will need to be brave. You will need to practice assertiveness. Without courage, you are doomed. And courage is not to be confused with fearlessness. Courage is the ability to be thoroughly terrified, but to still function with self-possession and intelligence despite the stress.

Classically, the twelfth house was related to *trouble* and *misfortune*. Astrologers, on seeing an edgy planet such as Mars there, often come up with some rather horrific interpretations. I'm not simply going to dismiss that perspective; we will get back to it. The bottom line here is that with Mars in the twelfth house, the stakes are indeed high. If we don't get it right, the results can be frightening.

So let's talk about how to get it right.

In its loftiest form, the twelfth house is mystical and spiritual. It references psychic phenomena and transcendent experience. It is the gateway to a realm of consciousness that lies beyond personality, beyond the realm of ego.

Since we are talking about a house, we focus on the sorts of behaviors and circumstances that reflect those interests. How might we act if we were motivated by a spiritual quest? Some of the answers are quite obvious: we might spend time in meditation. We might keep vigil. We might fast or chant or sit on a mountaintop. We might pray. Historically, the twelfth house referred to monasteries or convents—and even though entering holy orders has become rare today, it also reflects similar interests and motivations.

All of those are, in the broad sense, positive twelfth house behaviors regardless of what planets lie there.

But how do we integrate these mystical behaviors with the god of war? When we think of monks, nuns, and meditators, we are likely to think of milder sorts of people—people who turn the other cheek.

Mars, however, is more inclined to punch you in the nose.

Any planet in the twelfth house stands between you and a higher state of consciousness. That is fundamental. When I say that it "stands between you and that higher condition," I don't mean to frame the planet as an obstacle. That's one possibility—but here is a more inspiring one: that planet operates as a *spiritual teacher* for you. It is as if it were your guru—although immediately we have to add that the planet is not a person, nor does it often represent one; it's a part of you. But it is a part of you that is charged with an incredible power: it can carry you, efficiently and rapidly, beyond the tyranny of your own ego.

With Mars in the twelfth house, we can say that "Mars is your guru"—that is, your guru is the god of war.

On the face of it, that doesn't sound like particularly good news. But here's the heart of the matter: as we know, the highest aspiration of Mars is courage. And that brings us to our core insight: you have reached a point in the evolutionary journey where the thinnest of eggshells stands between you and a higher state of consciousness. And the substance of that eggshell can be defined in one single word: *fear.*

To break through to the next evolutionary level, you must face that fear.

Imagine you spontaneously begin to have an out-of-body experience. Yikes, your consciousness is exiting your flesh and bones! Your inner monkey immediately squeals, "Uh oh—*death!* Abandon ship!"

And in a flash, you've snapped right back into the physical world. You didn't even have to think about it—fear made the decision. Fear was the reflex.

If you desire an out-of-body experience, you'll have to overcome that reflex.

We are a million miles from making out-of-body experience the goal with a twelfth house Mars, nor do I even want to frame such experiences as particularly important or desirable. The imagery simply focuses the larger issue: we glibly speak of spiritual experience—but the truth of it is that as we advance on the path, things can get pretty weird. We aren't talking here about the Thursday night meditation group or church on Sunday. We're talking about full-blown transcendental experience.

And the line between that kind of experience of "opening up psychically" and flat-out madness is notoriously fine.

How would you feel if every time you looked at a friend, you immediately had insights into how that person would die? Or perhaps you might have similar insights about yourself when you looked in the mirror.

To paint spirituality as frightening is not the point here. Spirituality has many other dimensions, and many of them are sweet, loving, and pleasant. The point is that *with Mars in the twelfth house, you personally have reached a point in the journey where fear stands between you and these higher states.* The soul-contract of your birthchart includes a commitment on your part to wrestle with that particular issue. You have signed up for it. And if you don't show up, Mars is going to come looking for you. Remember what happens if you don't choose Hunter…

We'll get to that darker possibility in a few moments.

How might you rise to the call of Mars in the twelfth house? Let me make a suggestion: *jump out of airplanes.*

On the face of it, to most of us, skydiving doesn't seem like a spiritual practice. But ask anyone who's ever done it—so many who have had that experience say that it changed their lives. There's something about the experience of "jumping to your death"—even if you do not actually die—that focuses the mind very directly on eternal questions.

These skydivers have also consistently told me one more thing, and it's not actually surprising at all: jumping out of airplanes gets easier and less frightening every time you do it. That thought brings us to the heart of the evolutionary path represented by Mars in the twelfth house. By doing things that frighten us—and doing them repeatedly—we become *desensitized to fear.* The result? The next time we begin spontaneously to have an out-of-body experience, perhaps the inner monkey is not so quick to grab the steering wheel and pull us back into the three-dimensional realm.

Let's look at the darker possibilities. What if we refuse to jump out of an airplane? What if, in other words, we do not practice the yoga of facing our fears? What if we do not accept the higher shamanic path indicated by Mars in the twelfth house?

That leaves us with the lower path.

At the beginning of the section, I mentioned that classically the twelfth house was related to trouble and misfortune. Having Mars there was seen as a particularly ominous configuration. The suggestion was often that there was a heightened risk of exposure to accident or violence.

I don't personally have Mars in my twelfth house, but I do have Scorpio on the cusp. With Mars as the classical ruler of Scorpio, there is a certain resonance with these archetypal ideas in my own chart. In closing here, I would like quickly to recount a personal experience that reflects the principles we're exploring.

Because of my commitment to teaching, I have spent a large part of the past three or four decades consigned to the tender mercies of the airline industry. Once, many years ago, the inevitable happened: I was on a flight that got into mechanical trouble in midair. The details aren't important; suffice it to say that for about ten or fifteen minutes, I was confronted with the immediate reality of my own death.

Obviously, everything turned out fine. When I got home and recounted the experience to my friends, I kept hearing, "That's terrible, Steve. What an awful experience." Those sentiments were, of course, unimpeachable.

But the reality is that I treasured the experience. I did not treasure it when it was actually happening—I was scared. But, realizing that I was about to die, I had come to a crossroads: I could die well or I could die in a panic. Hunter or Prey. Sitting on that "doomed airliner," faced with the reality of my death, a kind of spiritual instinct took over: I got centered. I prepared myself as best I could to exit this world with whatever grace and faith I could muster.

Without that experience, I wouldn't have known for sure how I might respond to such a radical stimulus. In retrospect, I'd received a fierce gift from the war-god. I treasure the experience to this day and pray that when my time actually comes, it will remain with me.

Telling this personal story could seem self-aggrandizing. The point is actually the polar opposite: I suspect the reality is that I had missed an opportunity to do something scary for the sake of my spirituality. Maybe I needed to go on a vigil in the mountains. Or maybe, God forbid, I actually did need to jump out of an airplane.

But I didn't do any of those things.

So instead of my willingly choosing to face fear, *Mars had to come and find me.* In the mysterious and endless synchronicity that animates the universe, I boarded an airplane that was headed for trouble. In the end, it worked out well.

But it was not my finest hour, nor an illustration of the highest possible response to Mars-energy in the twelfth house.

PART THREE

MARS, THE SUN, AND JUPITER THROUGH THE TWELVE SIGNS AND HOUSES

Nothing in astrology exists in a vacuum. Each configuration derives its human meaning largely from its context. A person might have Mars in Aries—and nine planets in Pisces. The human meaning of that Arian Mars will be mightily impacted by the larger Piscean agenda—and will operate very differently from that same Mars in Aries were it in a more Fiery chart.

In the chapters that follow, I provide some point-of-departure suggestions for the interpretation of our three Fire planets in the context of each of the twelve signs and houses. Please take this information as a starting point for a more integrative and holistic analysis.

That is how the magic happens.

9

MARS IN THE TWELVE SIGNS

MARS IN ARIES

Underlying Agenda: I resolve that fear will never grab the steering wheel of my life. That is not to say that I will never be afraid; it is that I will not allow fear to stand between me and doing what I feel is right for myself. I resolve to accept the fact that life entails risk, and that no one gets out of here alive. I will protect myself and those I love.

Strategy: I commit to doing things that frighten me. Some of these brave actions will be physical; I understand and accept that putting my body on the line is one method for my full engagement in this particular evolutionary effort. I also understand and accept that this process unfolds on levels other than those requiring physical courage; I will be truthful about expressing my emotional needs and my feelings, even when that might lead to conflict in my relationships.

Tools: Into this world I bring a reflex of courage under fire. Compared to most people, I have a relative immunity to panic, even though it might take the right circumstances for me to become aware of this steady quality in myself. My nature is honest and direct, and I am fiercely loyal to those whom I love.

Dealing with the Shadow: I resolve to be wary of my temper. I will not pretend that my anger and resentments are always "righteous indignation."

I will reflect on the possibility that at times forgiveness or even surrender might be the right course.

MARS IN TAURUS

Underlying Agenda: I accept the fundamental paradox of my life: that I must constantly fight for peace. I am not weak, but I choose solace; I prioritize serenity above everything else. I understand that battles lie ahead of me on my way toward those safe and natural harbors. I will courageously face those battles, fearing nothing and no one—and simultaneously I will scrupulously avoid being sucker-punched into battles I do not need to fight.

Strategy: I resolve to establish a reasonable level of physical security in my life, understanding that peace cannot arise if I feel constantly embattled or under practical stress. I will enter the natural world in a spirit of adventure and I will derive solace from it. I will be fiercely loyal to any animal companions that join me in my journey. I will take comfort in music. I will carefully monitor the feedback I receive from my own physical body, and thus keep my stress levels down to reasonable levels.

Tools: I have come into this world with a no-nonsense set of instincts about what is truly important and what is simply excess. I will prioritize that which is essential to my survival and well-being, while distancing myself from the mirages of mindless materialism and vain display. My body speaks loudly, clearly, and eloquently to me. I value it and I listen to it.

Dealing with the Shadow: I resolve to be wary of lassitude and sloth. I affirm that happiness derives more from wanting what I have than from getting what I want. I do not pretend that I am without desires, but I recognize that every desire comes with a price tag, in that every moment spent chasing after it can erode my serenity. I make those choices mindfully.

MARS IN GEMINI

Underlying Agenda: I resolve that I will never let fear silence my voice. I am becoming brave enough to claim my right to be heard. I recognize that while courage is the critical ingredient here, it is not the only one—to find my voice, I must first have something to say. And I resolve to discover the worthy content of my voice through a commitment to wide experience and endless learning. I bravely pursue whatever triggers my curiosity or my interests, no matter what perils such a journey entails.

Strategy: When adventure calls, I answer. That applies to mental adventures too. I resolve to cultivate an open mind. When I feel intellectually intimidated, I dive into my studies and thus develop confidence in my knowledge. When reasonable fear stands between me and an experience that appeals to me, I never give fear the final vote. When I feel afraid to speak, I take that as a signal that it is time for me to speak. I will become confident in argument.

Tools: I have been blessed with a penetrating mind, capable of cutting right to the heart of any matter. I can quickly and intuitively grasp the essentials in any situation. I am formidable in argument. I can convey not only information to people, but also enthusiasm and passion about that information.

Dealing with the Shadow: I am aware that I can win arguments even if I am wrong. I can be unintentionally abrasive. When I set out to be verbally defensive, I can effectively defend myself against growth or the possibility of ever learning anything. I can express myself with too much vehemence, to the point that no one wants to listen to me even if they agree with me. I resolve to be conscious of these qualities and to try to minimize their hold upon my behavior.

MARS IN CANCER

Underlying Agenda: I resolve to cultivate the courage to heal my inner wounds. Some people behave bravely by distancing themselves from their feelings of fear or insecurity; I will never do that. I will let my heart speak and I will be vulnerable, always, to its message, no matter how threatening that message might be. Like a warrior, I will face the reality of my own heart.

Strategy: I recognize that I need time alone, in silence and safety. I resolve to make space in my outer life for my inner life. I defend those necessary borders fiercely. I recognize that nothing so reveals the reality of my heart as committed relationships: this means partnership—but it also means my family in the larger sense of the word. I claim the enormous courage that is necessary for committed "no exit" love and friendship.

Tools: I have a passion for inner work. My heart speaks loudly to me; I cannot help but listen to it. There is no warrior in the forest like mama bear when she feels that her cubs are threatened; I am like mama bear. I defend my home, my hearth, and my clan. I have no desire to die for them, but I would do that if necessary, without a moment's hesitation. That is the quality of the love I offer.

Dealing with the Shadow: I accept the fact that life is inherently dangerous; there are limits to how effectively I can defend myself. I accept that fact. I recognize that my innate caution can grab the steering wheel of my life, robbing me of vitality in the name of security. This creates a paradox: in my zeal to be safe and secure, it is possible that I might fail to live. I will not let that happen.

MARS IN LEO

Underlying Agenda: I resolve that I will not exit this world before I have left in its hands some evidence of my inner life. I will somehow express my values concretely—my sense of what is beautiful, what is sacred, what is worth living for. I am not afraid to roar like a lion. I will impact the community around me; people will know I was here. They will be touched by me. I am not afraid to be seen.

Strategy: I seek avenues of creative, personal expression. These creative avenues might take the form of art, but they are not limited to art. I will leave the stamp of my soul upon institutions, events, and people whom I meet. Even when I am frightened, I step out on the stage of life and I sing my heart out. Vulnerability does not scare me.

Tools: I have flair; I have charisma and presence. My passionate engagement with life radiates magnetically from me. I can perform. I can step out on the stage. I have the ability to trigger in other people an identification with me. I can ask for what I want. I am not afraid to shine.

Dealing with the Shadow: I am aware that I am not the center of the world. I cultivate fascination with other people and sensitivity towards them. I can as easily be a good audience as I can be the performer who is the focus of everyone's attention. I accept the fact that the critical ingredient in my self-expression must always be the authentic baring of my soul. It must always entail that kind of vulnerability, and I resolve that it will never descend into mere posturing. I will not become a dancing monkey calculating how to create the response of applause; I will not fear the risk of being nakedly honest even if people don't like it.

MARS IN VIRGO

Underlying Agenda: My spiritual survival depends upon my finding some kind of work that matters. Whether or not I am paid for this work is not the issue; what matters is that in the end I can honestly know that I polished and fully expressed the skills and abilities with which I was born. I understand that my pursuit of these crafts entails facing my own fears and insecurities. I will not let them stop me. I am a warrior in service to my community.

Strategy: I will allow nothing to stand between me and the training I need in order to fully develop and express my potential. "Training" in this context might refer to school, but the intention is broader: life itself can educate me, so long as I engage with it bravely. I understand that my particular path through this world entails encounters with *masters* of various sorts. I am part of a lineage; I will receive guidance from those who have gone before me—and I will repay the debt by passing on these skills to those who come after me.

Tools: I am not afraid of hard work; I understand self-discipline; I can focus; I can sustain concentration over long periods of time. I am not intimidated by complexity or detail. I can hammer away long after others, who might perhaps be more talented than me, have given up and gone home.

Dealing with the Shadow: I understand that sometimes "perfect" is the enemy of "good enough." I can accept that I have done well, declare victory and go home to my bed and sleep. I know that I am a worrier; I understand that worry can sap my energy, robbing me of the juice that I need in order to live my life as I want to live it. I carefully distinguish natural, healthy *concern* from needless, vitiating worry. Simultaneously, I resolve gracefully to accept the imperfections I accurately perceive in others.

MARS IN LIBRA

Underlying Agenda: I accept that my major aim in life is to achieve genuine intimacy—and "intimacy" here refers to all close human relationships, not only to the ones based on sexuality. I accept the fact that such authenticity of connection is inherently frightening. To be honest—and to create the space for a partner also to be genuinely honest—is true warrior work. I understand that conflict is not the opposite of love; it is part of authentic love, woven into the very DNA of genuine intimacy.

Strategy: I resolve to cultivate the skills of the intimate warrior. As I learn to express my needs and any pain I might feel in a relationship, I will not lose sight of my compassionate, respectful, three-dimensional *perception* of my partner. I do not fight to win; I fight to achieve fairness. Diplomacy in service of loving honesty is the craft I am developing.

Tools: I have an innate sense of how other people are different from me. I celebrate that reality, I am not surprised by it; I expect those differences. To intimacy I bring an open-minded sense of discovery. Without being foolish or ungrounded about it, I am a romantic. I accept that fact about myself, and I do not apologize for it. Love is important to me; I am willing to bravely commit to it and to do the work of sustaining it.

Dealing with the Shadow: I will never let diplomacy eclipse my honesty; instead, I express my honesty diplomatically. I resolve to be aware of this critical distinction. Harmony in relationship is valuable to me, but I will not participate in creating a false harmony that derives from my hiding who I am, what I need, and what I genuinely feel.

MARS IN SCORPIO

Underlying Agenda: Mars—which is to say, passionate intensity—is maximally powerful here, being the classical ruler of Scorpio. Therefore, I came into this world with my heart on fire. I came into this world, saying, "give me some truth." I am looking for a naked, unvarnished relationship with my own stormy heart. Once I have established that, I can seek similarly deep connections with a few other equally brave souls in this world.

Strategy: When something smells bad, people naturally turn away from it. My instinct, however, is to go toward the smell. What that means is that I am doing deep Shadow work in this lifetime. I trust my fascination with everything taboo; I may edit my behavior, but never my actual consciousness. I think anything, feel anything. Above all, I am true to my sexuality, knowing that its instinctual, mysterious compass needle points me unerringly to my path.

Tools: I can smell a lie from ten miles away. I can look anyone straight in the eye. I can handle intensity and drama. I understand that life is short and uncertain; this gives me an impatience with game-playing and superficiality. There is heat in my blood; people who cannot accept that tend to be afraid of me and go away. Let's celebrate their departures rather than lamenting them.

Dealing with the Shadow: Even without my intending it, my honesty, bluntness, and directness can hurt people. Because of that, when I was young, I was probably punished or criticized for those very qualities. Paradoxically, this could lead me to hide my honesty, bluntness, and directness. Internalizing those energies only hurts me; I could become isolated, resentful, and depressed. I resolve to not let that happen: I seek alliances with people who celebrate my intensity.

MARS IN SAGITTARIUS

Underlying Agenda: I resolve never to let fear compromise my fidelity to my gypsy soul. I seek wide experience and I resolve to live my life passionately. I am not afraid to make mistakes nor to learn things the hard way, if that is the deepest way to learn them. I hurl myself into experience in a spirit of faith and adventure. I am on a quest for *meaning* in life; I will not sacrifice that search on the altar of "practicality"— or of anyone else's agenda for me. When I come to the end of my life, I will have few regrets. I will not look back and say that I missed my chance to live.

Strategy: I will travel and be open to cross-cultural experiences. I learn from people who are different from me, socially or culturally. I live to stretch my horizons in every way possible—I accept the fact that this kind of stretching includes physical adventures, but also opportunities to learn and to immerse myself in anything I have never seen before.

Tools: I am fascinated with everything foreign or alien; I trust that feeling and let it motivate me. I am plucky. I bounce back from adversity. My faith in life is bulletproof. By reflex, I say yes rather than no. I express myself straightforwardly and directly. People will know who I am; they are free to make their own decisions about whether to like me or not.

Dealing with the Shadow: I am wary of how I can be blinded by my own passionate opinions. I know I can be wrong, even when I feel I am right. I temper my spontaneity with an awareness of other people's sensitivities or wounded places. My good-hearted desire not to do harm to anyone must be enhanced by constant mindfulness of my own Fiery nature.

MARS IN CAPRICORN

Underlying Agenda: Half fish, half mountain goat—Capricorn is a strange piece of biological engineering. But in the world of symbolism, it represents absolute mastery: the ability to swim the widest ocean and climb the highest mountain. With my Mars in Capricorn, I resolve to do exactly the same thing: with my courage married to my innate relentlessness and self-discipline, I have come into this world to accomplish Great Works. I seek only mountains worthy of my strengths, my values, and my highest aspirations.

Strategy: Looking at the astrological house in which my Mars lies and taking into account the aspects it makes, I perceive and define the exact nature of those "worthy mountains." Perhaps one is a professional accomplishment; just as easily, another could take the form of some inner work, creativity, or the perfection of an intimate relationship. With single-pointed focus, an absolute commitment to integrity, and monumental self-discipline, I ascend the peaks.

Tools: I was born with the ability to steel my nerves in the face of daunting circumstances. I am blessed with focus and a capacity for sustained concentration. I am efficient; I can sense priorities correctly and organize effective strategies for attaining them. I can put my ego and my insecurities aside and focus one-pointedly upon the goal. I am at my best in situations where other people are giving up.

Dealing with the Shadow: I resolve to be mindful of life's softer side, both in myself and in other people. When I am tired I will sleep. When I am hungry I will eat. I will take time to treat my own needs and the needs of others with tenderness and respect. I recognize that the blinders which allow me to maintain my focus might also blind me to life's unexpected wonders and sweet compensations. I resolve not to fall into that cold trap.

MARS IN AQUARIUS

Underlying Agenda: I accept that I must fight to be free. No one has granted me a right to express my individuality; instead, I must assert myself and claim that right. The experiences that actually nourish my inner warrior are experiences which others might try to forbid me to have. My distorted social training began early in life, so brave inner work is required as I sift my real desires from what is merely internalized social conditioning. I resolve to heed my inner voice, to follow its guidance—and to face down anyone who tries to make me wrong for being true to myself.

Strategy: Setting boundaries is not enough; I must learn to *defend* those boundaries as well. I will undoubtedly attract petty tyrants into my life—people with plans for me, and even if they are well intended, these are plans that would render my life meaningless. Faced with them, I resolve to stand my ground. I will question authority. I will doubt the "received wisdoms" of my generation and my society. I bow to no one unless they have proven themselves worthy of my submission.

Tools: I have been blessed with an ability to think outside the box. If we understand "genius" as the ability to ask questions no one before has even thought to ask, then I acknowledge I possess a certain genius. I have a warrior's instinct to defend minority viewpoints and the rights of those whose voices are not heard. I can argue effectively; I have the ability to pry open closed minds.

Dealing with the Shadow: I affirm that life is multidimensional, full of paradox, and inhabited by other human beings with hearts and souls as deep and authentic as my own. I will not become lost in abstraction; I will not turn people into symbols. I cultivate kindness and forgiveness in myself. I remember always to laugh and to love. I honor tenderness.

MARS IN PISCES

Underlying Agenda: I recognize that the thinnest of barriers stands between me and a fundamental breakthrough in the depth of my consciousness and my spirituality. I recognize that the exact nature of that barrier is fear. The divine mystery is not "safe" in some churchy sense of the word. I have reached a stage in my evolutionary journey in which the next steps will launch me upon some stormy—and rather shamanic—seas. I boldly surrender to the Mysteries.

Strategy: I am learning to steady my nerves in the face of psychological and spiritual experiences that frighten me. While the ultimate application of this skill lies in my inner work, I can strengthen it by facing almost any kind of scary adventure. Riding a roller coaster can thus be understood, for me, as a spiritual discipline. Walking past the graveyard alone after midnight can be even more effective. In a nutshell, I face my fears—and especially those fears that derived from the opening of my psychic faculties.

Tools: I was born with a natural attunement to the edgy dimensions of the psychic realms and astral worlds. The archetype of the spiritual warrior arises naturally in me; I understand it intuitively, even if no one has ever explained it to me. When I tune into my deep self, I quickly connect with the part of my consciousness that has no fear of death—the part of me that knows that my consciousness will survive it. The more I meditate upon that place in myself, the more fearless I become.

Dealing with the Shadow: I fight passivity. I am cautious about the "transcendent" parts of myself—which are also the parts of me that could let life slip through my fingers. "What will this matter in five hundred years" is a wise statement—but also a dangerous attitude when contemplating a committed relationship, or a decision to pursue a career, or choosing to embrace a system of beliefs. I will not become a ghost in my own life.

10

THE SUN IN THE TWELVE SIGNS

SUN IN ARIES

Evolutionary Aim: I resolve to follow the soul-path of the spiritual warrior. Emphatically, this does not mean that I intend harm to anyone. Instead, it means that I resolve never to let fear shape my decisions. I will have something beyond myself to live for in this lifetime. I will stand for my principles and I will be loyal to those whom I love. Being true to this path is the source of my energy, my self-respect, and my recuperative powers, as well as the foundation of my spiritual sanity.

Core Values: Above all other virtues, I value courage. I do not confuse this quality with fearlessness, which I rightfully consider to be a psychotic condition. When I am frightened, I admit it; by courage, I only mean that I do not let panic grab the steering wheel of my life. I am appropriately assertive; I set boundaries and I am capable of defending them. I am fiercely loyal. I do not glorify martyrdom—but I pity people who have nothing in their lives for which they would willingly die.

Strategy: I will intentionally do things that frighten me. I will recognize that taking reasonable physical risks is part of my evolutionary strategy. Equally, I will recognize the efficacy of my taking emotional risks as I develop the spiritual virtue of courage: I bring up difficult subjects with the people in my life even when doing so might trigger conflict.

Tools: I am good under pressure. Compared to other people, I have a relative immunity to panic. Faced with pressure, I tend to not fall apart, but rather to keep my head. I appreciate directness and honesty, and I tend to offer those gifts myself. I expect the same. I am loyal; if I am your friend, you can count on me.

Dealing with the Shadow: In situations of conflict or disagreement, I resolve to use sufficient force, but never too much force. I am passionate, but I resolve not to be controlled by my passions. I am wary of drama. I understand that my intensity might frighten some people; I therefore moderate it when it would be pointless unkindness not to do so. There are battles I do not need to fight. Sometimes I win by walking away.

SUN IN TAURUS

Evolutionary Aim: In this lifetime, I resolve to achieve a peaceful heart. I humbly acknowledge the tension and woundedness present in my soul. I take no shame in that reality; I realize that the origin of this pain lies in the mysteries of who I was before I was born into this body. I resolve to realize that now that I have won the ancient war, I must win the peace. I seek and deserve the solace I need. Being true to this path is the source of my energy and my recuperative powers, as well as the foundation of my spiritual sanity.

Core Values: I value serenity of spirit above all other virtues. I value naturalness and simplicity. I appreciate silence. I trust my instincts. I recognize that achieving existential stability and material security supports my spiritual quest; so long as I seek them primarily for that single reason, they serve me well. I honor my inner animal-self, and always listen to its wise voice.

Strategy: I resolve always to heed the messages of my body. I will learn to trust my guts. I will spend time immersed in silence and in nature. I will listen to music; it calms my spirit. I value physical touch. I will celebrate my relationship with animals; they know things I need to remember. I will avoid unnecessary drama and psychological complications, along with the kinds of people who foment them. I will cultivate inner silence.

Tools: I was born with an earthy, grounded nature. I can navigate the practical world with little fuss or confusion. I am not squeamish. My instincts guide me unerringly, if I only take time to listen to them. My ability to reason in a grounded way is powerful too. I see through pretense and posturing. Animals like me and I like them; we understand each other and support each other.

Dealing with the Shadow: Life is change; I accept that reality. I realize that consistency is often simply my right to be just as stupid next year as I was last year. I avoid rigidity and judgment. While I recognize that achieving material security is part of my strategy for achieving peace, I also recognize that I could pay too much for my money; I do not confuse material security and predictability with inner peace.

SUN IN GEMINI

Evolutionary Aim: I resolve to cultivate "a beginner's mind"—that is to say, I celebrate questions more than I celebrate answers. I accept the principle that whatever I might see, the truth is beyond that—in other words, the wiser I become, the greater my area of contact with the unknown becomes. I celebrate that too. I realize that, in pursuing such questions, I find my true voice. Being true to this path is the source of my energy, my self-respect and my recuperative powers, as well as the foundation of my spiritual sanity.

Core Values: Listening teaches me more than talking ever does. I would rather learn something than to be considered an expert. I am drawn to people who surprise me and stretch the boundaries of my understanding. I celebrate the deep energetic mystery behind even a simple conversation—the way what might be called "small talk" weaves energy bodies together, if only we are mindful of what is really happening behind the words.

Strategy: I will resolve to avoid boredom, even when it comes cleverly disguised as practicality, responsibility, or maturity. I will pack the experience of many lifetimes into one lifetime. I will speak up—but I will also listen carefully. I am energized by questions; I am thrilled when confronted with paradox, the inexplicable, or the miraculous. I seek them. I recognize that when I am proven wrong, while the experience is unpleasant, it is the portal to higher wisdom.

Tools: I was born with restless, insatiable curiosity. Language skills arise in me without much effort. I am a natural student and a natural teacher. I am energetic; my mind quickly engages with anything novel or unexpected.

Dealing with the Shadow: I recognize that my natural curiosity can scatter my attention in too many directions. I cultivate focus, strategy and my capacity for linear thought. I strive to make a distinction between serendipitous curiosity and simply being distracted; I make a conscious effort to stay on the correct side of that line. I am happy to talk, but I try to spend an equal amount of time listening.

SUN IN CANCER

Evolutionary Aim: In this lifetime, I resolve to cultivate an open heart. I aim to become fully vulnerable to my own humanity. I do not edit, restrict, or judge my feelings. As I accomplish these aims, I am healing an ancient wound in myself. As I progress in that healing process, my capacity to heal others increases proportionately. Ultimately, I am here to be a Healer of some sort—but I recognize that in order to accomplish that aim I must first heal myself. Being true to this path is the source of my energy, my self-respect and my recuperative powers, as well as the foundation of my spiritual sanity.

Core Values: Quiet, along with freedom from outward distraction, are crucial to my inner work; I value them above material rewards, the applause of this world, and all outward stimulus. I value home and hearth; I value family in any sense of that word, so long as the relationships are functional, kind, and respectful of human diversity. I honor introversion and recognize it as a spiritual path.

Strategy: I will defend my heart; I understand that only when I feel safe can I fully open myself to my inner life. For that reason, I value walls: these might be the walls of my physical home that hold the craziness of the world at bay. Just as easily, these might be walls that I place around my own heart in order to protect it from those who might do it harm. I make time in my life for quiet.

Tools: Even though I was born with an enormous sensitivity on both the emotional and the psychic levels, I know that I am fully capable of defending myself. I do not need to be afraid. The volume is turned up inside of me on all psychological processes—and by "psychological processes," I mean my direct attunement to the raw energies of my emotional life, not just the fancy labels one might encounter in a PhD "psych" program.

Dealing with the Shadow: While I recognize that it is imperative that I defend my sensitivity, I also recognize that I can defend it too well: I can shield myself from life. I can hide inside my shell. I further recognize that my kindness towards others, especially those in pain, can trap me in a role of endless, draining nurturing behavior. I recognize that this "caring" role is yet another shell in which I can hide myself from life.

SUN IN LEO

Evolutionary Aim: I resolve in this lifetime to cultivate four virtues: joy, comfort, trust, and forgiveness. I relish being alive. I am comfortable and trusting relative to other humans, and I strive to forgive those who have hurt me. I recognize that underlying these intentions is a wound of rejection that I sustained in a prior lifetime. Somehow, I was hurt or betrayed by the human family. It still haunts me, and makes me feel more afraid than I look. There was no joy for me—and probably a lot of the opposite. That's a lot to forgive. Being real about all of this and true to my path is the source of my energy and my recuperative powers, as well as the foundation of my spiritual sanity. I aim to become easy enough inside myself that I can achieve authentic vulnerability without effort, self-consciousness, or strain.

Core Values: I value sincere, courageous, honest self-expression. Performance and loud applause do not count; there must be actual risk, actual vulnerability, in what I express. I do want attention; there is no shame in owning that need. But the part of me that prospers spiritually from that attention is my soul. If merely my hair or my bank account get the attention, nothing of lasting value comes to me from those kinds of accolades.

Strategy: I resolve to perform. That performance can take many forms so long as they are sincere and express what is in my heart. Perhaps I paint, or sing, or write poetry; equally, I might leave the stamp of my soul upon an institution or an event. I will find an appreciative audience and express myself, and thus reclaim my ability to feel comfortable and trusting in the human family. Further, I realize that if I reveal my heart and no one cares, I am in the wrong crowd. I then simply move on.

Tools: I have presence. Like a king or a queen, I radiate quiet dignity. Perhaps I am charismatic, or maybe a better way to say it is that I possess *gravitas.* That distinction depends on the tone of the rest of my chart. I am creative. I am a natural performer. I can hold people's attention and get them to identify with my point of view or with what I am feeling.

Dealing with the Shadow: Healing, for me, takes the form of a loop: I express my soul, while people express their appreciation of my soul. For it to work, it must be a two-way street. If I express something other than my soul, no matter how loudly they clap their hands, I am living on a diet of cotton candy. My soul is not nourished at all. For this reason, I renounce my attachment to any form of applause that is not connected to my vulnerable heart with absolute sincerity. I also resolve quickly to exit any situation or relationship where I am not understood and appreciated—there's no loop there either.

SUN IN VIRGO

Evolutionary Aim: I resolve to learn to love myself and I resolve to accomplish that aim in the most difficult of conceivable circumstances: *a radically honest mind.* I will never take refuge in false pride or delusions of grandeur; I will see myself clearly, and I will work on myself relentlessly. I also resolve to take the talents and skills I have been given and polish them; I will then offer them as a meaningful service to my community. Being true to this path is the source of my energy, my self-respect and my recuperative powers, as well as the foundation of my spiritual sanity.

Core Values: I value skill and competence; I value precision. I value honesty, humility, and clarity. I respect people who work hard and are good at what they do. I respect people who do what they say they are going to do and who then do it well. I value neatness, order, and a job well done.

Strategy: I will take an inventory of my natural skills. Once I have identified them, I will zealously develop them. To accomplish that, I will seek appropriate teachers and role models; I will seek education in some sense of the word. As I express these skills in the world and I am appreciated for them, dignity, self-love, and self-respect arise naturally in me. These three virtues stabilize my fierce evolutionary intensity; they save me from sabotaging myself with self-doubt.

Tools: I am not afraid of hard work, either in the world or on myself. I am not afraid to take a fearless inventory of my weaknesses and delusions, and to work on improving them day by day until I have resolved them. I am a realist; I see the world clearly. Through my capacity for sustained self-discipline, I can often outperform people who might have more innate skill than I do.

Dealing with the Shadow: Perfection is a harsh master; I strive for the high standard—but I resolve not to punish myself for falling short of it.

I judge myself by the intensity of my effort, not against the standard of something unreachable. I recognize how I can drain myself with worry and self-criticism. I also recognize how endless preparation can prevent me from ever actually doing anything.

SUN IN LIBRA

Evolutionary Aim: I resolve to achieve a condition of harmony, ease, and balance in my consciousness in this lifetime. I recognize that I was born in a state of tension; I understand that the source of this tension is unresolved trauma from a prior existence. Recovery—the attainment of serenity of spirit—is my overarching aim in this lifetime. Nothing else matters nearly as much. Remembering that and being true to this path is the source of my energy and my recuperative powers, as well as the foundation of my spiritual sanity.

Core Values: I resolve to let life be as complicated as it is; in other words, rather than resisting them, I expect and tolerate paradox, irony, and ambiguity. I know that justice is symbolized by the balance-scales. I also appreciate beauty, whether it is the beauty of nature or the beauty of art. I value harmonious intimacy with graceful, sensitive human beings. All of these gifts have one effect: they calm me down.

Strategy: As I immerse myself in the perception of beauty, something wonderful happens: the harmonies of colors, shapes, and sounds harmonize my inner states. Thus, the immersion of my senses in beauty works for me as an evolutionary strategy. I will not wrestle against the actual nature of reality. That means that as I recognize that all stories—and all truths—have at least two sides, I free myself from the cognitive tension that is inherent in any form of dogmatism. As I reach out to others in a spirit of fascination and discovery, I internalize the comforting solace of true friendship and intimacy.

Tools: I was born with an expectation of paradox in all my perceptions. I accept the fact that the opposite of a great truth is always another great truth. I have taste; faced with any form of art, I am an intelligent, engaged audience. If I choose to create beauty, I find peace in the process. I see other people as independent centers of the creation of values and dreams—in other words, I do not assume that everyone is like me; instead my instinct is to discover what is surprising and unexpected about the other person and then to enjoy our differences.

Dealing with the Shadow: I seek true inner harmony; I will not settle for mere appearances. I have the diplomatic skills necessary to placate people, but I understand that if I allow those skills to run my life, it just becomes a political game that no one wins. Furthermore, maintaining such a fictional appearance of harmony is exhausting; there is no peace in it. It is only in shared truth that I will find the serenity I seek; I will express my truth diplomatically and gracefully—but I will never compromise it.

SUN IN SCORPIO

Evolutionary Aim: I resolve in this lifetime to make my unconscious mind conscious. I will turn away from no truth, no matter how threatening it might feel. In this lifetime, I will wrestle honestly with the fundamental questions of life and death. I celebrate my sexuality for many reasons, including for the complex questions it raises in my life. The inner journey is a warrior's journey; it requires courage. I accept that. In fact I revel in it. Being true to this path is the source of my energy, my self-respect and my recuperative powers, as well as the foundation of my spiritual sanity.

Core Values: I value the struggle toward honesty, both within myself and in my relationships with others, above all other virtues. I am most comfortable with people who look me right in the eye and do not turn away when I do the same with them. I know we are all human, which means we all have a dark side. I judge no one for that; the only thing for which I do judge others is hypocrisy and taking cheap refuge in intentional shallowness.

Strategy: I will seek close friends with whom I can be relentlessly honest, and appreciated for it. I recognize that most people cannot handle my intensity; I do not criticize them for that; I simply seek human connections elsewhere. When anything makes me feel uncomfortable or tempts me towards denial and rationalization, I seek to get to the bottom of it.

Tools: Into this world I have brought depth and a penetrating mind, along with a naturally psychological style of consciousness; that is to say, I have a mind that naturally looks beneath the surface of behavior and appearance, seeking its roots. It is difficult to lie to me—I may not know the truth, but I usually sense the presence of a lie. I am not squeamish; I can handle rawness, drama, and intensity. I recognize that a sense of humor is an essential tool for surviving my own intense inner processes. Laughter gives me strength.

Dealing with the Shadow: I acknowledge my most vulnerable quality: *I am capable of getting deeper faster than I can handle.* I have depth and penetration, but I do not always maintain clear perspective. Without that perspective, I can spiral down into moody, heavy spaces. To keep balance, three blessings are essential: humor, humility, and a few really good friends.

SUN IN SAGITTARIUS

Evolutionary Aim: I resolve to pack the experience of seven lifetimes into one lifetime; I aim to live my life with no regrets. I say yes to experience; I am not afraid to make mistakes—that is how I learn. I will stretch my horizons in every sense of the word: culturally, intellectually, and physically. Above all, I seek *understanding*: Why are we here in this world? What is really going on before my eyes? Being true to this Questing path is the source of my energy and my recuperative powers, as well as the foundation of my spiritual sanity.

Core Values: I value a plucky, open-minded sense of adventure. I value a willingness to take chances. When in doubt, I say roll the dice and let's see what happens. In my core, there is a fundamental faith that life can be trusted. In my core, there is a fundamental faith that life is meaningful—and that our purpose here is to discover and embody that meaning. I value being true to my principles above all practical concerns. I cannot be bought.

Strategy: I will stretch my horizons by immersing myself in cross-cultural experiences, and internalizing them. One way for me to accomplish that is simply to travel; equally, befriending people from different backgrounds has a similarly beneficial impact. Underlying this strategy is the realization that my perceptions have been limited by my own society and its cultural training. The liberating, empowering truth I seek is on the other side of that boundary. Education in the broadest sense of the word can help me accomplish that aim. I resolve to spend my life learning. Some of that learning may happen in classes, or from books—but much of it arises simply from my embracing life.

Tools: I was born with a philosophical nature; I have always been motivated to wrestle with big questions. I have an intuitive ability to connect the dots of my experience and draw conclusions about the basic laws and principles of the universe. I am plucky; I bounce back from adversity. My faith in life is resilient; I don't mind a bumpy ride some of the time, if that is the price of living my life the way I want to.

Dealing with the Shadow: I recognize that sometimes I might be too quick to connect the dots. I might jump to conclusions—sometimes wrong, but never in doubt. I guard myself against this kind of oversimplification by making sure that my senses are constantly flooded with more experience—wide experience being the sovereign remedy for dogmatism. I recognize that my spontaneity and transparency, while well-intended, can sometimes hurt people. That is not my intention, so I am mindful of my Fiery nature and I temper it with judgment, patience, and a compassionate sensitivity toward other people's vulnerabilities.

SUN IN CAPRICORN

Evolutionary Aim: I resolve to make my appetites, personal needs, and fears subordinate to my higher intentions. My will-power, not my appetite, shapes my life. Every other aspect of my being has its place of honor and acceptance, but it is always secondary to my sense of mission in the world. I have reached a stage in my evolutionary journey in which I know I must perform a Great Work. Being true to this path is the source of my energy, my self-respect, and my recuperative powers, as well as the foundation of my spiritual sanity.

Core Values: I value single-pointed focus and self-discipline. I value the ability to avoid distraction from my goals. I value resourcefulness—and I abhor waste and inefficiency. I value integrity and personal honor. Emphatically, I do not value self-punishment—but I recognize and accept that maintaining integrity and personal honor may create the appearance of self-punishment.

Strategy: I search my soul for a goal that is a worthy match for the enormous efforts of which I am capable. Once I have identified that worthy goal, it becomes "the pearl of great price:" no sacrifice is too costly for achieving it. I set priorities and stick to them; I make rational plans; I inventory my resources; I waste nothing—most especially my time.

Tools: I was born with enormous self-discipline. I keep my eye on the prize. I am resourceful; I can make ten beans last for two weeks if I have to. I have a high tolerance for solitude—in fact I need at least some solitude every day in order to keep my existential batteries charged. I can sustain long trains of logic. I think in paragraphs rather than in sound bites.

Dealing with the Shadow: I acknowledge that my goal-driven nature can estrange me from the natural self-monitoring mechanisms of my body, mind, and soul. I resolve to improve my ability to notice those kinds of signals: to register, for example, when I am tired, or lonely, or hungry. Above all, I recognize my vulnerability to internalizing goals and values that have their origin in other people's intentions rather than in my own. I will not harness my enormous capacity for self-discipline to a dream that did not arise in my own soul.

SUN IN AQUARIUS

Evolutionary Aim: I resolve above all to be true to myself. That is, I resolve to sort out who I really am from everything I have been trained or conditioned to believe that I am. I recognize the dilemma: half of what I am is actually rooted in my soul, while the other half is merely a product of my society, the age in which I am living, my family of origin, and so on. I resolve to sort out which half is which, and to follow my own path no matter what costs, criticisms, or judgments arise. I will not be duped into living a life that is not truly my own. Being true to this path is the source of my energy, my self-respect, and my recuperative powers, as well as the foundation of my spiritual sanity.

Core Values: I value the kind of true independence that arises from authentic self-knowledge. I value the ability to follow one's own path in the face of threats, attacks, payoffs, or simple misunderstandings. I honor geniuses and rebels—and I understand that they are often labeled as criminals, at least for a while. I aspire to follow in their footsteps. I aspire to be impervious to the pitiful human need for the approval of others.

Strategy: I will be wary of the bribes this world offers me for betraying myself; I cannot be bought that way. Similarly, threats do not intimidate me. I will think outside the box; I will follow the road less traveled; I will accept the fact that the more I am true to myself, the more unusual I will look to most people. Being called "weird" does not bother me.

Tools: I am inherently innovative. I have a reflexive tendency to question authority. When I hear the words, "Everybody knows..." I instinctively suspect that what follows is incorrect. Compared to most people, I am hard to manipulate. No one can buy me. I prefer to be liked; but I do not need to be liked. I can breathe the thin, cool, stratospheric air of true individuality, and I can thrive on it.

Dealing with the Shadow: I acknowledge that one of my survival strategies has been to protect myself from manipulation by maintaining a posture of distance or aloofness; this has been necessary; I have no shame about it. But I also recognize that as I become more secure in my own identity, I need to develop warmer, more vulnerable, people-skills. I also resolve to recognize that mere contrariness, idiosyncrasy, and stubbornness must never be confused with the inner path of discovering my true individuality.

SUN IN PISCES

Evolutionary Aim: I resolve to attain and explore a significantly higher state of consciousness in this lifetime. I resolve increasingly to separate my consciousness from my personality, and to become more identified with consciousness itself. I accept the fact that I am positioned for such a breakthrough—that in this lifetime I might, with skillful effort, become significantly more transparent to the Divine. Being true to this path is the source of my energy, my self-respect, and my recuperative powers, as well as the foundation of my spiritual sanity.

Core Values: I am, above all, committed to following a spiritual path, however I choose to define that journey. I value mysticism and a sense of magic; I find value in spiritual teachings, and perhaps in religion. I value compassion. I am suspicious of mere materialism and I am profoundly aware of the limitations of three-dimensional, time-bound, logic. I value the idea that reality has more in common with a dream than with a machine.

Strategy: I will take time regularly to sit quietly, to open my awareness to the vastness of Mind itself—and for a while not be preoccupied with the affairs of my ego or my personality. I may call this time "meditation;" just as easily, I might call it fishing—or sitting quietly in the garden, or watching the Sun go down. The words do not matter; what matters is my "logging hours" in that altered, transcendent condition. In a nutshell, every day I will find time to sit and think about exactly what is looking through my eyes.

Tools: I came into this world with a sense of magic. I came into this world with what might be called a sense of the presence of God. Ever since

I was young, I have had inexplicable experiences: knowing things that I had no rational way of knowing. I was born, in other words, with psychic sensitivity. My imagination has always been vivid; my ability to visualize inner worlds is extraordinary. When I close my eyes, I enter a world of infinite mystery.

Dealing with the Shadow: I acknowledge that I was born with more psychic sensitivity than I know how to handle. I can be overwhelmed by it. When that happens, the first side effect is that I tend to become absent-minded. I lose my focus in this world. Next, I might potentially be tempted to move in escapist directions. I need to be careful of those kinds of pitfalls. I also acknowledge that my more transcendent reflexes could put me in a position where I fail to defend myself or to claim what I actually need. Faced with other people's intensity, ego, or neediness, I could lose sight of my own path. Down that lonely road, I could become a ghost in my own life. I resolve not to do that.

11

JUPITER IN THE TWELVE SIGNS

JUPITER IN ARIES

The Prize: To achieve meaningful victory—and "meaningful" is the key word here. Aries energy is the astrological equivalent of nuclear power; when allied with the expansive qualities of Jupiter, it is essential to maintain some restraint and clarity of intention, lest we leave a trail of blood behind us. Self-knowledge about *what is actually good for you* must underlie your decisions. With this configuration, there is a good chance that you will get what you want.

Never Underestimate... your courage under pressure. Your ability to snatch victory from the jaws of defeat. Your ability to bounce back from adversity. Your resilience. Your ability to improvise strategy and tactics in the face of unforeseen circumstances.

Beware of Inflation... arising from the marriage of ego and anger. The intoxication of winning and the single-minded fixation upon victory can blind you to their costs. Make sure the victory is one that is worthy of you—and worth its costs.

Your Gift From the Gods: Pluck and resilience.

Helpful Wisdom: Wise old karate masters tell us that sometimes the most effective strategy is simply to walk away from the fight.

JUPITER IN TAURUS

The Prize: What is more precious than a serene heart? Your wisest aim in life is the achievement of an abundance of peace. To relax. To know that enough is enough—and to recognize "enough" when you see it. Silence is precious. So is a healthy relationship with your physical body. Real friends, natural beauty, a freedom from trivial distraction, and above all, time to immerse yourself in them—these are the true prizes.

Never Underestimate… the therapeutic impact on your soul of quiet, of physical touch, and of listening carefully to the promptings of your physical body. Never underestimate the wisdom of your instincts. Trust your animal friends: they have something important to teach you.

Beware of Inflation… regarding the hyped, empty promises of this commercialized world—glamour, money, fame, and so forth. They promise far more peace than they ever actually deliver.

Your Gift From the Gods: If you are truly quiet and listen carefully to the still, small voice within, you have utterly reliable instincts.

Helpful wisdom: 'Tis a Gift To Be Simple

JUPITER IN GEMINI

The Prize: A life of endless fascination, a life in which you are never bored, a life of wonder and miracles—that is the prize. Endless learning is pivotal; but do not confuse that with dry academic pedagogy. This is about intellectual passion. It is about the mental appetite that we call curiosity curating a feast of epic proportions.

Never Underestimate… the simple fact that you have something important to say in this world. Never underestimate the benefit of education in the broadest sense of the word. Never underestimate your powers of persuasion; you can convey not only information, but contagious enthusiasm for that information.

Beware of Inflation… regarding your estimate of other people's fascination with your opinions, along with your certainty about the veracity of those opinions. Mark Twain wrote a windy letter to a friend that began with an apology: "I am sorry this letter is so long. I didn't have time to write a short one." Remember that sometimes it is best to "write the short one."

Your Gift From the Gods: Curiosity. Persuasiveness. Skill with language. Educability—you can learn anything.

Helpful wisdom: Never fail to take full advantage of an opportunity to keep your mouth shut.

JUPITER IN CANCER

The Prize: Home Sweet Home—and that familiar phrase has many levels of meaning, all of which can potentially constitute an enormous source of joy for you. Any planet in Cancer reflects an inward agenda of self-healing, and, pursuant of that, a pleasant, quiet, safe place to live is always helpful in that process. But a house is not a home; domestic love is a critical ingredient here—but that love need not take a traditional form. It is about people upon whom you can count, people who share the road of life with you in a spirit of commitment. Framing these human treasures as the grand prize in life, and valuing them above all other distractions, is the right use of this energy.

Never Underestimate... the healing, deepening impact on you of quiet time in a safe place with people you love. Recognize that much good comes to your soul while you are sleeping, so make sure you get enough of it. Sleep heals more than the physical body. Never underestimate the healing impact your faith has on people around you.

Beware of Inflation... regarding other people's definitions of your duties and responsibilities toward them. Beware of the endless insatiability of family; do not allow yourself to be devoured by them. Beware of defending yourself too much against life.

Your Gift From the Gods: Sensitivity. A big, generous, nurturing heart. A full-time guardian angel watching over your domestic environment. Luck finding a good place to live.

Helpful wisdom: As Leonard Cohen said,"Put your hat on your headache and dance."

JUPITER IN LEO

The Prize: Spontaneity. A feeling of being at ease with your own vulnerability; expressing it without hesitation under the assumption that you will be appreciated. You are here learning to walk like a king or a queen in this world, confident, with your head held high, and comfortable with your valued place in the human family. To attain the prize, you must offer a rich gift: leaving some sincere evidence of your inner life in the hands of your community.

Never Underestimate... your creativity, your capacity to perform, and your personal magnetism, especially when you are taking chances regarding self-revelation. Trust your sense of drama and your ability to hold the attention of an audience, small or large—and never underestimate the charm of your sense of humor.

Beware of Inflation... regarding your own capacity to endlessly fascinate people. Other people's appreciative attention can be intoxicating; enjoy a glass or two—but not three or four.

Your Gift From the Gods: Star-quality.

Helpful wisdom: Seasoned performers say you should make your audience happy once, but not twice—in other words, they should be happy when you step out on the stage, but they should not be happy when they see you leave it.

JUPITER IN VIRGO

The Prize: In the long run, is there any prize more worthy of pursuit than feeling that we actually made a difference in the world? Your prize, in a nutshell, is to find work and responsibilities that truly matter. You revel in skill and competence; you shine when you are appreciated for your well-honed skills.

Never Underestimate... what you are capable of achieving in terms of prestige in your field—not that prestige itself is the point, only that prestige arises naturally when you spread your wings and truly claim the highest levels of your potential skill-set. You are capable of more than you imagine.

Beware of Inflation... regarding other people's ever-expanding definitions of your alleged duties and responsibilities. You are here to help people; but you are not a public utility. We are talking about *self-expression through service*, not having your life defined by other people's whining.

Your Gift From the Gods: The ability to master complex skills; the ability to harness your intelligence and press it toward the far limits of its potential development.

Helpful wisdom: Your prayer: God grant that today I do work that matters.

JUPITER IN LIBRA

The Prize: A life of grace and elegance, for sure—but, to keep perspective, immediately contemplate the graceful elegance of a gazelle, and compare it with crass, tasteless ostentation, especially when it is fueled by wealth. Go for the gazelle, in other words! This is about a single rose in a vase on your kitchen table. This is about poetry and music, and the company of the sorts of friends who appreciate them. You claim your true prize when that external grace and elegance sink into the marrow of your bones. That is more likely to happen if you are not seeking to keep up with anyone or trying to impress anyone.

Never Underestimate... your aesthetic instincts; they unerringly lead you to the creation of an environment that soothes your spirit. Trust your creative impulses and invest generously in their development. Never underestimate the benefit to you of the company of people who can be moved to tears by a sunset or a fading rose or a piece of haunting music.

Beware of Inflation... regarding the generation of the outward appearance of position, prosperity, beauty, or personal importance. Be as beautiful as you can be; enjoy that. But be wary of vanity, both physically and socially.

Your Gift From the Gods: The ability to harmonize colors, shapes, contradictory ideas, and different kinds of people. The ability to present yourself attractively to many different sorts of people.

Helpful wisdom: As the Navajos say, "May you walk in beauty."

JUPITER IN SCORPIO

The Prize: Imagine, on one hand, the fiercest, most psychologically threatening truths you can muster—and on the other hand, meeting them with joy and faith. That marriage of apparent opposites is the prize here. We are talking about looking "the devil in the eye"—and smiling, even laughing. In this configuration, we see evidence of a soul finding itself on the cusp of achieving victory over an ancient wound—dancing triumphantly on its own grave from a past life.

Never Underestimate... the ultimate power of truth to liberate you from despair. And never underestimate the strength that enters the human spirit when we let humor be one of our tools. Laughter is a healing force. Eventually on this path, you can even learn to laugh at the feebleness of death itself.

Beware of Inflation... regarding the dramatic gravity of your own wounds and issues, and your "Tell-All" narrative about them. Even when they are real and legitimate and you are facing them honestly, recognize that they can hypnotize you. You have a real capacity for psychological penetration—but do guard your sense of perspective. Be wary of a subtle, creeping vanity in regard to your own depth.

Your Gift From the Gods: The ability to maintain faith, humor, and spiritedness in the face of life's genuine darkness.

Helpful wisdom: Some people say angels can fly because they have wings, but angels fly because they take themselves lightly.

JUPITER IN SAGITTARIUS

The Prize: A complete commitment to living your life as a Quest, and doing so unabashedly, and enthusiastically, and without shame. This involves a deep integration of the idea that there are ultimately no mistakes, only experiences to be digested. We are talking about faith, but not in a narrowly religious sense—it is more like faith in the fundamental goodness of embodied existence, and an enthusiastic willingness to dive into it. Your basic goodness is being forged into wisdom in the cauldrons of experience.

Never Underestimate... your luck. Here is another way to express that idea: you have a guardian angel who has vowed to protect you so long as you maintain your commitment to being fully alive. Not comfortable with the idea of angels? Then let's say the same thing a third way: you are plugged into the synchronistic fabric of the universe in a way that favors risk and audacity.

Beware of Inflation... regarding "being right" all the time. In your enthusiasm for understanding, you can jump to conclusions. And about that fabled "luck" of yours—it operates in service of your Quest, not in service of greed or stupidity.

Your Gift From the Gods: A primal enthusiasm for life; an ability to find meaning in chaos.

Helpful wisdom: Experience brings wisdom; a lack of wisdom brings experience.

JUPITER IN CAPRICORN

The Prize: The dignity, self-respect, and personal *gravitas* that arise from genuine accomplishment. It is as if the universe has challenged you, "Show us excellence.

Show us the Great Work of a lifetime. Make something that outlasts you. Leave some substantial evidence of your existence, your vision, and your integrity behind you in this world."

Never Underestimate... your capacity for sustained discipline and focused concentration over long periods of time. Never underestimate the fruits of persistence. Like the tortoise and the hare, slow and steady wins the race.

Beware of Inflation... regarding your own self-importance. Be hesitant and generous in your judgment of others: not all those who wander are lost. Cultivate sensitivity to your own needs; learn to sleep when you are tired, to eat when you are hungry—and to play in the mud when you are becoming too "adult" for your own good.

Your Gift From the Gods: You can keep your eye on the prize long after others have become distracted. You are hardwired for accomplishing great works.

Helpful wisdom: Moral values and integrity are everything; take care to define them for yourself rather than accepting external, conventional definitions of them. Harness your strength to your own heart, not to the values of strangers.

JUPITER IN AQUARIUS

The Prize: A magnificent life that is truly your own; a free-spirited existence guided by your own stars; a unique story that has never been lived before by anyone else. To have enough faith in your own perceptions that you need no one else's validation, agreement, or approval. To breathe deeply in the intoxicating stratosphere of true individuality and genuine freedom.

Never Underestimate... the validity of your own perceptions, even if no one else shares them. There is an element of genius in your makeup; never doubt that. Never underestimate the soul-crushing power of any vestige in you of a need for other people's approval—and never underestimate your ability to resist that deadening force.

Beware of Inflation... regarding the sanctity of your quirks. You have a natural right to be different, but those differences do not make other people wrong. Do not be afraid to learn from others: you can spend a long time reinventing the wheel, only to find out that it was already done a few thousand years ago.

Your Gift From the Gods: an ability to think outside the box; an ability to see possibilities that no one else has ever imagined.

Helpful wisdom: As Oscar Wilde said, "I put all my genius into my life; I put only my talent into my works."

JUPITER IN PISCES

The Prize: There are prizes we must forfeit at the moment of death and there are prizes that, once we have won them, remain ours for eternity. Your prize is in the second category: it is nothing less than a breakthrough in consciousness. It is a major step in the direction of wisdom, even the potential attainment of something akin to sainthood. Only with spiritual discernment can anyone even recognize this precious prize—learn to pursue what your soul truly values.

Never Underestimate... your evolutionary potential. You have already earned the right to a spiritual breakthrough. Take heart from that fact, and go about your life expecting miracles. In this lifetime, you will be kissed by an angel. Do not fail to notice it.

Beware of Inflation... regarding your spiritual and psychic accomplishments. Recognize that these developments are not happening in your ego; they are happening because your ego is becoming transparent to your larger self. Do not allow mere pride to debase this gift.

Your Gift From the Gods: Psychic sensitivity. No matter what path you take through life, you will feel the presence of higher powers—of God, of angels, of energies: the words do not matter; it is the experience itself that is the gift from the gods. The world might call this perceptual phenomenon "faith," but it is more direct than that.

Helpful wisdom: Earth is not the most prestigious address in the galaxy.

12

MARS IN THE TWELVE HOUSES

MARS IN THE FIRST HOUSE

Battlefield: Forks in the road of life; fateful choices that require a lot of courage. Assertiveness training. Critical decision points, which are often characterized by insufficient information. Binding vows made in an imperfect world. Painful choices. Leadership, in situations where others who are incapable of defending themselves are counting on you. Meeting resistance with appropriate force.

Strategy: To accept the challenge. To recognize that "fear is the mind killer." To avoid panic. To be willing to burn bridges behind you. To use sufficient force—but no more than necessary. To protect that which is worthy of protection—and sacrifice the rest.

Objective: To truly *lead* a life rather than have it happen to you. To recognize that fear—and only fear—blocks your path. To find your inner warrior.

The Shape of Failure: Cowardice. Allowing yourself to become the designated victim. To let fear make your decisions. To surrender your freedom to the will of petty tyrants. Alternatively, to become cruel and tyrannical yourself. To let anger rule your life.

MARS IN THE SECOND HOUSE

Battlefield: Challenges that afford you an opportunity to prove yourself to yourself and to others. Winning despite limited resources. Financial stress: either too little money—or too much. Gaining confidence in your inner warrior and his or her ability to come out on top despite the odds.

Strategy: Feel the fear, but do it anyway. Rise to challenges. Prove yourself to yourself by facing people and situations that intimidate you. Be willing to bet on yourself financially, taking money risks in order to fulfill your dreams and aspirations. Be willing to "die with your boots on." Accept the risks entailed in claiming the resources and tools that you need for your journey.

Objective: A fundamental, elevating transformation in your level of self-confidence and warrior dignity.

The Shape of Failure: Being afraid to follow the path with heart. Looking back on the life you did not live. Giving your need for material security too much power in shaping your decisions. Attracting a pattern of financial stress.

MARS IN THE THIRD HOUSE

Battlefield: Finding your voice. Expressing your passion. Standing up to intellectual intimidation. Trusting your own perceptions even if others tell you they are incorrect or heretical. Claiming your right to an education in every sense of that word. Learning to be effective in argument.

Strategy: Speaking up. Expressing yourself with passion and convincing vehemence. Trusting your curiosity. Seizing experience that has been forbidden to you. Not allowing yourself to be silenced. Recognizing that you do some of your most penetrating thinking while in physical motion—that is, while walking, driving, or traveling.

Objective: To claim your right and your ability to speak passionately, confidently, and persuasively on any topic, even in the face of judgment or intimidation.

The Shape of Failure: Allowing yourself to be silenced, your voice shut down by others whom you have allowed to overpower or overshadow you. To betray your own best truths by leaving them unsaid. Alternatively, to become compulsively argumentative, defensive, bitter, and damagingly sarcastic.

MARS IN THE FOURTH HOUSE

Battlefield: First and foremost, this configuration is about developing the emotional courage necessary for all inner work—facing the truth of our own souls is frightening. Psychological wounds are often connected to family dynamics, and these kinds of issues figure prominently here. Anger, resentments and repression linked to domestic life arise and require resolution.

Strategy: Contemplation of the Warrior archetype, leading to the integration of the inner warrior into the shape of the outward biographical life. Bringing your fierceness, passion, and heat to the surface where others can see it. Finding the strength and courage to claim one's natural home and to protect it against any assault.

Objective: A passionate *soul* is not enough; the aim here is a passionate *life*, lived in the right location and shared with the right people.

The Shape of Failure: To harbor seething resentments or frustrations without a ripple on the surface. The bomb detonating inside the steel room. Domestic or familial conflict endlessly repeating and never resolving.

MARS IN THE FIFTH HOUSE

Battlefield: Stepping onto the stage of life and belting out your song, whatever that means for you. The courage to express yourself honestly and creatively. The courage to be sincere to the point of genuine vulnerability. Performance. Facing stage fright. Feeling confident and legitimate in the behavioral expression of your sexuality. Passionate love affairs, with the ghost of unresolved karma hovering over them.

Strategy: Finding your natural instrument of self-expression and polishing your skills with it. Committing yourself to a life of creativity and taking the emotional risks that path entails. Using sports to gain confidence in your warrior-body. Trusting your lust—but first, making sure that it is trustworthy.

Objective: Total unselfconscious self-expression at every level.

The Shape of Failure: Being ruled by your inhibitions and your fear of ridicule. Turning away from your passion; allowing others to shame your sexuality. Remaining in unresolved, karmically-based relationships with people who hurt you.

MARS IN THE SIXTH HOUSE

Battlefield: Finding the right work. Independently defining your own responsibilities and executing them decisively. Seeking mentors who embody courage and who show you the right use of force. Learning to compete mindfully. Protecting those who legitimately depend on you. Forcefully defending your right to self-care.

Strategy: Letting no one and nothing stand between you and the path that leads to meaningful work—and being brave enough to strike out on your own independent career or vocation. Seeking teachers who instantly fill you with respect for them. Finding a place for competitiveness in your life, one that does not leave a trail of blood behind you. Defending your right to take care of your health at every level.

Objective: Mastery. Finding the right vocation. Developing the skills that underlie meaningful victory. Seeking your teachers—and later defending your students.

The Shape of Failure: Working for a boss who was "Attila the Hun" in a prior lifetime. Accepting abuse, internalizing shame that derives from the niggling criticism of minor tyrants. Stress-related disorders, both physical and mental.

MARS IN THE SEVENTH HOUSE

Battlefield: Intimacy in all senses: marriage, friendship, partnership. Passionate connections. Difficult relationships—including those that are worth the trouble. Accepting the fact that some element of conflict is endemic to all human interdependency, along with the development of mindful skills for dealing with it. Facing the seductive, slippery dangers of numbing familiarity and mechanical ritual in long-term relationship; defeating those dangers.

Strategy: Learning the art of intimate conflict resolution. Being direct and truthful rather than harboring tensions under the banners of tolerance or forgiveness. Most critically, learning to discern and select partners *who would immediately understand the previous sentence.*

Objective: The maintenance of genuine passion in long-term intimacy.

The Shape of Failure: A chronic attraction to people whom you do not actually like or respect. Endless drama—or endless therapy—that goes nowhere. Fights that are not about what they appear to be about; mere venting and needless, pointless emotional bloodshed.

MARS IN THE EIGHTH HOUSE

Battlefield: The behaviors that arise from all of the complex emotions, instincts, and issues that are triggered by the process of coupling or mating. Unresolved psychological wounds and how we deal with them—or how they deal with us. The unconscious mind manifesting in our intimate behavior. Human mortality—that is to say, our psychological and spiritual relationship to our own deaths and to the deaths of people with whom we share life.

Strategy: Above all, honesty—the inner behavior of truthful self-examination, along with the outward behavior of penetrating interactions with people with whom we have deep bonds. Committed sexuality as one path of the spiritual warrior. Lifelong preparation for the spiritual adventure of death.

Objective: Making death our counselor—which is to say that in the light of our mortality, much becomes very clear. We then understand what is important and what is not important. Bringing that wisdom to bear upon the entire length of life. The wasteful futility of lying to ourselves or lying to anyone with whom we are pretending to be intimate. Our objective is to live each day as if it were our last and to love with that kind of transparency, intensity, and nakedness.

The Shape of Failure: Belief in the illusion of a "magical partner" with whom we can remain in a fairyland of passion forever without making any evolutionary effort; the inevitable cycle of disappointments that follow from such an erroneous belief. Acting as if we think that we will live forever.

MARS IN THE NINTH HOUSE

Battlefield: The endless, passionate search for meaning and understanding in life. Adventures of all sorts. Travel that requires courage; cross-cultural experience. Education, both in the formal and the experiential sense. Robust religion and philosophy tempered and deepened by a willingness to hurl oneself bravely into life.

Strategy: Going where we are drawn to go but afraid to go. That includes travel, but also crossing cultural or social boundaries closer to home.

Assertively claiming our right to learn or to achieve education. Testing our beliefs against reality and being willing to renounce the ones that fail the test, all the while accepting the social consequences of walking that talk.

Objective: A warrior's path of endless stretching and adventure that leads to a personally convincing and utterly honest sense of the meaning of life. A feeling of having been set free in the world, able to move confidently through various cultures, social strata, and exotic places.

The Shape of Failure: The armchair adventurer eating potato chips in front of a television. Angry religious or philosophical fanaticism and dogmatism impervious to information. Preaching. The need to convince others of that which, in truth, we do not fully believe ourselves. Willful ignorance.

MARS IN THE TENTH HOUSE

Battlefield: Your mission in the world. An independent, adventurous career. A colorful reputation. Bravely affecting the myths and symbols of your community. Forcefully making a difference in the world. Standing up publicly and being counted. Enemies and competitors. Two dogs and one bone. Public conflicts where compromise is not available or possible.

Strategy: To be willing to pay the price and face the stress of accepting your legitimate public mission in the world. To cultivate autonomy and independence as you shape your lifestyle. To recognize that others' fates are dependent upon your being courageous. To accept that it is your path to protect entities—that is to say, people, ideas, even creatures—which are incapable of protecting themselves.

Objective: To have a mission in life so passionately meaningful and so transcendently important to you that you would die for it—not that you are eager to die for it, but that you would if you had to. Waking up each morning with that kind of vitality. A fire in your belly to go to work in the morning.

The Shape of Failure: Endless stress in meaningless work or social situations, typically characterized by oppressive, unfair, or angry authorities above you. Being defined as the natural victim or scapegoat—everyone's favorite punch.

MARS IN THE ELEVENTH HOUSE

Battlefield: The search for your natural tribe. Networking; teamwork—often with difficult people. "Herding cats." Soul-clans characterized by stressful karma—enemies, class struggle, social conflict. Meaningful aims involving experiences that can only be attained via cooperation with other people. Passionate devotion to long-term goals and projects. Battles in the second half of life; the "call of destiny" coming in maturity.

Strategy: Setting goals which require courage—and accepting them and committing to them long-term. Relentless devotion, with the eye on the prize. Once such goals are set—and only then—the seeking of the team or the human network necessary for reaching them.

Objective: To devote the first half of life to embodying a warrior-spirit worthy of the mission that emerges in the second half of life; to assemble the network of allies who allow you to fulfill that mission. To keep the faith that you have something important to contribute to your community despite the slow emergence of the circumstances that call for it.

The Shape of Failure: Empty, pointless alliances. Stressful, fruitless social over-extension. Gossip; petty wars and rivalries; "court intrigue." Endless interpersonal politics. Exhausting inner tension or frustration boiling over in the second half of life, often taking the form of an existential explosion—or a depressive surrender to exhaustion.

MARS IN THE TWELFTH HOUSE

Battlefield: Consciousness itself; the psychic realms; the spiritual path. What stands between you and a major breakthrough in those categories is simply *fear.* You have reached the stage in the evolutionary journey where you will either make a breakthrough or you will break down. Thus you attract everything scary, from apparitions of the lower astral planes to brushes with physical danger in this world.

Strategy: You are training your nerves to remain unflappable and steady in the face of strange, unsettling, or weird psychic stimuli. Facing specific fears of any sort, even physical ones—repeatedly, over time—*desensitizes your response to panic.* Thus, for example, you might contemplate the possible spiritual benefits of skydiving, spelunking, or mountaineering—or if you are an old woman in a walker, contemplate the possible spiritual benefit of walking across the street.

Objective: Staying centered no matter what happens. An absolute, self-possessed sense of presence in the eternal now, no matter what manner of stimulus arises. Spiritual courage. Alignment with the archetype of the spiritual warrior.

The Shape of Failure: Accidents and misfortunes arising as the law of synchronicity presents you with frightening growth opportunities from which you turn away—in other words, it is better to embrace those scary experiences rather than fleeing them and thus forcing them to manifest in a more negative way. Spiritual stasis; being stalled on the cusp of evolutionary breakthrough. Vague, unspecified fears and free-floating anxiety; the specter of madness.

13

THE SUN IN THE TWELVE HOUSES

SUN IN THE FIRST HOUSE

Necessary Action: Leadership—both in the sense of leading other people and in the sense of independently leading your own life. The development of willpower and decisiveness, especially in situations characterized by uncertainty and requiring quick thinking. Self-reliance; autonomy. Influencing other people and attracting followers, whether they are desired or not. Choosing a path and committing to it, even in the face of insufficient information; trusting intuition when actual facts are lacking or contradictory.

Words To Live By: You can't make an omelette without breaking some eggs. The buck stops here. Burning bridges behind you. Not looking back. The die is cast. Crossing the Rubicon. Sometimes selfishness is necessary—and sometimes selfishness is simply a shaming, manipulative word aimed at a person who is only taking care of herself or himself.

Synchronistic Correlates: Forks in the road of life; choice points. Difficult decisions that bind you to a specific future. Situations in which you are more frightened or uncertain than you are perceived to be. Unintentionally eliciting psychological projections, positive or negative, from others. Being thrust into situations of responsibility.

The Shape of Failure: Actual selfishness or insensitivity toward the needs, values, and diverse natures of others. The belief that everything revolves around you. Bad choices—or "choices" illustrating the principle that sometimes indecision is a decision.

SUN IN THE SECOND HOUSE

Necessary Action: Concrete, real-world accomplishments through which you win your own self-respect and self-confidence. Proving yourself to yourself. Acquiring the critical resources that support such efforts: skills, alliances, tools, education—and sometimes money. Never forget that the second house represents the material basis of survival, not just finances. Money is popular because it buys food and shelter—discernment and decisiveness may be necessary in securing them.

Words To Live By: You miss 100 percent of the shots you don't take. Never fear failure; failure sometimes teaches us more than success. Don't put yourself in the position of looking back on the life that you did not live. It is possible for a person to pay way too much for his or her money.

Synchronistic Correlates: Financial and material ups and downs; good weeks and bad weeks, money-wise. Self-employment—or work based on commission rather than a reliable salary. Issues generated by poverty—or by wealth. The universe seems to be asking you, how much power do you want to give to money? How much time do you want to spend concerned with it? In a strong response, we develop skills that enhance our faith in our ability to improvise our survival; money itself then fades in importance.

The Shape of Failure: "I would love to do that, but I can't afford to"—sometimes those words are simply true—but how often are they a clever disguise for our fear of failure or our lack of confidence in ourselves? Failure here looks like the flower that never opened, the novel that was never written, or the soul-mate who was never approached.

SUN IN THE THIRD HOUSE

Necessary Action: The development of your own voice. Working with media—which includes the spoken word, but also writing, film, and all other methods by which humans tell their stories, converse, share, or teach. The development of such a "voice" is nourished by an endless diet of fresh perceptions—and so we see here an avid desire for experience in the form of learning, traveling, and a general willingness to throw a monkey wrench into the humming gear-works of a mechanically predictable life.

Words To Live By: Questions teach you more than answers. You learn more with your mouth shut than with your mouth open. Whatever you presently see or understand, the truth is far beyond that.

Synchronistic Correlates: A lifelong pattern of chaotic, unpredictable circumstances—and the question is, do you surf those waves of unpredictability or do you just deal with one damn thing after another? The experience of many lifetimes lived in a single lifetime. The opportunity—and the pressure—to speak up. Connections with teaching, publishing, the Internet, and the world of media.

The Shape of Failure: Running around in circles, distracted by everything, never achieving excellence in any one area. All tactics, but no strategy. Compulsive chatter. Jittery, nervous, scattered energy.

SUN IN THE FOURTH HOUSE

Necessary Action: Creating outward circumstances that are conducive to inward reflection—quiet, along with a feeling of safety and uncontested privacy. "Majoring in psychology." The search for your natural soul-family—and remember to extend the definition of "family" to include non-traditional possibilities. The establishment of lifelong commitments, including deep friendships. The search for your natural home. Living together. Wrestling with the power that the family myth holds over you.

Words To Live By: A house is not a home; a house is simply architecture until we see committed love in some form under one roof. "I will never leave you." Shared memories; the long, shared story. The ground in which my grandparents' bones are buried. Practicing the presence of one's ancestors.

Synchronistic Correlates: Complicated family dynamics; domestic responsibilities; a demanding or otherwise highly impactful family. Heritage; the psychological presence of your ancestry. Circumstances that vector the attention inward, perhaps toward history and ultimate origins: for example, the presence in your life of psychologists, genealogists—or astrologers.

The Shape of Failure: To be completely dominated and overshadowed by the expectations of family or clan. To be defined and limited by the place and culture of your birth. To have your individuality buried under the weight of being "the son of" or "the daughter of." To become self-indulgent, so mesmerized by your inner life that you never manifest a meaningful outward life.

SUN IN THE FIFTH HOUSE

Necessary Action: The cultivation of an unabashed, pagan attitude towards your natural appetites. To embrace the pleasures and celebrations of life. To find a creative outlet—some medium whereby what you personally hold to be sacred or beautiful can be expressed, seen, and applauded. To perform. To play. To step out on the stage of life. Perhaps to have children—and to let them teach you how to be a child again.

Words To Live By: In life, everything boils down to either pleasure or pain. We have a characteristic human reaction to each of them—we open our hearts to pleasure and we shut down in the face of pain. In prior lifetimes, you experienced some terrible hurt. In this lifetime, you are in recovery from that injury. In light of all that, *you are here on Earth to have a good time.* As trivial as that comment sounds, it is central to any understanding of the purpose of your life. That is how you recover.

Synchronistic Correlates: Opportunities to develop creative skills: music, dance, painting, and so on. Opportunities to participate in sports—and by sports, we mean not only football and basketball, but also non-competitive ones such as hiking or boating. The presence of children in your life. Love affairs—which often actually mean finishing up unresolved karma with people who seem "strangely familiar." Playmates. Toys—which is to say, objects that invoke playfulness, remembering that "the difference between men and boys is the price of their toys."

The Shape of Failure: An unbalanced obsession with physical pleasures to the point that it eclipses the joys of mind and spirit. Addiction; a compulsion to dive into oblivion. Never growing up. An inability to resist temptation. Making a fool of yourself in order to attract attention.

SUN IN THE SIXTH HOUSE

Necessary Action: Finding right work and right responsibilities. That means identifying and polishing your innate gifts and skills. You can accomplish that aim through training and education, with a particular emphasis on establishing personal relationships with worthy mentors. Cultivating the humility needed to surrender to teachers. Balancing self-care with caring for others.

Words To Live By: An ancient Egyptian prayer: "God grant that today I do work that matters." I accept that I am on the path of service; it is more blessed to give than to receive. I resolve to become the kind of person who genuinely does not hate Mondays.

Synchronistic Correlates: Responsibilities, often of an extremely demanding nature, arise. You attract genuine mentors who are precious to you and pivotal in your development—but you can also attract petty tyrants who attempt to control you with outright intimidation, the abuse of authority, endless demands, shaming, or piteous whining.

The Shape of Failure: Slavery. Meaningless work that is not rooted in the essence of your psyche. Your actual, substantial gifts and talents going to waste, rotting on the vine. Turning your back on your true mentors. A life defined by external demands and orders, especially the demands of those who lord it over you. Some of them might try to dominate you from actual positions of power—but others do it by accessing your conscience, and thus manipulating you with their weakness and desperation.

SUN IN THE SEVENTH HOUSE

Necessary Action: The establishment of active evolutionary relationship with your natural partners. These partnerships may be intimate, but they also include lasting friendships, creative partnerships, even business connections. The point is that you cannot do what you have come into this world to do all by yourself. These relationships are typically characterized by affection—but even more central is a sense of equality, mutual complementarity, and the possibility of the connection enduring until the end of your life.

Words To Live By: No man (or woman) is an island. Some truths are so large that it takes two people to hold them. If we agreed all the time, neither of us would ever learn anything. People falling in love always say, "you and I are so alike." People actually in love always say, "you and I are so different." That latter conversation leads you directly to your evolutionary path.

Synchronistic Correlates: Fateful meetings that change the course of your life. Receiving and internalizing impactful counsel. Relationships with strong-willed "solar" types of people. Playing with half a deck of cards—and finding the person who holds the other half.

The Shape of Failure: Going into orbit around another person, thereby losing track of the natural thread of your own life. Codependency masquerading as interdependency. Endless intimate drama. Attracting arrogant, self-important, or egomaniacal partners, incapable of loving you.

SUN IN THE EIGHTH HOUSE

Necessary Action: Intense inner work; making the unconscious mind conscious; facing primal wounds and fears. For most people, sexuality lies at the heart of this effort—and by sexuality, we do not simply mean sexual intercourse, but rather the complex psychological processes triggered by mating, bonding, or the formation of a committed couple—a process which is sure to bring all of your issues to the surface. Being mindful of death is fundamental here; at the highest level of response, a conscious, lifelong preparation for death is indicated.

Words To Live By: If your goal is to imagine that you are perfectly sane and have no psychological issues left to work on, then never stay in a physical relationship with another human being for more than about six weeks. That's because intimacy reveals the naked truth of who you are. We always hurt the ones we love. An Englishman was going to be hung in the morning. Someone asked him how he felt about that. He responded, "It composes the mind most excellently." In other words, no one gets out of here alive, so let death be your counselor.

Synchronistic Correlates: Dramatic, psychologically-complicated relationships. Grand passions, which prove transformative—or at least "instructive." Close brushes with death serving as spiritual wake-up calls. Biographically significant deaths in the intimate circle: for example, the death of a young friend, the early death of a parent, the death of a sibling.

The Shape of Failure: Choosing partners who make you feel crazy; learning nothing from them, while remaining in the toxic framework that you jointly create. Endless psychodrama. A life dominated by dark moods. Letting your "little head" do all the thinking, while ignoring the wisdom and experience of your big head.

SUN IN THE NINTH HOUSE

Necessary Action: Stretching your horizons in every sense—embracing cross-cultural experience, a commitment to ongoing, lifelong education, and a willingness to frame your existence as a Quest for Meaning. Leaving home. Going off to seek your fortune. Recognizing the provincial nature of your origins, wherever you were born. The shock of internalizing another cultural perspective and recognizing that it is as legitimate as the one in which you were initially trained—your sense of reality cracks wide open in that moment.

Words To Live By: Not all those who wander are lost. As Napoleon once said, "History is a lie agreed upon." We might say the same for "reality:" it too is nothing but a social construct. Let this be your mantra: *Beyond, beyond the beyond—and beyond that too.* As the Zen masters say, "Religion is a finger pointing at the moon." Follow the finger if you like—but remember that it is the moon itself that you are seeking.

Synchronistic Correlates: Opportunities for travel. Contact with foreigners or with people from different social backgrounds. The doorway to education (in the broad sense of the word) is open. Religion, in its healthy and unhealthy forms, often plays a role in the life. Moral dilemmas arise, complicating—and perhaps ultimately clarifying—your sense of the fundamental laws of the universe.

The Shape of Failure: Wasting your life and your energy in defense of limiting belief systems and narrow cultural perspectives. Xenophobia. Slavery to your own opinions. Abdication from learning. Defending your right to be just as dumb next year as you were last year. Rigid fundamentalism in any category: religion, politics, science.

SUN IN THE TENTH HOUSE

Necessary Action: Following the threads of omens and synchronicities that lead to the discovery of your true public mission in life. Finding the right career. Figuring out a way to get paid for being yourself—which is to say, being recognized and appreciated socially for your solar nature. (Look to the Sun's sign and aspects to focus this insight.) Making a difference in your community; touching the lives of people with whom you do not have personal karma.

Words To Live By: To say that "we all want to leave the world a better place" might sound trite and formulaic, but it is a primal human drive—a point easily proven by a brief meditation upon the following curse: *may you have a job that pays you only money.* Man shall not live by bread alone—which means that your work needs to provide a sense of meaning in your life, along with a paycheck. You want more from your work than the sustenance required to get up the following morning and do it all over again.

Synchronistic Correlates: The call of destiny: signs and circumstances arise that guide you in the direction of your mission. As you follow the evolutionary path defined by the Sun in your chart, you become a living answer to a question that is synchronistically arising in your community.

The Shape of Failure: Focus on mere mechanical careerism and ambition rather than the more uplifting idea of mission. Opportunism ungrounded in the actual nature of your psyche. Career arising without self-examination. A life defined by the prosaic and unquestioned expectations implicit in the culture of your birth. An exaggerated concern with appearance, status, and reputation.

SUN IN THE ELEVENTH HOUSE

Necessary Action: Setting meaningful goals and aspirations. Establishing and—with brutal honesty—ranking/ordering your priorities. For one hard example, while we all want both love and purposeful work, which one of the two will actually take precedence in your life? Are you coming home at 5:00 o'clock—or staying in the office until 7:00? Human existence is not so black and white—but it is short, and strategic choices must be made. With that accomplished, then you must establish tactics for achieving them, pay the piper, and stick to those tactics no matter what the cost. One fundamental skill here is the establishment of *helpful alliances*—hence, the old astrological idea that this is the "house of friends." If you want to be an artist, hang out with artists. If your goals are spiritual, where is your spiritual tribe?

Words To Live By: To get what you want, you need to know what you want. Trust your natural passions; let your soul be your pilot. Keep your eye on the prize. A balanced life can be a dull life. The great work of your life is not the work of a young person; your work as a young person lies in gathering the experience that underlies your wisdom in the second half of life.

Synchronistic Correlates: Projects and ambitions requiring long-term commitment. Spiritually catalytic experiences which can only be accessed in the context of group activity: no one can be a football player all by himself; no one can play third violin in Beethoven's Ninth Symphony without the help of an orchestra. Deep conversations with strangers whom you never see again.

The Shape of Failure: Drifting into social alliances and obligations without an underlying and unifying sense of your aim in life. The dark side of "living for the moment," which boils down to all tactics, but no strategy. A life defined by unending "politics"—in the sense that whenever three or four are gathered together, we soon have politics.

SUN IN THE TWELFTH HOUSE

Necessary Action: Climbing to the mountaintop and sitting on it. You naturally feel a strong spiritual impulse—so what should you do about it? What actual actions and behaviors contribute to the expansion of your consciousness? There are a variety of good answers; pick the ones that feel right and act on them. Meditation, prayer, contemplation, chanting, retreat, periods of solitude, ritual, walking the labyrinth, entering the monastery—the list is long. That is your menu; eat what you want—but eat heartily.

Words To Live By: As St. Francis said, "what we are looking for is what is looking." As you turn your attention inward toward the nature of consciousness itself, what is this luminous emptiness that is gazing out through your eyes? The phrase "you can't take it with you" does not apply to spiritual accomplishment. Once you have made progress in that direction, there is no force in the universe that can take it from you.

Synchronistic Correlates: No one has to suffer in order to grow spiritually; never believe that this configuration is "unlucky" despite much astrological lore to that effect. But if you *need* suffering as a spiritual reminder, the universe will be generous with it. *Attachment triggers loss*; that is the main clause in the soul-contract you signed with your first breath. Therefore, it is wise to constantly question any worldly attachments that arise in your life. You can, of course, love the things of this world and its inhabitants—but never forget the real reason you are here.

The Shape of Failure: Spiritual laziness, resulting in a life that feels as if it were unfolding under a curse or a jinx. Resignation; withdrawal from life.

Self-numbing escapism in any of its myriad forms: drunkenness, addiction, floating off into *La La Land*. Hypersensitivity; being overwhelmed by your own psychic openness, rather than learning how to explore and celebrate it.

14

JUPITER IN THE TWELVE HOUSES

JUPITER IN THE FIRST HOUSE

Above All, Believe… that it is your destiny to be some kind of leader and to have a positive impact on the lives of other people. That leadership can take many forms, starting with simply being an influence on others. From there, it runs right up to a substantial capacity to shape the future of your community or your profession.

Never Underestimate… your impact on other people, even when you simply walk into the room. Trust your charisma and your "star-quality." Never underestimate the magnetic charm invoked by your sense of humor and your generosity of spirit.

Your Gift From the Gods: In a word, magic. The power of your Will is not only strong in obvious ways, but it also possesses a subtle higher harmonic: what you intend or desire often tends to crystallize before your eyes. That is especially true when your benign intentions are aimed at impacting other people—when you are in a position of leadership, in other words. People probably think you are "lucky." Whatever that word actually means, it is fair to say that they are not wrong.

When Ego Grabs the Steering Wheel: You can become haughty, seemingly expecting to be treated as rock-star royalty. You might not even intend that effect or feel that way, but that appearance arises and creates bad reactions in other people. You might lose your sense of humor about yourself—but don't worry: if you fall into that trap, others will supply the humor behind your back.

JUPITER IN THE SECOND HOUSE

Above All, Believe... in yourself. You have set the bar of success quite high in this lifetime. The conventional standards by which people generally define a successful life are not sufficient for you. You have been born to accomplish something of greater significance. Exactly what? The answer to that pressing question lies in the larger logic of your birthchart as a whole.

Never Underestimate... your resourcefulness nor your capacity for relentless effort once you have your eye on the prize. Never underestimate your ability to attract the resources you need in order to fulfill your destiny: allies, tools, and sufficient financial fortune to do what you are here to do.

Your Gift From the Gods: A destiny that, if you choose to accept it, will give meaning to your life until the end of your days—and probably beyond them. All that—plus the gods have made you a promise: no matter what path you take, you will always have rice in your bowl. You are protected financially and materially.

When Ego Grabs the Steering Wheel: You turn away from your best self and your higher calling, and instead chase after mere glitz: money, prestige, the enthusiastic support of shallow people. Your magic is such that you can have those things too, if you are crazy enough to want them. They promise abundance and deliver emptiness.

JUPITER IN THE THIRD HOUSE

Above All, Believe... that you have something important to say to this world. You bear a much-needed message of encouragement—perhaps of spiritual encouragement—that many people need to hear. You have the ability to express it compellingly; they are depending on you to deliver it.

Never Underestimate... your powers of persuasion. You are capable of conveying not only information, but also enthusiasm for the information. Never underestimate your potential for developing these communicative skills. If you are thinking of whispering, that probably means you need to shout. If you're thinking of a short story, that probably means you have a novel in you.

Your Gift From the Gods: Some degree of eloquence. The ability to convey ideas appealingly, so listeners enjoy *hearing* you—or perhaps they enjoy *reading* your words. You have the gift of gab; you have the gift of humor. You can get behind people's defenses. You can convince skeptics. You can learn anything.

When Ego Grabs the Steering Wheel: You talk too much. You become enamored of your own voice and your own opinions, overestimating their appeal to your listeners. You can jump to conclusions; you can fail to see real obstacles and genuine problems. Positive thinking potentially has a dark side: it can blind you to uncomfortable truths, especially ones about yourself.

JUPITER IN THE FOURTH HOUSE

Above All, Believe... in the power of your big heart to attract the sweetness of a rich inner life to you, along with the gift of a happy home. A major evolutionary focus in your life lies not with the larger world, but rather with the people in your intimate circle—those with whom you share life's long story. You are here to make a real difference in their lives. Your generosity of spirit plays a pivotal and encouraging role in their journeys.

Never Underestimate... the long-term transformative power of your sustained faith in the people whom you love. Never underestimate the spiritual significance of a life that the larger world ignores or about which it never even knows. Not all soul-victories are for public consumption. Never underestimate your ability to recover from loss or adversity; you are resilient.

Your Gift From the Gods: A certain magic when it comes to finding the perfect place to live. Angels seem to watch over you in that department. Family is another gift from the gods—but here, although we might be thinking conventionally of your kinship group, we are actually referring more reliably to the great blessing in your life of your soul-family. Celebrate them—and thank the gods and goddesses for them by prioritizing time spent in their company.

When Ego Grabs the Steering Wheel: You can experience an inflated desire for an impressive physical home. You might become too attached to your family name, your ancestry, or your social circle. It is better to impress yourself than to impress everyone else.

JUPITER IN THE FIFTH HOUSE

Above All, Believe... in your creative capacities. Quite probably, you were born with some genuine artistic or performance talent—but we intend the word "creativity" more broadly than that. You have the ability to leave the stamp of your soul upon people, events, materials—or even businesses. Believe, above all, in your profound capacity to engage people's attention and to capture their imaginations.

Never Underestimate... how contagious your spontaneity and humor can be. When you are brave enough to step out on the stage without a master plan, magic happens. Never underestimate how a good performance or a skillfully-wrought work of art can sneak behind people's defenses and take root in their hearts.

Your Gift From the Gods: Creativity—and along with it, the capacity to trigger in other people a psychological identification with you. Thus, you can invoke cathartic experience in any audience. When you are brave enough to shine, people feel what you are feeling and think what you are thinking.

When Ego Grabs the Steering Wheel: Your personal life becomes the stage of a soap opera and you find yourself cast in a silly role which embarrasses you. Your soul is better than that, and you know it. Down that road, you succumb to various excesses—too much food or alcohol, a vast collection of shoes you never wear...

JUPITER IN THE SIXTH HOUSE

Above All, Believe... that you have the ability to become superlatively proficient at some skill that makes a real difference in the lives of others. What skill? The shape of the answer lies in the context of the larger, integrated interpretation of your birthchart. It will have something to do with offering encouragement, support, and blessing to those who partake of your gifts.

Never Underestimate... your potential impact on other people's lives. You are part of a *lineage*; trust your teachers and your mentors, and seek them out. Never underestimate your ability to master difficult talents, procedures, and tools. Never doubt that your destiny lies on the path of service.

Your Gift From the Gods: With your skills, you are capable not only of helping people in concrete ways, but also of restoring their damaged faith in life itself. Your faith brings them faith. You are blessed with role models: men and women who have gone before you on a road similar to the one you are traveling. They care about you; their example and teaching are one of your gifts from the gods.

When Ego Grabs the Steering Wheel: You find yourself drowning in a sea of ever-expanding, meaningless responsibilities. You have bitten off more than you can chew. The demands on your time and energy outpace your human limits; people seem to think of you as a public utility.

JUPITER IN THE SEVENTH HOUSE

Above All, Believe... in the uplifting, transformative impact of love—and here we use the word "love" in an inclusive sense: marriage and similar partnerships are on the list, but so are deep, long-lasting friendships. You are not alone; other familiar souls have accompanied you into this world. Some of them "owe you one" and are eager to repay the debt; accept their help without feeling like you have to offer anything in return—this frees them as well as supports you.

Never Underestimate... your own level of spiritual and psychological sophistication. This is a critical point, because if you do underestimate yourself, that error will manifest as destructive intimate choices—specifically, you might give yourself to people who are unworthy of you.

Your Gift From the Gods: Friends who believe in you more than you believe in yourself. Their faith in you triggers your ability to reach for the higher ground and the far limits of your human potential. The humor, affection, and support of these soul-allies are your gift from the gods.

When Ego Grabs the Steering Wheel: You choose partners and associates based on their appearance or status, without listening to your own heart. The "decorative" lover or the prestigious "close personal friend" are a sugar diet; they only nourish the ego, not the soul.

JUPITER IN THE EIGHTH HOUSE

Above All, Believe... in your insights. Have faith in your X-ray ability to see into your own wounds, and above all, have faith in your ability to triumph over them in this lifetime. Trust your insights into other people as well, even when faced with resistance, denial, or anger. Believe in the mutual healing impact of honest intimacy. Believe that by the end of this lifetime, if you follow the path of your destiny, you will laugh at the illusion we call death.

Never Underestimate... yourself regarding your choice of an intimate partner. You need someone who is worthy of you—and that worthiness proves itself by his or her ability to hold the helpful mirror of truth before you in a spirit of love. Never doubt the insights that are arising in you regarding the lessons—and the fierce blessings—deriving from human mortality. Death is your guru.

Your Gift From the Gods: The ability to maintain a plucky, positive spirit in the face of life's fiercest truths. You have no need to take refuge in any metaphysical or "spiritual" fantasyland; you can look life's darkness straight in the eye and still smile. You know that you are bigger than it is. Your faith can digest life's harder truths.

When Ego Grabs the Steering Wheel: You become uncritically governed by your own passionate nature; you begin to take too much pride in your intensity and your honesty, to the point that you lose sight of humility, a sense of humor about yourself, and your ability to surrender to the kinds of people who are actually good for you.

JUPITER IN THE NINTH HOUSE

Above All, Believe... that the ultimate purpose of your life is a quest for meaning. Everything else is secondary. You were born with the seeds of genuine philosophical wisdom. Never lose sight of the fact that if you boldly follow the adventurous path of your destiny, by the end of this lifetime your wisdom will be seven times deeper.

Never Underestimate... the triggering impact on your consciousness of contact with other cultures and other systems of belief. The expansion of your wisdom in this incarnation depends on encounters with exotic thoughts and ideas, along with exotic societies and people who represent alien perspectives. These experiences nourish you. Predictability does not.

Your Gift From the Gods: You intuitively and quickly figure out how to build bridges across cultural divides. You are a good traveler. You have a genuine enthusiasm for learning; you enjoy it and are motivated to live a life of endless education. Life offers you these opportunities; they seem to fall out of the clear blue sky into your lap.

When Ego Grabs the Steering Wheel: You become convinced of the absolute validity of your own opinions. You become, in your own mind, an expert. In place of intellectual expansion, you experience intellectual stasis. Behind your back, people warn each other, "Don't get him (or her) started..."

JUPITER IN THE TENTH HOUSE

Above All, Believe... that you were born with a larger mission in this world. If you follow the path of destiny, you will energize and illuminate the lives of people whom you do not know or with whom you do not have personal karma to work out. You are here to do something big—do not doubt that. Many souls are depending on your getting this right.

Never Underestimate... what you are on this earth to accomplish, nor your ability to accomplish it. Humility is a virtue, but you need to be wary of it: if you are unwilling to "think big" about your mission, your imagination will fail to encompass it correctly.

Your Gift From the Gods: The capacity to plausibly play the role of the "star" or the hero, and thus embody some principle in which you believe on the public stage—and to embody it in a way that inspires enthusiasm for that principle in anyone watching you. Your magic can open doors for you. You can gain the ear—and the trust—of people in positions of power.

When Ego Grabs the Steering Wheel: You succumb to the cotton-candy temptations of power, position, or fame. The gratification of your ego becomes more compelling to you than the mission itself. One way of saying this is that "the devil" fears the good you will accomplish if you rise to your actual mission, and so he is inclined to "make you an offer too good to refuse..."

JUPITER IN THE ELEVENTH HOUSE

Above All, Believe... that the great work of this lifetime for you is not the work of a young person. If you are young, you must keep the faith—and pursue the experiences that lead you toward the bright future in mid-life and beyond for which you were born. If you are older, it is time to step up to the plate and find some way to make a gift to the world of your hard-earned wisdom. Above all, believe that you play a pivotal role in a soul-tribe and that its members recognize you and are counting on you.

Never Underestimate... the sweet fruits of faith, persistence, and of keeping your eye on the prize over the long haul. Never underestimate the power of a noble dream. Furthermore, never doubt that you have *help* in all of this—that you are not alone; others, who believe in you, have accompanied you into this world. Never mistrust your feelings when you have that sense of recognition; you know the members of your own soul-clan when you see them.

Your Gift From the Gods: An ability to dream big, uplifting, long-term dreams. You also have the ability to generate strategies for making those dreams real. You can absorb the big picture and see the subtle shapes unfolding in the present—shapes that prophesy the nature of the future. And you are gifted with a soul-tribe, here to support you in fulfilling those big dreams.

When Ego Grabs the Steering Wheel: You find yourself mired in social overextension, dealing with tedious, draining relationships that seem to offer you very little in return except possibly glitter. As you enter the second half of your life, while you may have the outward appearances of success, you have the feeling that somehow you have lost the thread of any real existential purpose—and you have.

JUPITER IN THE TWELFTH HOUSE

Above All, Believe... that you are poised for a major breakthrough in consciousness in this lifetime. You have earned it; meritorious actions in prior lifetimes have put you in this position today. All that is required to trigger this breakthrough is that you place a big bet on yourself in terms of some audacious bid for spiritual catharsis.

Never Underestimate... the impact of a single bold move. Do you quit your job to go on a year-long spiritual retreat? Do you do a vision quest or a pilgrimage? Do you actively seek a spiritual teacher? *Ask and ye shall receive*—all you need in order to pick the lock on this spiritual treasure chest is absolute faith in those words.

Your Gift From the Gods: There are many ways to translate the following idea, but here is one wording: *you have a Guardian Angel.* Something or someone is watching out for you in this lifetime, making it safer for you to take the spiritual risks you need to take. All you have to do is to supply the audacity.

When Ego Grabs the Steering Wheel: You become spiritually complacent, even arrogant, to the point that you fail to make the bold moves that precipitate the spiritual breakthrough you have incarnated in order to experience. Down that road, you detour into a familiar *cul-de-sac*: spiritual pride.

Part Four

SEEING POSSIBLE FUTURES

Even if your astrological makeup is as Watery as the Atlantic Ocean or as Airy as the wind beneath the eagle's wings, you will go through Fiery periods in your life.

What signals their arrival? How can we best prepare for them? How can we use them intentionally rather than being buffeted by them?

Against the backdrop of your natal chart, there is a constant flux of moving points: transits, progressions, and solar arcs. They provide the key to mapping the dynamics of our day-by-day, year-by-year, evolution. Sometimes these astrological triggers move into Fire signs or into the "Fire" houses. Sometimes they form aspects to Mars, the Sun, or Jupiter.

Count on this—those will be "hot" periods in your life.

Meanwhile, those three Fire planets are themselves moving through your natal chart, hitting sensitive points via their own transits, progressions, and solar arcs.

These types of astrological events mark the onset of Fiery chapters in your journey. These are times when your elemental vitality can be renewed—or sapped, if you miss their point.

In the past, astrologers were expected to "make predictions." Many still do; some are even correct sometimes. But we are not puppets dangling from planetary strings; we are human beings, endowed with the magical powers of creativity, learning, aspiration, and—just possibly—wisdom.

In the pages that follow, we throw away the astrologers' traditional crystal ball. Instead, we use these Fiery events to predict questions and to help us sug-

gest the answers—which is to say, the conscious choices—that lead to the higher ground.

You have many possible futures. Astrology can help you navigate wisely among them. There is, however, one possibility that does not exist: that these astrological events will not impact you at all. Their energy has been created; it cannot be destroyed, only changed in form. What actually determines the form these celestial events will take is your own choice—and your own responsibility.

Meanwhile, your ace in the hole is your own magic. You do not have the power to evade these archetypes—but you do have the power to shape your response to them.

15

THE FIRE FAMILY AND ASTROLOGY'S CRYSTAL BALL

In astrology's deck of cards, the Sun is the ace. All the other symbols are significant in their own ways, but everything ultimately revolves around the Sun. That is just as true astrologically as it is astronomically. In looking at astrology's foundational document—the birthchart—this simple guideline, *always give priority to the Sun,* will never seriously mislead you.

But in the astrology of transits and progressions, there's a twist. Sometimes the Sun takes second place—or third, or fourth. Sometimes another planet is taking its turn in the spotlight. In astrology, even Mercury can eclipse the Sun, at least symbolically.

The principle behind this idea is utterly simple: *everything depends upon the speed at which the planet is moving.* In a nutshell, slowness generally equates with significance.

We can summarize this twist with a brief reflection upon a seemingly simple question: *which is the more life-shaping astrological event, a transit of the Sun or a progression of Mars?*

In this case, that progression of Mars is the right answer.

Here is why: a transit of the Sun over a sensitive point is a passing event; it will only last for a few days. It therefore does not have much *time to develop depth and complexity of meaning*. A progression of Mars over a sensitive point, on the other hand, will forcibly engage your attention for at least a period of two or three years, and maybe much longer. Such a Mars event can potentially reorient your life in very fundamental ways—ways we'll explore in great detail a few pages from now.

The key insight here is simply that you and progressed Mars, unlike you and the transiting Sun, are going to have plenty of time for a very long conversation.

This point pivots on a second elemental astrological principle: emphatically, astrology is not simply about the planets; the planets are only half the picture. Astrology works because of the *interaction* between two factors: on one hand, the archetypal fields those planets represent, and on the other hand, your own consciousness.

Sleep with someone in a spirit of love for ten years. Have a meaningful hour-long conversation with a stranger. Which experience sinks more deeply into your bones?

It is as simple as that.

PAPUAN LORIKEETS

The transiting Sun conjuncts your natal Uranus. Uranian-fashion, an odd event happens out of the clear blue sky, something that you never would have predicted. In a ten-day period, for example, three of your friends independently announce their intention of buying Papuan lorikeets—*Charmosyna papou*, in case you were wondering.

You give the weird pattern some amused or befuddled thought at the time. Is the universe trying to tell you something? Maybe it has something to do with synchronicity. But what is the symbolism of Papuan lorikeets, and what does it have to do with you? You scratch your head. By the next day, you've let the question go. Messages from the universe can be very cryptic sometimes. Who could possibly decipher them all?

That event was truly Uranian—no one could have foretold that three friends would be attracted to the same species of pet bird in the same ten days. But what does it matter? Synchronicity is real; maybe there was some hidden meaning there—but God only knows what that meaning is.

In other words, you forget about it.

At the other end of the spectrum, over a period of a few years, a drama involving progressed Mars unfolds in your life. Perhaps you are courageously and nervously starting your own business; perhaps you are going through a litigious divorce. Maybe you're mounting an expedition. You have plenty of time to contemplate Mars from every angle; it has *enough time* to become a critical page in your biography. Big questions arise: when does courage cross the line into stupidity? What is the right use of force? When have you gone too far—and when have you not gone far enough? How much power do you want to assign to anger in your life? What about fear?

Big questions indeed!

It's not that progressed Mars is more *powerful* than the transiting Sun; it's simply that it *endures* long enough to develop that famous "depth and complexity of meaning."

Let's add another perspective: during the few days that the transiting Sun is activating your natal Uranus, looking at it hour-by-hour, the effects might be spectacularly obvious—how often do three of your friends decide to buy Papuan lorikeets in the same ten-day period? The critical point is that, minute to minute, the solar transit is not *weaker* than the Mars progression. But it doesn't stick around; again, you soon forget about it. In the long run, it has only a minor impact on your life.

These principles underlie the practical application of all predictive theory in astrology. Everything boils down to one point: all the planets, nodes, and angles move through your chart at varying speeds. And in predictive astrology, *slowness equals power and impact*. Speed, in contrast, equates with transitoriness. Planets in slow motion establish the grand thematic scheme of a life, while the fast-moving ones operate as triggers, precipitating these themes as specific events.

THE RHYTHM OF THE SPHERES

Just in case you're new to astrology—transits are the actual motions of planets in the sky. If, for example, Saturn is in Aquarius by transit, that's true for everyone. Transits are external factors; they're like the weather. Everyone shares the same rainy day, although some people find a gray day gloomy, while others may find it poignant and romantic. It's the same with transits. They are like a Rorschach test for your personality, just like the weather.

Progressions are more like an internal biological clock. For one thing, they are unique to you; while your Mars is progressing through Scorpio, my Mars might be progressing through Pisces.

The theory behind progressions sounds strange, but it works quite reliably: *days become years.* If you want to know the positions of your progressed planets on your fortieth birthday, you find out where those planets were literally forty *days* after your birth.

Those are your progressed positions at age forty.

Solar arcs are really just a subset of progressions. We see how far the Sun has progressed and then we add that same "arc" to the rest of the planets. The Sun progresses approximately 1° for every year of your life, so when you turn thirty, it has moved about 30° ahead of where it was when you were born. To calculate your solar arcs, we would then add that same 30° to the position of your Moon, your Mercury, your Ascendant, and so on. Solar arcs are thus slaved to the Sun; they have the Sun's nature—which is to say they are very biographical and outward in their manifestations.

(One quick technical note: Earth's orbit around the Sun is elliptical. The effect is that we are moving more slowly during the northern hemisphere summer and more quickly six months later. The idea that solar arcs move 1° per year is a useful approximation, but your mileage will vary slightly. The average annual motion of the progressed Sun is actually 59'08". If you were born in the northern hemisphere summer, on your thirtieth birthday, the Sun will have progressed a bit less than 30°, and *vice versa*, if you born in winter.)

We will soon explore all three of these techniques interpretively in relation to the Fire Family. Discovering the life-giving meaning of the transits, progressions, and solar arcs of the Sun, Mars, and Jupiter is the heart of the rest of this book.

In this present chapter, our focus is more astronomical than astrological. Cycles have rhythms; before we can do any effective interpretations, we need to get with their beat.

As we saw a few moments ago, speed of these planetary rhythms is a critical factor in our application of predictive theory. Our bottom line is that by progression and solar arc, planets move slowly—so they all have time to become important. With transits, it is more complicated: the Moon passes through all twelve signs in a little less than a month, while Pluto takes 248 years to get around your chart. In looking for the big themes of a biography, you can therefore forget about the transiting Moon—meanwhile, you could write the whole story around the transits of Pluto.

My second book, *The Changing Sky*, covers this territory in great detail. You might want to bone up there if this material is unfamiliar to you. I don't want to repeat all the details, so let's cut to the chase…

MARS IN MOTION

The further a planet lies from the Sun, the greater the diameter of its orbit. The circumference of a circle is its diameter multiplied by *pi*; so those more distant planets have far longer roads to follow before they get back to their starting points.

There's a second factor in play: the further a planet is from the Sun, the more slowly it moves. So not only does it have further to go, its cruising speed is less. Earth, for example, is moving around the Sun at about 18.5 miles per second, while Mars, which is the next planet out from the Sun, is a bit slower, advancing at a more stately 14.5 miles per second. By the time we get out to Pluto, we're down to an average speed of just under three miles per second.

Let's focus on Mars. Two factors come together here: the Red Planet is not only moving more slowly than Earth, but it also has further to go to get around the Sun. So naturally its "year" is significantly longer than our own.

For Mars, a year lasts about 22.5 months.

While we are at it, let's add one more definition: Earth and Mars align relative to the Sun every 780 days. That is called their *synodic* cycle.

All of this observational astronomy is complicated by the fact that we're watching Mars from our own pony on the cosmic merry-go-round: the planet Earth—which is moving too. Because Earth is faster than Mars, sometimes we "pass" it, exactly the way we might pass a car on the highway. When that happens, that slower car seems to be going backwards for a few moments. Mars works the same way, and so do the rest of the planets. That is why planets display *retrograde* motion.

During its approximately two-year orbital cycle, Mars will spend somewhere between fifty-eight and eighty-one days in this retrograde mode. As it approaches its *station*—the point where it stops and turns around—it slows down very gradually, then speeds up very gradually in the opposite direction.

The practical astrological effect of all this is that if Mars "makes a station" on a sensitive point in your chart, it will have plenty of time to develop that "depth and complexity of meaning" we explored a few paragraphs ago.

On the other hand, transiting Mars might be far from a station and thus moving at maximum speed. Then it will whip through that same sensitive point so quickly that you might barely notice it. The conversation is very brief.

All of the foregoing material describes the actual motion of the planet Mars as we observe it in the heavens—or see it reflected in our charts. It's all been about Mars *transits*, in other words.

But what about the progressions of Mars?

Remember, with progressions, days turn into years. Therefore, everything slows down dramatically. The progressions of Mars are languorous; sometimes, in fact, they're so slow that they're almost unusable astrologically. Like watching kids growing up, we hardly notice the process—until one day we register that somehow they've become adults.

Here's a quick illustration of the slowness of progressed Mars: On July 4, 1776, when the United States of America was born, Mars was in 21°23' of Gemini. When will progressed Mars complete its turn around the chart and return to that same degree? The answer is June 8, 2487.

That is 711 years later: *slow!*

In average terms, the forward motion of progressed Mars runs about half a degree per year. But remember: Mars slows down even more as it approaches a station.

For practical purposes, if you happened to be born anywhere near the date of a Mars station, *by progression* the planet will barely move in the course of your entire lifetime. For example, in the USA chart, Mars made a station and turned retrograde on July 16, 2006, at 18° 42' of Libra. Today, as I write these words about twelve years later, where is America's progressed Mars? The answer is 17° 50' of Libra—in other words, Mars has moved less than 1° in a dozen years. And it will not turn direct again until 2086.

Bottom line, working with progressed Mars is an extremely individual affair. While everyone responds vigorously to the transits of Mars, the progressed Mars might be near a station at birth and therefore almost irrelevant for practical purposes.

Furthermore, even at its cruising speed of half a degree per year, Mars might spend decades passing through a relatively dead zone in a person's chart, and thus have very little active relevance for much of his or her lifetime.

On the other hand, maybe you were born with a tight square aspect between your Sun and your Moon, with Neptune opposite your Sun and thus also in a square to your Moon. When progressed Mars triggers any one of those points, it's hitting all the others at about the same time. Stand back! That one is going to really get your attention—and if that progressed Mars is anywhere near a station while this is happening, we are basically looking at the story of your life.

With the progressions of Mars, in other words, you really have to take it case-by-case.

By solar arc, Mars is straightforward; as with all the other solar arcs, Mars marches to the beat of the same drummer, moving forward in lockstep with the Sun at the pace of approximately 1° per year. Solar arcs, by the way, are always direct, never making stations or turning retrograde. Their speed varies very little.

Later we will go deeply into how to interpret Mars periods in your life. For now, here's our practical takeaway about these Martial planetary rhythms:

* By transit, Mars is relatively fast, so therefore it operates as a trigger, precipitating some kind of fierce action connected with the larger developmental patterns revealed by slower theme-building astrological events.
* By solar arc, Mars always signals major epochs in a person's dance with the Fire family. At 1° per year, it has plenty of time to develop depth and complexity of meaning.
* By progression, working with Mars is a highly individual experience. Typically, it is a theme-builder, just like solar arc Mars. But sometimes progressed Mars stalls; if it stalls near a sensitive point in your chart, that point will be highly stimulated over decades of time. This is a real and powerful affect—but it lasts so long that

subjectively it begins to feel like a "permanent installation" in your life. On the other hand, maybe Mars is progressing very slowly through an area of your chart where it is not making any significant aspects. Its importance then fades, eclipsed by more pressing developmental matters.

THE SUN IN MOTION

Compared to Mars, working with the Sun is easy. By transit, it moves about 1° per day (think: 365 days to get through 360°). Thus its passage through an aspect, even given a generous 7° orb on either side of exactitude, will only take a couple of weeks—seven days in and seven days out. During that time, the impact of the Sun on your affairs or in your attitudes is unmistakable—but, to use our famous phrase yet again, two weeks is not long enough for the transit to develop "depth and complexity of meaning." Therefore the transiting Sun operates as a trigger rather than as a true theme-builder.

Here's an example of how we might usefully employ the transiting Sun in astrological counsel. First, set the stage: maybe progressed Mars is conjuncting your natal Venus. Some major—and presumably uncomfortable—adjustments need to be made, bravely, in at least one of your major relationships. That progressed Mars event will be in effect for a few years, so there will presumably be many individual "episodes" in this period of evolutionary adjustment.

Knowledge of that progressed Mars event sets the stage. It provides the backdrop for understanding a specific transit of the Sun. For example, when the Sun transits into your seventh house, specific intimate events unfold connected with that larger Mars event. It might, for instance, be "time for the big scary talk." You might sit down with your partner and say, "There is something we need to discuss."

The underlying idea is straightforward: the Sun's transit draws its meaning from the broader developmental context indicated by progressed Mars conjuncting the natal Venus.

The progressed Sun and the solar arc Sun are the same, always in exactly the same position. Their motion is that familiar 1° per year—plenty of time for them to develop depth and complexity of meaning. These two faces of the Sun are in fact the kingpin of the entire predictive system.

Roll the drums: in a word, the progressed—or solar arc—Sun reflects the *evolving self.* I cannot imagine doing any kind of effective developmental astrology without reference to this solar factor. There is nothing more important or central.

We will soon explore its personal impact in detail. Right now, we're still in astronomy class, with one subject still to go.

JUPITER IN MOTION

Jupiter takes about twelve years to get around the Sun, conveniently spending about one year in each sign of the zodiac. In common with the rest of the planets, its orbit is elliptical, so sometimes, it's moving a little faster or slower than at other times. Its actual orbital period is 11.88 years—eleven years and a bit over ten months.

Like Mars, Jupiter will sometimes make a station and turn retrograde. The rhythm of its stations is somewhat variable—generally speaking, Jupiter will be retrograde for about four months, then direct for about nine or ten.

In working with Jupiter's transits, watch out for those stations! If Jupiter stands still while it's sitting on a sensitive point in your chart, its effects are multiplied dramatically.

Conversely, when Jupiter is moving at maximum speed and briefly contacts a sensitive point, you might barely notice it. Jupiter then sort of blows through without having time—you guessed it—to develop depth or complexity of meaning.

All planets seem to have their "amperage" increased when they are stationary, but for some reason, that effect seems particularly pronounced with Jupiter. Again, if Jupiter makes a station on a sensitive spot in your chart... well, enter some contests.

Another practical wrinkle I've discovered in working with Jupiter transits is that a *whole sign* approach seems to be indicated. In other words, say that you're born a Gemini—and it does not matter if the Sun lies at the beginning or near the end of that sign. The entire time that Jupiter is transiting through Gemini will bear that synchronistic, jovial fingerprint. The exact degrees, normally so critically important in transit theory, don't seem to matter quite as much with Jupiter. I'm not sure why that's true, but it is something that I've observed. I encourage you to take it into account.

Transiting Jupiter usually moves slowly enough that I would call it a true theme-builder—although it can also operate as a precipitating trigger, especially when it is midway between stations and thus moving faster than usual.

By solar arc, Jupiter moves at the universal pace of about 1° per year, and so it, too, is a theme-builder, as are all the solar arcs.

By progression, Jupiter moves too slowly to be of much practical use. As I write these words, I'm approaching my seventieth birthday. In my own chart, Jupiter has only progressed about 15° in all that time, having made only three major aspects since the day I was born. I can relate to those aspects meaningfully, if somewhat abstractly—but each one remained within reasonable orbs for a couple of decades. I didn't even register them at the time. It is only now, looking back on seven decades of life, that I can discern their broad strokes.

It comes down to the proverbial question: what does the mayfly know of the glacier? I can helpfully suggest to a client experiencing an influx of Jupiter energy that risk-taking and audacity will be rewarded "this year" or, even better, "this July." But if I make the same suggestion for "the next twenty years," it is of little practical use and is soon forgotten—in one ear, and out the other.

That's the problem with the progressed Jupiter. It moves so slowly that we barely notice it. Therefore, for our practical purposes in this book, we will ignore it.

As we contemplate the application of Fire Family theory in predictive astrology, we will also need to think about the rest of the planets as they move through the Fire signs—Aries, Leo, and Sagittarius—along with their motions through the first, fifth, and ninth houses.

We will save those subjects for later; for now, let's start by diving into the meaning of Mars as it steps into the spotlight.

16

A FRESH LOOK AT THE ASTROLOGICAL ASPECTS

Aspects bind a chart together—but they aren't the only technique that does that. If, for example, a person has Mercury in opposition to Neptune in her natal chart, *her perceptual function is bound to her psychic functions*—thus, we might helpfully speak with her about developing her skills at psychic visualization. But let's say that another person is a solar Gemini with Mercury conjunct his Sun and with Neptune in his third house. Even if Neptune makes no aspects to his Sun or his Mercury, any helpful reading of his chart must include a similar synthesis of his perceptual function and his capacity for psychic visualization.

Ultimately, you have only one head between your ears. Everything in the birthchart is interactive with everything else even without any aspects in the mix. Aspects are only one mechanism by which we spotlight the most vigorous interactions in a birthchart. As astrologers, we must master aspects—but we must also never forget that there are other processes at work as well.

ALL ASPECTS ARE ABOUT INTEGRATION

If you forget everything else and simply let that single integrative principle guide your thinking, then your work with aspects will be helpful, accurate, and profound. And if you forget that all aspects—even the so-called "bad" ones—are about integration, you lapse into a far more limiting, depressing, and far less sophisticated form of astrological work.

I emphasize this principle in order to counter the ubiquitous and terribly distorting idea of "good" aspects and "bad" aspects. We still see this idea everywhere in the astrological literature, and it's never once helped anyone become wiser or more self-accepting.

Good and bad aspects are not useless concepts, but I would love to declare a ten-year moratorium on astrologers using the words. It is far more accurate—and really just as simple—to say "easy aspects" and "hard aspects."

And let's remember that "hard" equals "bad" only for lazy people. We've all done hard things that were good for us. We've all even done hard things that we enjoyed doing. Why would anyone explore the Arctic? Why would anyone read James Joyce's *Ulysses*? Why would anyone learn to play the piano?

The pivotal concept here is not some pop-psychological stricture against using judgmental words. It's simply that when two planets are in aspect, the reality is *always* that they are trying to work together. They are trying to integrate their energies.

If they're linked by a so-called "bad aspect," that integration is indeed more difficult. If it's an "easy" aspect, the integration is easier—but there's also a danger of laziness or a lack of pressing motivation.

Bottom line, my suggestion is that when you're confronted with any astrological aspect, organize your thinking as follows:

* Start by contemplating the energies the planetary archetypes represent. Realize that if they are linked by any aspect at all, they're trying to cooperate—and your evolution depends on getting them to work together.
* Imagine what such an integration might look like if it were successful.
* Pay attention to what it would look like if the planetary partnership became unhealthy—that's always a possibility too.

Notice that what I've said so far is totally independent of what aspect we are talking about—it could be a trine, a square, or a sesquiquadrate; so far, it doesn't matter. Regardless of the aspect, it's all about integration, always.

* Next, for the first time, consider the actual nature of the aspect itself. Are we talking about friction or complementary tensions between the two archetypes? That's how the hard ones work. Or are we in the realm of the easy aspects? Are we thus talking about mutual enhancement and support—and the possibility of laziness, a lack of motivation, and dark collusion?

In a nutshell, put the planetary integration first and the nature of the aspect last.

ASPECTUAL ORBS

There's nothing rigid about the orbs of aspects—except perhaps astrologers' opinions. Some of us use tight orbs in order to strategically reduce the number of aspects in a chart and thus focus narrowly on the most pressing ones. Other astrologers use wider orbs—and thus have more aspects—in order to paint a more subtle portrait.

Two general principles reliably guide us as we consider how we might best relate to orbs:

* Aspects are not all equal in strength. Use wider orbs for the more important ones. Here, in my experience, is the hierarchy of aspectual strength in descending order of power: conjunctions, oppositions, squares, trines, sextiles, quincunxes—followed by sesquiquadrates, quintiles, semi-sextiles and the rest of the minor series.

(Another astrologer might list them differently, especially as we get further down the list. I don't mean to sound dogmatic here; these are just my impressions.)

* The more charged the astrological planet or point, the wider the orb it casts. Almost universally, astrologers use wider orbs for the Sun than they do for, say, Mercury. But be careful here; other factors intervene—if, for example, Gemini is rising, then Mercury rules the chart. That strengthens the Mercury a lot, dictating wider orbs for any aspects it makes. But where exactly is that Mercury placed and how central is it? Is it conjunct the Midheaven, or hiding out in a corner somewhere? Those questions affect its strength too.

In other words, many factors come together to determine the power of a planet, and thus we understand that any hard and fast rules about the orbs of aspects represent a dangerous oversimplification.

TAILORING ORBS TO FIT YOUR OWN COGNITIVE STYLE

Your own cognitive style is a major factor here too. It is wise to include that kind of self-knowledge in your considerations about how you choose to work with aspects and their orbs. Here's what that means: As we mentioned earlier, tighter orbs mean fewer aspects. That approach might suit you very well. Your nature might dictate that you will be a more effective astrologer if you go deeply into a few aspects, having narrowed your list down to the most pivotal ones via the simple device of using tight orbs.

On the other hand, you might be the sort of astrologer who can surf integratively over large sets of data, with your intuitive function pulling it all together. Then by all means go ahead and use wider orbs; naturally, you will have more aspects—but your consciousness is wired to be able to handle that kind of complexity.

Let us immediately blow the trumpet for respecting both of these approaches. It's a question of style, not of skill or intelligence.

I suspect you're beginning to have a sense of why I shake my head when I read an astrological text that tells me authoritatively—and completely erroneously—that trines should have an orb of 7°, while sextiles should have an orb of 5°, and so on. Reality is simply not that rigid—and furthermore, such a dogmatic technocratic approach completely ignores the critical factor of adapting aspects to one's own cognitive nature.

WHOLE SIGNS VERSUS GEOMETRY

Be sensitive to "whole sign aspects," no matter what the orbs might be. Anything in Leo is going to experience some "squaring" by anything in Scorpio. That situation gets very interesting when a planet in 29° Scorpio "trines" a planet in 1° Leo. We call that an *out of quality* trine—that is, one that involves planets in the "wrong" signs.

Out of quality aspects are always tricky to interpret because you have two incompatible principles interacting: the geometrical aspect and the whole sign aspect. My approach is to pay attention to both perspectives; each of them will make itself felt in life and in consciousness.

IS IT A QUINCUNX OR IS IT A QUINTILE?

Similar ambiguity can arise when aspects overlap. We might have two planets separated by 147°. Do we call that a 150° quincunx—or a 144° bi-quintile?

As with the previous "squared trine" example, both interpretations can cast light on the experienced reality.

APPLYING VERSUS SEPARATING, WAXING VERSUS WANING

Applying aspects feel like an in-breath and separating ones feel like an out-breath. Applying ones are more urgent, active and intense, while separating ones are more reflective, cautious, and passive.

Similar statements can be made about waxing aspects in contrast with waning ones. To determine waxing/waning status, a good starting point is to take the slower body as the anchor point. In other words, since Venus moves faster than Mars, see if Venus is waxing relative to Mars—that is, between 0° and 180° ahead of it in the zodiac. But that simple principle breaks down with the Sun. Even though it moves faster than most of the planets, it makes the most sense to take it as the anchor point. We can make a similar case for the Moon.

None of this is exactly rocket science, as you can see. Once we get past aspects as they're presented in an initial six-week beginning astrology course, the waters become murky, just like life.

ASPECTS IN A NUTSHELL

Aspect	Separation	Action
Conjunction	0°	Fusion. Formation of one single "meta-planet"
Semi-sextile	30°	Clash; annoyance. Waning: Letting go.
Semi-square	45°	Fighting for freedom; awkward transitions; endings
Sextile	60°	Mutual excitation and stimulus
Quintile	72°	Creativity; inspiration
Square	90°	Blocking; challenge; contradiction
Trine	120°	Mutual enhancement; support
Sesquiquadrate	135°	Tension; breakthrough or breakdown; sacrifice
Bi-quintile	144°	Demands toward transcendence; "the Call"
Quincunx	150°	Adjustment; shared creativity; romance
Opposition	180°	Polarization or Complementarity

17

CELESTIAL NAVIGATION I: MARS TIMES, ARIES TIMES

Mars is a planet, Aries is a sign, and never the twain shall meet. They are related, but different—just like you and your chimpanzee cousins. With the apes, we all have to admit a certain familial resemblance, but we appreciate not being put in the same cage. Our astrological vision becomes clearer if we are mindful of the distinctions between planets and signs.

Planets can be understood as "circuit boards" in your head. Freud modeled the human mind as composed of ego, superego, and the unconscious (sometimes called the *Id*), while astrologers employ a more granular system: in astrology, your mind is structured around Mars drives, Venus drives, Jupiter-drives, and so on.

In either case, Freudian theory or astrology, what we have is a map of the mind.

Meanwhile, the signs of the zodiac provide those planets with particular underlying agendas, interests, and motivations. That remains true regardless of whether we're talking about configurations in the natal chart or more transitory astrological events. In both cases, the twelve signs are universally present. They add uniqueness, style, and individuality to our basic mental circuits. The fiery energy of Mars, for example, can be motivated by a *desire to be number one* (Mars in Aries), or by a *desire for peace and fruitful partnership* (Mars in Libra), or perhaps by a *desire to be left alone to get on with one's work* (Mars in Capricorn).

And those comments can cast light on an entire lifetime if we are talking about configurations in the natal chart, or upon a particular chapter in one lifetime if we are talking about transits, progressions, and solar arcs.

So planets and signs are not the same. We should not confuse them. Still, the spirit of Mars and the spirit of Aries share a lot of symbolic DNA. The language we use in describing them overlaps quite a lot. This is, of course, the basis of the astrological idea of "rulership"—that Mars *rules* Aries, the Sun *rules* Leo, and so forth.

In this chapter, we build upon that kinship, recognizing that there are certain experiential commonalities that arise regardless of whether we're talking about Mars moving by transit or progression into the spotlight or about any one of the planets entering Aries.

At some point, chimpanzees and humans became different branches on the evolutionary tree. In similar fashion, for our purposes here in meditating on the connections between Aries and Mars, we focus initially on the trunk of that tree, looking back into the primal roots of the symbolism before they split off into planets and signs.

In subsequent chapters, we'll do the same thing with the dyad of the Sun and Leo, and later with Jupiter and Sagittarius.

Down the road a little further, we bring in the parallel question of transits, progressions, and solar arcs impacting the first, fifth, and ninth houses: our three "Fire houses," which complete the life-giving Fire Family Tree.

A STORY

With the Fiery "Warrior" symbolism of Mars and Aries, it's easy for our metaphors to become too pyrotechnical—too full of "battles to save the galaxy." Sure enough, if anyone is ever going to get into a big fist fight or to go bungee jumping, you will very likely see some kind of Mars or Aries element implicated in the astrological symbolism of the time. That extreme and very colorful face of Mars is a reality—but so are softer, more human expressions of the energy. Pursuing that softer road, let me tell you a true story from my client files…

A woman with whom I worked astrologically was born with Mars in Gemini and the Moon in Cancer. At the time of this story, Mars had progressed into a conjunction with her Moon. What follows is a tender, complicated tale, one that embraces cautionary elements as well as a glimpse of the higher ground.

This woman—let's call her Jane—had a teenage son. One day after doing the laundry, Jane was putting her son's socks and underpants back in his dresser drawer. She found a plastic baggie pushed to the back, poorly hidden. It was full of herbal material that resembled tobacco, but did not smell quite the same. She suspected, correctly, that it was marijuana. This was twenty-five years ago, before legalization swept the nation. In the conservative mainstream of culture back then, there was a lot of fear around illegal mind-altering substances.

Jane loved her son; she had a naturally protective feeling toward him. She interpreted marijuana as a major threat to his future, not to mention to his survival. She had visions of him turning into a junkie in an alley somewhere, with a needle stuck in his arm. What's a mother to do? She panicked.

When her son got home from school, she confronted him aggressively, transferring her panic directly to him. She forbade him from ever smoking marijuana again; she forbade him from seeing the particular friends whom she judged to be the source of the temptation: they were the "bad influences." She grounded him; he was not to be out after 6:00 p.m. for the next month. After that, they would talk about it some more.

These were the laws Jane laid down—but her son was seventeen years old, on the verge of adulthood, and naturally motivated to defend his autonomy and his emerging individuality. Plus, Jane's panic was contagious: her son quickly caught it too. He blew up; he did not accept his mother's rules. Just like his mother, he overreacted.

A terrible argument ensued. As the war escalated, it spun out of control. This is the eternal logic of rage—and the dark side of Mars and Aries.

The upshot of it all was disastrous; the son slammed the door, left home, and went to live with one of his friends in a rat-trap apartment across town. He dropped out of school. Needing to support himself somehow, he found part-time scut work.

For a while, it looked as if the young man had destroyed all of the good future possibilities in his own life, while his mother, in her over-the-top fury, had lost her son.

Just to complete the story, within a few weeks they buried the hatchet. The son returned to school and to his home, and it all worked out. But the ending might not have been that way; it could have been an emotional and existential catastrophe for both of them. Jane could have, in essence, created the very reality she most feared.

Let's analyze what we can learn here. What exactly was the mother's mistake? It's not an error for a parent to want to protect a child—and remember that Jane had the Moon in Cancer, which enormously underscores those protective instincts. And it's not a mistake to recognize that young people, lacking the judgment that experience brings, are prone to getting themselves into trouble. Knowing that, parents do have a duty to try to protect their children. Furthermore, the "person whose life has been destroyed by drugs" is a familiar figure, straight out of central casting. Addiction is an ugly, nightmarish reality.

And that nightmare is what Jane thought she found in her son's dresser drawer. After that "understanding" arose, she let fear make the rest of her decisions.

In Mars and Aries times, that's mistake number one. To say that we "should not be afraid" in such times is psychologically unrealistic; times like that are indeed often frightening. The great virtue of the Warrior, always necessary under such stimulus, is courage—but courage is not to be confused with fearlessness, courage is the ability to be scared half to death and still think clearly. To not let fear grab the steering wheel. When Mars and Aries step to center stage, we need to fear one thing above everything else: that is *panic.*

Jane panicked and it was a disaster.

We can learn even more from this painful Mars story. When Jane grounded her son and forbade him to see his friends, *she was acting as if she had the power to actually accomplish that.* She did not. The truth is, this young man was an autonomous being, nearing adulthood. He felt, with arguable accuracy, that his mother was behaving like a tyrant. He refused to knuckle under. The results were briefly cataclysmic for both of them—but what happens to a young person who fails to stand up to tyranny and defend his or her own natural right to autonomy? *What kind of disasters does that acquiescence invite further down the road?*

Our takeaway: when Mars and Aries knock on your door, *know the limits of your powers.* Operate within those limits. Do not let panic, self-righteousness, or adrenaline distort your sense of reality. Do not make threats you cannot carry out. Do not become drunk on anger or fear, as Jane did. Assess the powers you truly have; use them skillfully. A good rule of thumb in such times is to use the least amount of force possible to achieve an acceptable aim.

How might Jane have responded more mindfully to discovering that bag of marijuana? This is hindsight, but it also illustrates the very practical way in which astrology can enhance our mindfulness and help us make better decisions. If, instead of blowing up at her son, Jane had come to me for counsel as progressed Mars conjuncted her Moon, here's the speech I would have made:

Jane, your son is on the verge of manhood. Like almost everyone at that stage of life, he is probably insecure, touchy, and feeling the need to prove himself. You cannot stop him from making his own decisions and his own mistakes, just as you and I have made them ourselves. Please realize that the period during which you could protect him from life is coming to an end. You need to accept that. You have done what you can. That acceptance is the next developmental stage in your journey as a parent.

Lots of people smoke marijuana and are none the worse for it; and of course some people become drug addicts, and that's terrible—but it is not within anyone's power to stop them if that is what they choose to do.

Accept that you can no longer control your son. That is simply a fact, like gravity. You have to deal with it.

So what can you actually do?

Sit down with your son. Talk honestly and vulnerably with him, like two adults. Tell him that you love him and that you're worried about him. Tell him that you found what appeared to be marijuana in his drawer—and make sure he knows that you were not snooping, you were just putting his socks away. Be clear about that. He needs to know his boundaries are respected, just like you do.

Tell him that you are afraid—but also tell him that you understand he can do what he wants. It is his life, not yours.

Ask him to talk to you about marijuana—and when he talks, listen.

Jane, the only true power you have in this situation is the fact that you and your son love each other. Everything else is a delusion. Do not waste the one power you actually have on some groundless bluff.

Ask your son, in the name of that love, adult to adult, to please reassure your human heart. That takes you right to the edge of your actual powers in the situation, and your power—the power of love—is a formidable one. Use it!

Would this approach to Jane's progressed Mars crisis have worked? What can we say? *Maybe...*

But one thing is sure: this measured, un-panicked approach,

capitalizing on the solid foundation of their love for each other, would surely have produced a more positive outcome than Jane's overdramatic, overheated blunder.

The moral of the tale: when Mars or Aries looms in your chart, don't panic—but accept that you might have to do battle. Resolve to win—but define victory soberly and realistically. Inventory your actual powers in the situation; never base your strategy on a power that you don't actually have. Fear only panic, along with the distortions that arise from passionate self-righteousness.

And never forget that classic karate move: simply walking away.

DRIVING DOWN THE ROAD

Transiting Mars is opposing your natal Sun. You're driving down the highway, in two lanes of traffic heading west. In your rearview mirror you see a big white pickup truck looking like it's doing about eighty-five miles an hour—and about to ride up your rear bumper. You decide to "fix that guy." You accelerate a bit, pulling up almost parallel to a Toyota *Prius* festooned with cool environmentalist bumper stickers. That guy is doing fifty-five in the slow lane, so together you're blocking out the aggressive moron in the pickup truck. In that smug fashion, you merrily cruise down the highway.

Meanwhile, the moron is switching lanes back and forth, riding your rear bumper, pounding his steering wheel, and experiencing a serious spike in his blood pressure.

Sweet revenge. "I may be slow, but I'm ahead of you."

Spend an hour on a freeway anywhere and you'll see a dozen examples of this kind of behavior. Humans are a competitive bunch; peace, love, and understanding do not always dominate our collective behavior, especially behind the steering wheel. "It's a jungle out there:" a cliché, of course, but often a useful one. It's an accurate reference to a dimension of reality—specifically, a dimension of reality symbolized by Mars and Aries.

We all live in that world sometimes. We must adapt to it. In the Fiery chapters of life, those realities press at you. They present slippery moral and spiritual questions, with very few of them susceptible to simple answers.

Back to the moron in the pickup truck. Why does it give you—and me—such joy to vex him? There are many possible perspectives on this question. All of them are potentially accurate and legitimate in a Mars time.

Let's ask a psychologist what's actually going on here. The psychologist tells us that the man in the pickup truck has probably come to symbolize powerful people who hurt you in the past. You are transferring your rage, for example, at your father onto this convenient target. You're in the grips of a psychological complex and you are allowing that complex to grab the steering wheel of your life—which is always a dangerous choice. Specifically, and for no very positive reason, you're risking your own life. You might become a victim of road rage. Perhaps the moron in the pickup truck is high on methamphetamines, just back from a combat zone, and armed with a semiautomatic pistol.

Maybe the psychologist is right—but before we take that pledge, let's ask an athlete what he thinks. And the athlete tells us that competition is fundamental to life and not necessarily a negative thing—and furthermore, competition is fun. We're just having a little bit of Mars-fun with the moron in the pickup truck. Let's hope he's having some fun too.

Is the athlete wrong? How can we know? It's just another legitimate perspective.

Finally, let's ask Gautama the Buddha for his opinion about our driving skills. By reflex, we might assume that the Buddha would pull over and allow the pickup truck to pass, "turning the other cheek," as his old pal Jesus taught.

That's possible—but here is another perspective that Gautama might entertain: the moron in the pickup truck is obviously driving dangerously, without regard to the lives of other people on the highway. Seeing him in the rearview mirror, the Buddha might immediately pull up parallel with that *Prius*—not to vex the driver of the pickup truck, but rather to protect the other drivers, not to mention protecting the moron from creating the karma that would arise from carelessly causing harm to another being.

In Mars-Aries times, all of these possibilities exist, and they all exist in potentially useful and honorable ways. They're all part of the spectrum. But the Buddhist perspective teaches us something very important here, something very central to the highest face of the Warrior archetype: at the most fundamental level, *Mars reflects a protective instinct.* The Warrior who kills in defense of the innocent or the defenseless is an impeccable character. When Mars hits a sensitive point or any planet enters Aries in your chart, you may be called upon to raise the sword to defend another being.

YOGA CLASS

A female yoga teacher brought a Mars problem to my attention. There was another yoga teacher in the community who appeared to be taking sexual advantage of some of his students. Relationships are volatile and breakups happen, but the pattern here bore the definitive signature of sexual exploitation. My client wondered if she should "do something" or if it might be wiser to simply let the karmic wheels turn.

Progressed Mars was in her tenth house (community) squaring her Sun; it was time for a battle. The integrity of the yoga community was worthy of defense. Her measured response was highly effective. She spoke with other yoga teachers; they too had become aware of this man's exploitative behavior. They staged an intervention with him, confronting him with his actions. He hated it, of course—but he got the message.

What happened was that he left town—and presumably he simply transferred his bad behavior to a different yoga community elsewhere. Did this leave the world a better place? Probably not—but it left the local yoga community a better place.

This is a very grown-up Mars story. Can anyone ever win a war? That's a slippery philosophical question. Perhaps the best we can hope for is to win a battle from time to time, to protect that which is under our care, and, hopefully, to do so in a way that keeps the corruption of rage out of our souls. In other words, during a Mars or Aries time, go ahead and block the moron in the pickup truck—*but try to change the form of the Mars energy in your head from displaced rage to the high Warrior path of protection.* Try not to be judge and jury; try instead to be the Guardian of those who cannot guard themselves.

ACCIDENTS HAPPEN

You're washing dishes by hand in the kitchen sink. Suddenly you notice the soapsuds have turned pink. You have broken a glass and gashed your hand.

It's not a big deal; the cut is already washed. You dry yourself off with a paper towel and dash to the bathroom for a *Band-Aid*. In a few days, the wound is healed and forgotten.

Meanwhile, in your birthchart, transiting Mars is crossing your Ascendant.

Accidents happen; we all know that. The cultural gloss over all this is simply that life is imperfect and much that happens is the result of random chance. No need to beat yourself up over a cut on your hand; it happens to everyone.

But Mars was on your Ascendant. There was nothing random about this accident. What was actually going on? What was the lesson your soul was potentially learning? And if you learned it, might you have not needed that *Band-Aid*?

Let's start by recalling that you've successfully washed dishes many times in your life without sustaining personal injury. Why did it happen now? As you washed those glasses, this time you were using a little too much force. That's why the glass broke; it was not a random event. Did you resent doing the dishes? Could you make a case that it was someone else's turn to do that work? If that were true and you weren't dealing with that issue consciously and directly, that might account for the accident. Perhaps the truth was not so simple: perhaps there was repressed resentment in some other category of your life, something that had nothing to do with dishes. Perhaps it was pent-up sexual energy—that's Mars too, as we saw in earlier chapters.

Maybe you have no idea at all about the origin of that tense Mars energy that's arising in your mind. From a psychological perspective, we might say that you need to delve down into yourself and figure out what's going on. That's a legitimate perspective—but astrologically, it is a Plutonian perspective, not so much a Martial one. Pluto loves psychological work; Mars is more ambivalent about it. Sometimes Mars "just wants to kill something"—or at least break something. Or make some noise. Or get all hot and sweaty.

Mars don't need no stinking psychologist.

There's something truly magical here, something fundamental to the mysteries of Mars: during a Mars period, far more than understanding, we need *energetic release*. Mindful, conscious work is always commendable—but if, before doing those dishes, you'd played your electric guitar loudly or danced until you were sweaty or made love as if you had just met... in any of those cases, those soapsuds wouldn't have turned pink.

WORDS OF WISDOM IN MARS TIMES

Time to stand up for yourself; don't be a doormat—it just fouls up your karma, not to mention the karma of the person who is stepping on you.

The universe is now manifesting to you as a course in assertiveness training; you have a right to see that your needs are met.

Worthy opponents—and petty tyrants—will arise. Ride out and meet them.

Use just enough force—and no more. Growl before you bite.

Fear panic.

Know the limits of your actual powers in a given situation; do not allow passion to trick you into thinking you have powers that you do not actually have.

Be the Hunter—or you will surely be the Prey.

No one ever gets angry; everyone gets "righteously indignant." What's the difference?

You are called upon to protect that which cannot protect itself.

Violence begets violence; use it as minimally as possible, given your responsibilities.

Do not become drunk on anger.

Repressed sexual energy turns to violence, resentment, and depression.

Trust your physical body; instinct may guide you more unerringly now than insight.

ONWARD...

In this chapter, we have explored some of the broad principles and synchronistic patterns that reliably arise when Mars raises its head in your chart or when we find some passing stimulus connected with the sign Aries. This is foundational material; it can manifest in diverse ways depending on the exact astrological context.

A little later, we'll explore some of those possible contexts in "cookbook" fashion. We will do that in two ways. The first is to consider how Mars—by transit, progression, or solar arc—interacts through the aspects it makes to the rest of the planets in your birthchart. The second is to consider what it means when each individual planet enters Aries—again, via any of those same three predictive methods.

Before we do any of that, let's put aspects on the evolutionary map. All astrologers speak of squares and oppositions and so on, but the understandings we've inherited regarding these planetary interactions tend to be marred by fatalism.

Let's see if we can make aspects sing from a new—and more evolutionary—hymnal. Once we've accomplished that, we'll add Mars to the mix, letting it dance with the rest of the planets through squares, trines, and so on.

18

ARIES TIMES, MARS TIMES: THE BUILDING BLOCKS

Mars can collide with the Sun or any other planet in three different ways: by transit, by progression, or by solar arc. Each of those techniques represents a distinct way of moving Mars around the birthchart, and each rings a distinct bell in your consciousness and in the synchronistic pattern of events you encounter during such a period.

Furthermore, those interactions can operate through any of the eleven aspects we just described. Again, each specific aspect will add its own tonality to the "negotiations" between the two planets, but the heart of the matter always remains the integration itself. Somehow, for everything to go right, Mars and whatever planet it is touching must strike a deal.

It would take an astrological encyclopedia to describe all of the possible combinations of Mars and the other planets, aspect by aspect—and even that encyclopedia would be incomplete: Mars making a quincunx to a Scorpio Sun in the tenth house presents a very different prospect than Mars quincunxing a Libran Sun in the fourth.

Our ace in the hole is to remember our guiding principle with all aspects: every one of them is about two distinct energies trying to find a way to cooperate. Regardless of the specific aspect involved, these two archetypal fields must find some kind of common ground in order for your journey to unfold on its proper course. In each case, we can be at least halfway to a proper understanding simply by thinking of how those two planets might look if they were cooperating successfully with each other—and how they might look if they were tripping over each other's feet. In this chapter, we explore exactly that, looking at some some specific guidelines about the aspectual integration of Mars with each one of the other planets—what it means, for example, when progressed Mars triggers Neptune, and so on though all the possibilities. What we will *not* consider is the difference between transiting Mars making a sextile aspect to natal Neptune versus progressed Mars squaring natal Neptune. Emphatically, those are different events—but trying to describe each of the eleven possible aspects individually brings us back to writing the encyclopedia. Here we concentrate on the heart of the matter: the transitory alchemical marriage of Mars and Neptune.

True astrological mastery arises only when we can skillfully hear all the grace notes and subtleties—houses, signs, and so forth. My hope is that by providing you with the basic integrative DNA behind all of these processes, I can help you make a good start in that direction.

As we contemplate Mars moving through an aspect with the Sun, we simultaneously learn something about what it might mean when the Sun moves into Aries—which is of course the sign ruled by Mars. These are different astrological events, but the synthesis of the two archetypal fields is rather similar.

While we're at it in this chapter, we will also explore the meaning of any planet moving by progression or by solar arc into the sign Aries.

What about the *transits* of these planets into Aries? Everyone on earth experiences Mars transiting into Aries at the same time; it is a universal event. For it to have personal meaning, Mars must simultaneously make some significant aspectual contact with your natal chart—that is, while it's passing through Aries, it must form an aspect to a planet in your birthchart. Otherwise it is not such a big deal for you at the personal level.

MARS CONTACTING THE SUN

Time To Defend Your Right… to exist and to thrive. To make your own choices. Actually to *lead* your own life for a change. To feed your natural passions and to satisfy them. To be bold. To be bawdy. To have adventures. To take risks. To do dumb or risky things if you feel like it. To make your own mistakes and learn from them.

Synchronistic Correlates: Opportunities for adventure. Risky situations. Bullies and tyrants appear—will you stand up to them or will you knuckle under? Accidents. Sexual opportunity or temptation. Festering situations boil over. Push comes to shove. Peaks of stress. Temper tantrums, arising in yourself or experiencing them in other people. Strenuous physical exercise. Challenges and dares at every level. Perspiration.

Beware of... the ways that passion, resentment, and anger can exaggerate your actions. Using too much force. Becoming drunk on your own rage and heat. Actions you will regret "in the cold light of dawn." Subliminal tensions leading to accidents and misadventure. Missing critical opportunities as a result of an excess of caution—be bold! Bottling up your fire and having it fester as resentment and depression.

MARS CONTACTING THE MOON

Time To Defend Your Right... to express your true feelings. To take time for your own healing and regeneration—and to defend your right to that time. To enjoy a domestic situation that meets your actual needs. To spend time with your soul-family. To not be materially productive. To sleep. To cultivate dream-time. To protect those whom you love.

Synchronistic Correlates: Signals from the emotional body indicating that it is time for some self-care. Similar signals from the physical body. Family events demanding attention; family crisis. Emotions boiling over. Hidden feelings revealed. An edgy mood. Touchiness.

Beware of... over-dramatization. The way passion exaggerates and distorts one's intended self-expression. Saying things in the heat of the moment that you later wish you could take back. Errors and accidents arising from a failure to monitor your own tiredness, frustration, or physical and emotional feedback. Irrational passion.

MARS CONTACTING MERCURY

Time To Defend Your Right... to speak your mind. To be clear and direct. To disagree out loud with other people's opinions. To ask hard questions and to follow up on them. To argue. To reject boredom and predictability in your life. To assert your right to learn and to educate yourself. To be witty, even if your wit does not please everyone.

Synchronistic Correlates: Situations of verbal confrontation; argument. The need to clear the air. Cutting through obfuscation and excessive politeness or diplomacy. Multitasking; juggling many balls at the same time. Shocking or surprising information emerging. Heart-to-heart conversations. Bringing up a dreaded subject.

Beware of... using hyperbolic and inflammatory language when simpler, more diplomatic statements would better serve your long-term aims. Unwittingly triggering defensiveness in other people. Attachment to winning arguments at any cost. Stressing yourself with overextension and worry. Nervous exhaustion.

MARS CONTACTING VENUS

Time To Defend Your Right... to have your intimate needs met. To speak from your heart in all your relationships. To be true to your sexuality and expressive of it. To not allow truly vibrant love to be eclipsed by caution, habit, or the psychological tyranny of personal insecurity. To live a passionate life. To initiate or precipitate intimate contact. To reach out assertively to possible new friends or partners.

Synchronistic Correlates: Moments of truth in ongoing relationships. Realizing that accepting conflict is sometimes the price of honesty. Trusting a relationship enough to give it space to evolve and change. Sexual adventures and misadventures. Encounters with art—music, film, and so on—that trigger cathartic emotional release.

Beware of... mistaking sexual passion for genuine intimacy. Confusing love and lust. Creating unnecessary conflict or drama in existing relationships. Thinking "with your little head." Being swept away by self-righteous anger in the course of working out a disagreement. Dynamiting the bridges that bind two people together.

MARS CONTACTING MARS

(Here we refer to Mars forming aspects to its natal position)

Time To Defend Your Right... to stand up for yourself. To be assertive. To claim things for yourself. To be number one. To have it be "your turn" for a change. To seize the day. To be colorful, controversial, and sexy. To win. To come out on top.

Synchronistic Correlates: Confrontations. Emotional situations, both internal and external, reaching critical mass; explosions. Breakdowns. Stressful situations peaking. Do-or-die moments. Facing fears. Accidents. Encounters with violence.

Beware of… your own hyperbolic, inflated responses. Letting fear make decisions for you. Missing opportunities because of hesitation. Intellect canceling out the wisdom of your instincts. Excessive meekness.

MARS CONTACTING JUPITER

Time To Defend Your Right… to expand your territory and enrich your kingdom. To take calculated risks; to bet the house. To achieve victory. To elevate and update your definition of success, and then not be afraid to make a bid for it. To celebrate your own passions. To claim what you have rightly earned already. To expect a miracle. To savor triumph.

Synchronistic Correlates: Opportunity abounds, but it requires bold and decisive action on your part to claim it. "Faint heart never wins fair maid." Adventure; risk. At this juncture of your life, admit it: you need a fresh victory; you need to raise your game to a new level. Gambles. Miracles.

Beware of… inflated, fantastical schemes that will never work. Dreaming instead of doing. Grandiosity compensating for insecurity. High-handed cruelty relative to the needs or rights of other people. Remember that you will meet the same people on the way down whom you met on the way up—and in either case, they will be waiting for you.

MARS CONTACTING SATURN

Time To Defend Your Right… to carve out time and resources in support of the Great Work of your life, whatever form it might take. To keep your eye on the prize no matter what the cost. To defend your solitude. To stand up for your integrity and values as you yourself define them. To make a stand; to hold your ground. To allow your sexuality to mature naturally.

Synchronistic Correlates: Challenges to your integrity. Moral temptation. Difficult decisions; points where the high and low roads separate. Enduring stress and criticism for the sake of your values and your self-respect. Sacrifices—both your own and those you must ask of others.

Beware of... defeatist thinking. The price of negativity. Concentrating too much on problems and not enough on solutions. Thinking the cup is half-empty; succumbing to feelings of impossibility and entrapment. Losing sight of the fountainhead of your true passions; failing to recognize that the nature of that fountainhead changes with the passing years—that which was formerly meaningful to you might no longer be so.

MARS CONTACTING URANUS

Time To Defend Your Right... to be yourself, and to do that without self-consciousness even if you are facing social pressures to pretend that you are someone other than who you really are. To go ahead and be "weird," if that is the word other people choose to use to describe you. To break away from the herd. To disappoint people, if that is the price of freedom. To do the unexpected. To growl at people who are trying to change you in ways that you do not choose to be changed. To let your sexuality be exactly what it is.

Synchronistic Correlates: Without your knowing it, a situation of unintentional hypocrisy has crept into your life; it is time to rectify it. Encounters with people who try to forbid your authenticity. Opportunities arise to break free of the pack. A chance to walk on the wild side. Life-changing sexual magic or sexual encounters.

Beware of... unreflective impulsiveness. Headstrong foolishness. Regardless of your age, beware of your "inner teenager." Contrariness; acting out. Three shots of tequila followed by what appears to be a good idea. Flying off the handle. Accidents. Unpremeditated idiocy.

MARS CONTACTING NEPTUNE

Time To Defend Your Right... to make time for your spiritual life. To be selfish or even fierce in service of your inner work. To withdraw temporarily from the world of action. To do what you must do in order to be receptive to a new vision. To position yourself in a way that allows "angels" to speak to you. To challenge your religion and your belief-system, knowing that if they are strong and true, they will survive the challenge. To integrate sexuality and spirituality and ride the waves they create together. To be courageous enough to face the great Vastness.

Synchronistic Correlates: A vision quest. A necessary crisis of faith. The path of the spiritual warrior; shamanism; psychedelic experience; sexual magic. Physical adventure arising as a spiritual path—illustration: skydiving, backpacking, or spelunking triggering breakthroughs in consciousness.

Beware of... delusional thinking defended passionately. Spiritual craziness. New Age excesses; Fundamentalist excesses. Jihad. The "flight into light." Sexual obsession, self-delusion, or escapism. Crusades; "killing for Christ." Confusing mere psychic excitation with true spirituality.

MARS CONTACTING PLUTO

Time To Defend Your Right... to do deep inner work, however much its revelations might threaten people around you. To ask hard questions of yourself and of others. To bravely ferret out the truth. To integrate sexuality and honesty. To look the devil straight in the eye. To bravely recognize the exact nature of your own woundedness. Then, with the foregoing steps at least partly accomplished, to confront the problem of evil, lies, and darkness in the world outside of yourself. To rise to your mission.

Synchronistic Correlates: Psychological crisis as a turning point in life as well as a point of illumination. You are now ready to face realities you were not previously ready to face. Intense interpersonal events, often sexual or otherwise passionate in nature, which bring challenging truths to the surface. The possibility of violence. Encounters with true evil or darkness. Soul-revealing contact with tragedy.

Beware of... the unintentional cruelty of trying to "help others see truths" which they in fact are not yet ready to see. Grandstanding; hyperbolic drama; extreme, overheated pronouncements. Unwittingly acting out your own woundedness rather than dealing with it psychologically, internally, and directly.

ENTERING ARIES

When a planet enters Aries by transit, progression or by solar arc, we are again faced with the need to integrate two archetypes: the specific nature of the planet and the Fiery agenda of Aries. The marriage might flow easily and harmoniously—or it might be a difficult and seemingly unnatural one.

Let's reflect for a moment on an example of the latter possibility.

Venus, for example, might've been peacefully progressing through Pisces in your chart for many years. Its underlying agenda has thus reflected the values that motivate Pisces—spirituality, romance, maybe forgiveness. Simultaneously, Venus has taken on a certain potential of vulnerability to the shadow-side of Pisces: perhaps too much of a tendency to turn the other cheek, or to sweep real issues under the carpet.

For many years, working all that out, in terms of finding the higher ground and navigating the shadow possibilities, has been your spiritual path.

As Venus progresses into Aries, all that changes. Suddenly the soul's lessons in intimacy—Venusian territory—become significantly *hotter.* It is time to learn to stand up for yourself, and to be more assertive about your intimate needs.

If you think that *you* are startled by these changes, just ask your partner how he or she feels!

Relationships very often weather these kinds of evolutionary steps and are even deepened by them. There's no need for fear—but it certainly helps to have the scorecard in your hand.

And that scorecard is your birthchart.

Earlier in this chapter we explored Mars interacting by aspect with all the planets. Here, let's investigate the bones of what it means when each planet enters Aries, whether by transit, by progression, or by solar arc. As we lamented earlier, this "cookbook" format precludes the inclusion of the vast array of astrological details that create practically infinite variation in the symbolism. So, once again, always remember that your personal experience will be flavored by the specifics of your own chart and your circumstances. Still, hopefully, these broad guidelines will cast some light on your own life and experience.

Note: The transits of the Sun, Moon, Mercury, Venus, and Mars are fast-moving astrological triggers. They do not have time to develop the depth and complexity of meaning that are characteristic of all progressions and solar arcs, along with the much slower transits of Jupiter, Saturn, Uranus, Neptune, and Pluto. In applying the material that follows, remember that the fast-moving planets operate as triggers while their slower counterparts are the theme-builders.

SUN ENTERING ARIES

Your New School: Assertiveness training. Time to "make things happen" in your life. The existential traffic light turns green; you've got a 400-horse-power sports car—and a moron in a pickup truck honking his horn behind you. Step on the gas. Claim what is yours. Your ego is your soul's vehicle, not your soul's enemy.

Don't Hold Onto... a form of Piscean "spirituality" that has become inappropriate for you—one that puts too much emphasis on passivity, surrender, and the acceptance of things as they are. Those were good lessons, but the point is that you have learned them and it is time to move on to some fiercer ones.

What To Expect: You will not lose the spiritual wisdom that you have gained; no force in the universe can take that from you now. But from this moment on, passivity will only lead to your feeling lost, as well as being vulnerable to victimization. Meanwhile, courage and audacity will be rewarded with meaningful experience.

The Shape of Failure: Allowing yourself to be intimidated or unduly discouraged by whatever challenges loom on your horizon. Holding yourself aloof from life, thus robbing the world of your gifts while robbing yourself of engagement, vitality, and the true pathway to meaningful evolution.

By Transit: Brief, emergent opportunities to assert yourself, be heard, and feel as if you matter in this world.

MOON ENTERING ARIES

Your New School: A deepening of your ability to trust your instincts and to act decisively and boldly upon them. Creating a social or familial network in which your needs and feelings matter; taking responsibility for shaping that network. Defending your home, family and your territory. Claiming your natural home.

Don't Hold Onto... ghostlike Piscean feelings of drifting passively through whatever experiences are presented to you. There is wisdom in beholding life as a dream, but the time for that particular wisdom is now finished. Don't dream it, live it.

What To Expect: You will attract opportunities to teach your heart courage. It might sound terrible to say that you should expect war and conflict, but there are wars worth fighting and conflicts worthy of your commitment: you may be called upon to defend something or someone you love—and it may be yourself.

The Shape of Failure: Emotional and existential paralysis resulting from fear; opportunities slipping through your fingers. The shame of not doing what you know you need to do. Dishonor.

By Transit: A transit of the Moon only lasts a couple of days. During that time, it will form aspects that emerge and disappear in a period of a few hours. Underlying that transitory mood is a motivation to defend your right to meet the specific needs of whichever planet is being contacted.

MERCURY ENTERING ARIES

Your New School: Claiming and defending your right to be heard. A quality of fire, directness, and intensity is integrating with your voice. You have a right to have access to information. You have a right to know exactly what is going on. You have a right to education. Trust your curiosity; it will lead you unerringly to the exact knowledge that you need. You are learning how to argue effectively, and thus to be taken seriously. Voice your demands.

Don't Hold Onto... a dreamy, unfocused, too-accepting attitude. Do not make a fetish out of Piscean intuition, imagination, or inspiration—they are truly magical virtues; you have them and you will not lose them, but what you need now is more intellectual discipline, analytic penetration, and cognitive rigor.

What To Expect: You will encounter situations that fill you with passion: injustice, unfairness—or finding precious new ideas about which no one seems to care. Opportunities to debate abound; rise to them and be heard.

The Shape of Failure: Two demons loom here. The first is being intimidated into silence. The second is the kind of stridency that defeats its own arguments.

By Transit: Differences of opinion arise; remember that it is possible for friends to enjoy them rather than allowing them to create interpersonal rifts. Annoyances and frustrations lead to opportunities for you to speak up and assert yourself.

VENUS ENTERING ARIES

Your New School: Passion—but that means dealing with passion's ancient enemy: the unresolved, unspoken tensions that often accumulate between people. Left unaddressed, they only create cold distance. In your new school, you are learning to keep "short accounts" with the people you love—that is to say, learning to put uncomfortable truths on the table before they have a chance to fester into those kinds of walls.

Don't Hold Onto... Piscean "forgiveness" or "transcendence"—they may have served a positive purpose in your life in the past, but now they are simply the disguises in which your truth conceals itself when it is afraid to be seen or heard.

What To Expect: Opportunities to be direct and honest. The condition of Venus is often reflected in the kinds of people we meet; you are likely now to encounter "warriors" of various stripes—colorful, adventurous people who look you directly in the eye and tell you what they think. People who expect the same from you.

The Shape of Failure: Allowing yourself to be intimidated, shamed, or controlled by another person. Alternatively, defending yourself from intimacy by intimidating, shaming, or otherwise controlling another person.

By Transit: Situations arise in which risking an honest conversation clears the air and saves you from more unpleasant conflict down the road.

MARS ENTERING ARIES

Your New School: Mars rules Aries, so this is a very pure and unalloyed expression of the Warrior archetype. Assertiveness training. Will you be the Hunter or the Prey? Competition. Adventure for the joy of it. High passion. Living as if each minute could be your last. A fascination with "the edge."

Don't Hold Onto... a Piscean fantasy life; it is better to have a real one.

What To Expect: Worthy opponents who potentially can bring out the best in you. Rivalry. Little Napoleons who try to intimidate you; paper tigers that appear to block your path. Competitive situations: two dogs and one bone; rivals for affection or for some other prize. The call of adventure. Situations with "no guarantees."

The Shape of Failure: Letting yourself be cast as the designated victim. Living with the realization that you voluntarily missed your chance because you were afraid. Internalized resentments; somatized stress. Dramatic overreaction to trivial annoyances. Self-righteousness.

By Transit: Doors open briefly, then suddenly close. Pass through them—or you miss your chance. Flair-ups in interpersonal situations. Opportunities to release tension through vigorous activity.

Note that from this point forward in the descriptions, we no longer include the section "By Transit." With the previous planets, their transits are relatively minor events. From here forward, we are looking at the kinds of slow, theme-building transits that can change your life.

JUPITER ENTERING ARIES

Your New School: Victory—and forging a truly personal, self-aware definition of the term. Finding the path of the inner King or Queen. Walking with your head held high. During periods of your life characterized by this combination of energies, you are capable of extraordinary accomplishments. Luck is on your side. The wind is at your back. Aim carefully, because you will get what you want. Do not underestimate yourself; the victory you must identify and secure is one that resonates with your soul, not just with your pride.

Don't Hold Onto... personally outdated Piscean attachments to humility, otherworldly forms of spirituality, or transcendent aloofness.

The Shape of Failure: Settling for mere glitter. The dubious triumph of having only impressed other people; being celebrated by people whom you do not respect. Counting victory strictly in terms of defeated competitors, missing the deeper, soul-centered possibilities of the word. Succumbing to the cold seduction of what amounts to a kind of bloodlust.

SATURN ENTERING ARIES

Your New School: Metaphorically, the prize of which you are worthy lies at the peak of a very steep and profoundly daunting mountain. The question is, *are you brave enough to climb it?* Saturnian "eye-on-the-prize" self-discipline is trying to merge with sheer Arian audacity. It is a powerful combination. "Warrior" responsibilities arise now: regardless of the odds, what honorable person would fail to stand up to those who would hurt his family or her children? As Aragorn said, faced with hordes of evil orcs in Lord of the Rings, "Ride out and meet them."

Don't Hold Onto... purely internal Piscean goals—with Saturn in Aries, the theater of your evolutionary work lies in this manifest world of concrete activity. It is time to actually "do something." In the end, if you are successful, you will have something to show for it—a prize that fills you with dignity and self-respect.

The Shape of Failure: Seeing the mountain you need to climb—and then turning away from it in discouragement. Instead, you need to show us what your best looks like; otherwise, you will remain trapped in the deadening responsibilities of maintaining a life that you actually outgrew years ago.

URANUS ENTERING ARIES

Your New School: Charting your own independent existential course. Bold moves, often undertaken without any external support. Sometimes you have to fight for the right to live your own life; sometimes you need to fight to be free. Standing up to figures of authority. Taking back your power from people to whom you have given it. Intrepidly trusting your own genius and seeing where it leads you.

Don't Hold Onto... "reasonable compromise" when in fact it is actually a compromise of your soul's intentions for this lifetime. Your Piscean inner life has laid a good foundation in consciousness and imagination; now it is time to manifest what you have imagined. Action, rooted in previous reflection, must replace mere reflection. You do not need the approval of anyone except yourself.

The Shape of Failure: Crankiness. Contrariness. Rebellion for its own sake. The urge to blow everything up without a corresponding vision for how to fill the resulting vacuum. Blaming other people for their "tyranny" over you, when in fact all that has been stopping you is your own lack of inspiration, *chutzpah*, and confidence.

NEPTUNE ENTERING ARIES

Your New School: Ego actually serving spirit; this implies an audacious willingness to claim specific experiences that expand your consciousness, even if in so doing you appear to be selfish. Spiritual adventures; facing fears connected with inner and astral realms. Recognizing that the spiritual path is not for wimps. Edgy states of consciousness straddling the fine line between wisdom and madness; staying on the right side of that line.

Don't Hold Onto... Piscean otherworldliness. Remember that this earth is just another plane of experience and that everything you do here echoes in eternity. Release any attachment to the Piscean notion that flesh is the enemy of spirit. Accept that your physical body is an evolutionary vehicle optimized for gathering the exact experiences that will trigger a higher state of being in you.

The Shape of Failure: Turning away in fear from a doorway to the higher spiritual ground. Placing too much value on "serenity" and "balance," not realizing that they are often the disguises worn by fear and evolutionary laziness.

PLUTO ENTERING ARIES

(Mostly irrelevant in the present era. As I write these words, Pluto is transiting through Capricorn [2008-2023/24]. Some babies born around now will experience the solar arc of Pluto into Aries in their old age. Many now-unborn kids with Pluto in Aquarius [2023/4 - 2043/4] will experience that solar arc—and so on. Pluto itself will not enter Aries by transit until 2066—and if anyone that far down the road is still reading these words... Hey, thank you!)

Your New School: Facing some specific soul-wounds, many of which have their origin in humanity's epochal love affair with violence. The origins of these wounds may lie in the present lifetime, or in previous ones. This process has two dimensions: the first lies in acknowledging and eventually healing memories and impressions of being victimized or hurt. The second dimension, far more difficult, involves facing your own complicity in humanity's endless war.

Don't Hold Onto... guilt or resentment. You are ready to release them both. Temper your natural fear of this inner work with the realization that you are now ready for it; what would have been too much for you in the past is now within the scope of your power to heal.

The Shape of Failure: War on every level, from the global to the interpersonal. Attacking outward symbols of the fears we have not been brave enough to face inside ourselves.

19

CELESTIAL NAVIGATION II: SUN TIMES, LEO TIMES

If someone needed my astrological help and I could know only one single piece of information about what was going on in his or her chart, I'd have my answer in one second: give me the current location of the progressed Sun. There's absolutely nothing more central or important in the entire system. I would long to know where Pluto and Neptune were. I would be curious about the progressed Moon. But I would choose the Sun. It is the undisputed *numero uno*; nothing else can compete with the impact of its message in any form of developmental astrology.

In the birthchart, the Sun is shorthand for the Self. By progression, we only need to add one adjective: it becomes the *Evolving* Self. As you let that sonorous term sink into your heart, you probably sense that it should be preceded by a drum roll and a trumpet fanfare.

The "evolving self"—ever so slowly, the lessons of life make it through our thick skulls. People rhapsodize about the "amazing changes" they experienced in a weekend workshop. At the risk of sounding a bit cynical, we often find that by Tuesday of the following week, their lives are pretty much where they were the previous week. *True fundamental evolutionary change typically happens at the pace of a glacier*. And that is the domain of the progressed Sun. As we saw a while back, its average speed is only about 1° per year. That is a literal, technical astrological truth—but it also serves as an excellent metaphor: at the stately pace of "1° per year," the Sun relentlessly and everlastingly chips away at our ignorance, our rationalizations, and our attachments.

Or potentially it does so—it at least triggers those kinds of evolutionary possibilities.

Learning to decipher the message of the progressed Sun is the single most fundamental skill required for mastery of the predictive branch of astrology.

A quick technical note before we dive into the complexities of this pivotal subject: by definition, the progressed Sun and the solar arc Sun are one and the same. The transiting Sun, by contrast, moves too quickly to develop much depth or complexity of meaning; in common with the other fast-moving points in astrology, it operates powerfully over a few days, functioning as a trigger for more fundamental developmental themes.

We will look at the transiting Sun—but the true behemoths here are its progressions and solar arcs.

THE EVOLVING SELF

A man has been merrily living a "pirate life," just like a character in a Jimmy Buffett song. He has done his share of "wasting away again in Margaritaville"—but he has also sailed the Caribbean, truly loved half a dozen women, and made all sorts of interesting mistakes in his life.

It's not our business to judge anyone, but let's say that from the angelic perspective, this fellow has been doing exactly what he needed to do for the feeding of his soul. His father may disapprove of him and he may worry his poor mother, but all that's their business, not his.

Looking at his chart, his natal Sun lies in Scorpio. But at the age of twenty-two—the very year he lit out for the islands—his Sun progressed into Sagittarius. His adventures began right on schedule.

Now, about thirty years later, the Sun is about to change signs. He is presently in his early fifties. What happens? His carefree Sagittarian life is beginning to pall; the prospect of yet another adventure does not energize and beguile him as much as it did in the past. He feels hungry to commit to something more substantial, to put down roots, to get serious.

Any astrologer would quickly see the mark of his Sun progressing into Capricorn.

A dogmatic person might misinterpret this gentleman's evolution as an "improvement" in his character. His change in attitude might be interpreted as him "finally, after all these years, growing up."

That's incorrect: he needed those Sagittarian experiences. But now he needs another, different set of experiences—ones that reflect his solar evolution into Capricorn.

Back in Chapter Four, we learned how the natal Sun correlates with our *values*. Similarly, we can think of the progressed Sun reflecting our *evolving* values. To bring this insight into full alignment with experienced reality, we need to add a critical variable: *human freedom*. We are all free to heed the message of these changing values and to harvest the multitudinous benefits of traveling wisdom's road. But of course we are free to ignore these changes—or to identify with distorted, even demonic, expressions of them. As astrologers, we never know what a person will actually do. That's up to him or to her; our job is only to point in the direction of the higher ground.

Down there in the Caribbean, our hero lived for three decades guided by the legitimate values of Sagittarius. There was no conceivable better use of his years in the world than doing exactly what he did. But as his Sun progresses into Capricorn, the Sagittarian values no longer serve his evolution. It's time for him to change his orientation to life.

His "Self" has evolved. To be true to himself, he must change.

ANIMAL VITALITY

If the Sun disappeared, life as we understand it would cease on earth. That apocalyptic scenario is a physical, scientific fact—but we don't need to be so extreme in our thinking in order to grasp the underlying astrological principle. A week of gray, drizzly weather will do the trick. After seven days like that, we all have the blues. When the Sun finally comes out, we are delighted to see it. The dogs are barking—even the flowers turn and face the Sun with their phototropic responses.

That "sunny" feeling—that vital hunger to get out of bed in the morning and seize the day—arises naturally in us when we are true to the values indicated by the Sun.

That last comment operates on two levels simultaneously: first, as we saw earlier in the book, it refers to the position of the Sun in your natal chart. That is the foundation. But in order to maintain vitality and engagement, we must also be true to the ever-changing values indicated by the position of the progressed Sun. They don't erase your natal Sun; nothing but death can do that. But they add some more dimensions to the mixture.

With this progressed Sun on the cusp of Capricorn, our Jimmy Buffett character felt enlivened by long-established reflex when a stranger he met in the bar in Nassau invited him to serve as first mate on a wooden ketch bound for St. Kitts at dawn the next day. Such spontaneity and openness to adventure energizes Sagittarius. But his Sun has just progressed into Capricorn; the value of keeping his "eye on the prize" now replaces the values of spontaneity and openness.

For a while, he is confused. A set of values that have worked for him consistently for thirty years seems to be running out of gas. If, out of the momentum of habit, he hops on that yacht leaving for St. Kitts, he'll feel lost, disengaged, and soul-tired throughout that voyage. The style of life that used to energize him now saps his animal vitality.

Naturally, this confuses him. When the progressed Sun changes signs, the underlying logic of life changes. What used to work for us no longer works. This is arguably the most fundamental change that astrological symbolism can represent. And all of us who make it to our thirtieth birthdays will have the experience of the progressed Sun changing signs. Most of us will experience it two or three times, possibly even four if you eat your organic vegetables.

A thirty-year habit has a lot of muscle; breaking it is a challenge. But these astrological archetypes are very powerful; their tides pull at our souls. No one needs to know astrology to experience them; they are hardwired into everyone's consciousness, no matter how unevolved or benighted that person might be.

Relatively few people use astrological language—but something deep down inside every one of us knows that "Capricorn follows Sagittarius." This is a law of nature; we're just using astrological words to describe it. In simpler terms, everyone knows that "after getting an education, we need a job." After developing wisdom through experience, we need to make a gift of that wisdom to our community.

That is Sagittarius evolving into Capricorn.

Deep in the consciousness of our pirate, these same ancient wheels are turning. Even if he knows nothing about astrology, as he comes to the end of his Sagittarian solar progression, an instinctual anticipation of Capricorn arises within him. His mind and heart naturally move in that direction—and very likely, even his dream-life begins to prepare him for this change.

Bottom line: despite the fact that a thirty-year habit is a formidable enemy, the human psyche has the tools needed to turn it around.

That is all true and perhaps even sufficient—but we have still another ace in the hole...

SYNCHRONICITY

Long ago, the late great Carl Gustav Jung noticed that there were too many coincidences for "coincidence" to be a reasonable explanation. Then he began to notice that there were *patterns* in the coincidences—patterns of meaning. Working with physicist Wolfgang Pauli, he coined the term *synchronicity,* which posits that events happen for either or both of two reasons: first, something makes them happen—simple causality, action and reaction.

And secondly, things happen because it is *meaningful* for them to happen.

Illustration: while passing time with an old *National Geographic* magazine as you wait in a dentist's office, you happen to read an article about Stonehenge. That night, unable to sleep, you flip on the television. You stumble onto a program about Stonehenge. Two days later, having lunch with a friend, she says, "Guess where I'm going next June?"

And of course the answer is Stonehenge.

Yacking away with your friend in the café, you light up, excited about her upcoming trip—and marveling out loud at how often Stonehenge has come up in your own life over the past several days. Ten minutes into the conversation, she pops the obvious question: Why don't you come with me?

Your line: *I guess I am supposed to.*

It never ceases to amaze me that synchronicity is actually, demonstrably, part of the way the universe works. We never learn about any of this in science class, but we see it everywhere in life once we begin to look for it.

Everything in astrology is synchronistic; in fact, to me, synchronicity provides the most plausible explanation I can imagine for how astrology works. I wrote in depth about all that in my book *The Night Speaks.* Here

I want to underscore a simpler point: while synchronicity pervades all astrological theory, it is nowhere more evident than in working with the progressed Sun. When the Sun hits a sensitive point, your whole external life lights up with signals, signs, and omens connected to what you need to do.

The Jimmy Buffett character in our example experiences the shift in his values and his self-image that correlate with the progression of the Sun into Capricorn. We saw all that a few paragraphs ago. Those are intrapsychic events, and quite central to our understanding of the meaning of this astrological passage. But through the principle of synchronicity, we must also anticipate the simultaneous emergence of "random" extra-psychic events that reflect and support these same changes.

That's how life works. That's synchronicity.

What happens for our adventurer? We can never foresee outward, objective events with rigid certainty. By bringing in the rest of the astrological details, we can narrow down the fields of possibility, but archetypal fields contain innumerable potential manifestations; all we know for sure is that a few of them will certainly materialize.

Maybe our pirate's beloved but judgmental father becomes ill. "Jimmy Buffett" returns to Illinois to help his mom out; maybe he winds up taking over the family business—and finds to his surprise that he has a taste for it.

Maybe he meets the love of his life and for the first time feels a strong desire to make a lifelong commitment to another human being. Maybe she has a child whom he finds he loves—there's the synchronistic dawn of another Capricorn responsibility.

Maybe on that voyage to St. Kitts, he spies a schooner built in 1938 that is slowly going to pieces in a backwater boat yard. It's for sale, cheap. He buys it as-is. He commits to a two- or three-year project of refitting the vessel, with an eye on starting his own yacht charter business.

In all of these illustrations, we observe one of the most benign and miraculous features of our existence in this magical, dreamlike universe: *the seemingly-random events of outer life always arise in a fashion that supports our inner journeys.* That's synchronicity again. And there is no way to understand astrology—and especially the progressions of the Sun—without keeping one eye on this principle. Just as the Sun's massive gravity holds the planets physically in their courses, similarly, its synchronistic gravity dominates, shapes, and overshadows everything that happens in our lives.

THE PROGRESSED SUN IN ASPECT

The progressed Sun changing signs is right at the top of the astrological food chain; with such an event, as we have just seen, our entire orientation to life experiences tectonic shifts. We can say the same about the progressed Sun shifting from one house to another—and we'll explore that in a few moments.

But first, let's think about the progressed Sun forming aspects to the rest of the planets in the birthchart.

Moving at 1° per year, if we live to be ninety years old, the Sun will have made it about 90° around the chart, give or take a little bit. It will not, in other words, have had time to make all of the possible aspects it could potentially make to all the planets. We would have to live to the ripe old age of 365 for that to happen. But by the time there are ninety candles on our birthday cake, the progressed Sun will have formed *some aspect* to every sensitive point in the chart.

When any such solar aspect occurs, *the evolving self must integrate that particular planetary function into its identity, values, and arsenal of evolutionary tools.* In order to go forward meaningfully and at full power in our lives, we need to deepen our relationship with that planetary energy. We need somehow to make an ally of it.

As we saw earlier, all aspects are about integration—the progressed Sun forming a square or in opposition to a natal planet is not a bad thing; it's just that the integration, while absolutely necessary, is likely to be more challenging. If we were to fail in that integration, the evolving storyline of our life would derail.

The same thing is true when, out of laziness, we sleep through a softer solar aspect. Again, "good" and "bad" are only useful words when we employ them discerningly to the evaluation of our *response* to a given progressed solar aspect, not to the aspect itself.

As an illustration, let's imagine a woman whose progressed Sun has formed an aspect to her natal Mercury. One simple possibility is that she's arrived at a point in her journey where, in order to go forward meaningfully, she must acquire further *education.* Perhaps when she graduated from high school, she immediately became a secretary. There's no shame in that, but she is now bored with her work. That boredom is a classic Mercury signature. To put the same thing positively, Mercury correlates with *curiosity*—and her present life as a secretary lost its fascination long ago.

Is it time for her to go to college? We can't be sure—but that is exactly the kind of illustration I would put on the table in an astrological counseling session. Going to college is pure Mercury—especially when it's an active choice rather than just another predictable passage in the journey of a middle-class youth.

If she *integrates her evolving solar storyline* with that Mercury, the positive energies of the planet enable her to go forward. If she fails to embrace that Mercury, we can imagine her feeling stuck, as if she's gotten lost in one of life's many *cul-de-sacs.* It's easy to make those kinds of mistakes; we all do it sometimes. It's often difficult to resolve them. We can do that too—our souls are resilient. But it is far better—and far easier—to get it right the first time.

TAKE YOUR MEDICINE

A few lines ago, I referred to one of the "most benign and miraculous features of our existence"—how, via synchronicity, "the seemingly-random events of outer life arise in a fashion that supports our inner journeys."

There are very few truths more fundamental than that one. But we need to understand it with a clear eye. The support synchronicity provides is not always welcome; sometimes it can feel pretty awful. But it is always the medicine we need.

One astrological example of that kind of "unwelcome help" is something we will explore later in this series, in *The Book of Earth*—when Saturn, for example, looms by transit or by solar arc, the soul is learning lessons of *endurance* and *self-discipline*. Who enjoys that? But the universe "cooperates" synchronistically: we encounter resistance, challenges, perhaps bad luck. What better environment is there for learning endurance and self-discipline?

Similarly, in Plutonian times, we often encounter dimensions of life which we might deem *tragic.* Synchronistically, we are then learning to face the raw, fragile reality of being human—and to do that in a spirit of radical honesty. We will look deeply into such Plutonian events when we get to the end of the series with *The Book of Water.*

Here, in *The Book of Fire*, we're exploring the Life-Givers. While, as we have seen, it is very possible to get into trouble with Mars, the Sun, or Jupiter, their energies tend to be more lively, even cheery, when compared to Saturn or Pluto. Their synchronistic correlates tend to reflect those happier, more upbeat kinds of moods. Typically, they open doors to enlivening experience.

In the next chapter, we'll explore in "cookbook" fashion the progression of the Sun through aspects to each of the planets. Here in this chapter, we are more concerned with internalizing the underlying principles and getting a feel for how to work with them.

Our next step in this exploration is to contemplate the meaning of the Sun progressing into a new house—an event which, as with the Sun progressing into a new sign, will happen to everyone who lives a normal lifespan two, three, or possibly four times. And, again just as when the Sun changes signs, we are looking at a massive change of orientation in life—the gravity of the synchronistic field has shifted to a new pole.

THE PROGRESSED SUN CHANGING HOUSES

When the progressed Sun enters a new house, the *circumstances* of life change. Our basic values and self-image, as illuminated by the *sign* position of the Sun, are now faced with a *novel environment, a fresh set of stimuli, and new behavioral possibilities.*

Another way to say it is that the "evolutionary school" we are attending suddenly begins to operate according to different rules. Our world seems to shift on its axis. That's because underlying everything is the fact that we are now learning a new set of lessons. No timely announcement of these changes arrives in your Inbox, but the message is displayed clearly in two places: your heart and your life.

Illustration: a woman is born with the natal Sun in the seventh house. She is therefore learning "lessons about trust" in this lifetime. As a child, she experiences a terrible blow to her ability to trust anyone: sexual abuse.

When her Sun progresses into the eighth house, events arise that trigger the long process of healing from that awful wound. Remember that the Sun progresses slowly—it will typically take three decades or so to pass through a house, although of course houses are quite variable in width. In any case, the woman's healing process will very likely be long and probably messy. Sexual abuse takes a long while to heal.

What happens?

With this solar progression, the circumstances of her life have now shifted into an eighth house context. Her behavior reflects her adaptation to that shift. What happens? What does she encounter? There are many possibilities, of course. Does she "act out" sexually? Does she attract predatory people into her life—clones of her abuser? Does she become asexual or unnaturally prim?

All of these behaviors and actions could happen. They are all on the table. We don't know which of them will be activated—but we do know that situations will arise that are conducive to any of these manifestations.

As the Sun advances in its progression through her eighth house, almost inevitably it will form aspects to various planets. Each one of those events will represent a potential evolutionary breakthrough in her healing process—that, or a disastrous behavioral expression of her wounded condition.

Typically, given the intimate nature of the eighth house, these progressed Sun aspects will correspond with *relationship* events.

Actual healing never happens automatically, but we can imagine that as the story of her Sun's progression through the eighth house unfolds, this woman will move gradually in the direction of wholeness. One possibility, among many other good ones, is that she enters effective psychotherapy.

She's now ready for that work; she heals.

And of course her Sun eventually progresses into the ninth house, where the orientation is much less toward psychology and more focused on outward experience. The energy that has so far gone into dealing with her wounds—or been wasted by the process of acting out her wounds—is now freed for other expressions. With her Sun progressing into the ninth house, she experiences a burst of vitality and a renewed sense of possibility. She feels a powerful urge to *expand her horizons*, perhaps through education, perhaps through travel, perhaps in the form of a more "questing" attitude toward her life. Perhaps she becomes bolder in the expression of her sexuality.

Because of synchronicity, as her Sun progresses into the ninth house, outward circumstances arise that reflect these inner changes in her evolutionary climate: perhaps she is offered a job in another country. Maybe an opportunity presents itself for her to go back to school and earn her master's degree.

The list of possibilities is practically endless: she gets her pilot's license. She spends a year in a monastery. She learns to speak Chinese. She hikes the length of the Pacific Crest Trail, all the way from Mexico to Canada.

As you reflect on the Sun's progression into a new house, I encourage you to marvel for a moment at the astonishing interplay of our inner journey and the nature of the outer experiences which we magnetize into our lives. That which our society would teach us to explain as the random "luck of the draw" is vastly more orderly and meaningful than we are led to believe.

This is the miracle of synchronicity—and it is nowhere so obvious as when we contemplate the progressed Sun in general, and most especially, its relationship to the astrological houses. That's because houses are about *manifestation*; we can always see them in action right before our eyes.

ENTERING LEO

What happens when a planet enters the Sun's natural sign, Leo? Certain "solar" possibilities will then animate that progressing or transiting planet. In other words, some of the ideas we have already been exploring in this chapter will make themselves felt in a slightly-altered form. As ever, we know how to keep perspective: the evolutionary impact of a Leo ingress is much more powerful if the planet involved is moving slowly.

Meditate with me for a moment on a simple phrase: when there's a significant Leo stimulus in your chart, *the time has come for you to shine.*

On the face of the phrase, what's not to like? We all like to shine—*or do we?* Stepping out on the stage of life can be frightening. To understand the evolutionary dynamic of Leo, try imagining yourself in this position: because of your hard work, you are about to receive a prestigious award. A gala banquet is held in your honor; three hundred people are in attendance. You are expected to stand at the podium in front of them and deliver a keynote speech.

How do you feel as you step onto the stage, faced with thunderous applause—and high expectations? You are the Person of the Hour—and everyone is expecting you to... shine.

Many of us would prefer a visit to the proctologist.

"Being seen" in this way triggers primal fears. One common example: a classic dream motif, especially prevalent during Leo times, is finding yourself naked in a public place. It is of course horrifying. You feel compelled to run away and hide. The inner experience of Leo is very much like that. As you step up to that podium, all eyes are on you. Can you be witty, engaging, and profound? Or will you make an ass of yourself? Either way, this is the moment of truth. The world is saying, "show us what you've got." Your vulnerability is absolute, and the emotional stakes are very high.

Let's say you nail it. People laugh at your jokes and nod meaningfully at your insights. As you leave the stage you receive a standing ovation.

What is the effect of that adulation? Obviously your ego gets a boost—and in thinking deeply about Leo, we need to have a little bit of compassion for the poor human ego. It is not the enemy of the soul; it's the *vehicle* of the soul—and in many ways it is quite fragile. In Leo times, your beleaguered ego needs some healing, and the method by which you obtain it is inseparable from your taking the risk of self-expression in a state of full vulnerability. This is what "shining" is about.

When a planet moves into Leo, you need to shine—and equally importantly, you need some applause. You need to be seen and appreciated; your soul needs to be recognized.

As ever in astrology, your own consciousness must willingly participate in the evolutionary process. Otherwise nothing positive happens—and, inevitably, the energy then gets tangled up in negativity.

A LESSON IN GROOMING

A man's Venus progresses into Leo. Translation: his attractiveness (*Venus*) needs a little polish (*Leo.*) What happens? If he gets it right, he trims his beard. He spends some money on new clothes. He visits the dentist. He gets rid of his collection of moth-eaten *Grateful Dead* T-shirts.

He senses that it's time for him to cut more of a figure in the world—to make a bid for some Venusian applause. It works too. Women who used to ignore him start to notice him. Friends tell him that "he's looking good." There's Venus animated by Leo—he's taken the risk of vulnerability, and he has received "applause" in return. The healing loop is cooking. Venus progressing into Leo means that his confidence in his own attractiveness in every sense of the word needed a boost; and he makes that happen.

Going deeper, in a spirit of vulnerability, our hero *owns the fact that he is lonely.* He owns the fact that he is beginning to feel like a sad clown. It's time for him to take the great risk of trying to be noticed, and perhaps to be loved. He rises to the challenge. He has responded wisely and courageously to the promptings of his own soul.

And he is enormously energized and re-invigorated by the process. Never forget our root principle: this is the Fire Family we are exploring. They are the Life-Givers.

How might our former Deadhead get this progression wrong? Well, for starters he might stick to the familiar safety zone of wearing those old, familiar *Grateful Dead* T-shirts. In a way, then *nothing happens*: no one tells him that he's looking good; women look at him as if he were a loaf of *Wonder Bread.*

In this version of the situation, we can accurately say that, at least in concrete terms, "nothing happened." In an outward sense, yes—there were no visible changes in his life. But from an evolutionary perspective, his better angels are shaking their heads. They do not think that "nothing happened." They think that he wasn't brave enough to take the Leo risk. He didn't make that vulnerable bid. No life-giving attention is heading his way.

There's a second way this fellow might make a mess out of Venus progressing into Leo. That is by overdoing it—going for glitz and trading on pretense instead of putting his soul out there on the butcher block. Down that road, he becomes all surfaces with no visible deeper content. In this dismal scenario, we see him in the uptown bar flashing his expensive watch and trying to pass himself off as James Bond.

Is anyone attracted to him? Perhaps yes—there are many people who are attracted only to surfaces. Such relationships tend not to survive beyond the half-life of hormones.

There are many critical comments we might make about this second unpleasant Leo behavior, but here's the heart of the matter: *he is not taking the risk of vulnerability.* He is all flash and posturing, without a drop of true unguarded sincerity in the mixture. What can we learn about the nature of his soul from these behaviors? Nothing, really—all we see is pathological insecurity and the pitiful, desperate need for approval.

As we saw earlier, when a major influence enters Leo, it is time to shine. Such a simple thing to say—but to truly embrace its meaning, we must celebrate the critical role played by that cardinal Fire virtue: *courage*. It takes a lot of courage to take off the mask and reveal the raw reality of our human hearts.

That, from the evolutionary point of view, is the meaning and purpose underlying anything moving through Leo.

20

LEO TIMES, SUN TIMES: THE BUILDING BLOCKS

The Sun can move through your chart in two ways. The first borders on trivial, while the second hits like a whirlwind. By transit, the Sun covers about 1° per day, and so it passes through an aspect in a couple of weeks, soup to nuts—not enough time to rock your world. You'll feel it when it's happening, but you will probably not be thinking about it six months from now.

By progression and by solar arc (again, with the Sun, they're the same), the Sun is the centerpiece of our whole system. If the planets were a naval fleet, the Sun would be the big aircraft carrier. If the planets were a football team, the Sun would be the quarterback.

In this chapter, we'll look at what happens when the Sun moves through an aspect with each one of the other planets—what it means, for one example, when the progressed Sun hits a square to Venus. I think you'll see that, while we can say helpful, relevant things about such an astrological event, there's much more information available if we take in the totality of an actual birthchart. Illustration: what if that progressed Sun is in the middle of Gemini, squaring a natal Venus in Virgo? Or what if the aspect is instead a Sagittarian Sun squaring a Piscean Venus? These are very different situations. As ever, it would take terabytes of data to cover all the possibilities and permutations.

Astrological mastery depends upon integrating many symbolic messages—houses, signs, and so forth. My hope is that these simple formulas help you make a good start in that direction.

THE SUN CONTACTING THE SUN

Watching the Sun progress in relation to its own natal position is a lot like watching the minute hand make its way around the clock. With a clock, you know that after fifteen minutes, the needle will be a quarter of the way around the dial. Similarly, with the Sun progressing 1° per year, when you're about ninety years old, the progressed Sun will square the natal Sun. Thus, these Sun-to-Sun aspects form a kind of universal developmental spine in everyone's life—in other words, everyone experiences them at more or less the same age.

Their specific meaning is flavored, as ever, by the larger astrological context. Still, here are some simple one-size-fits-all points we can reliably make...

Sun semi-sextile Sun (about age 30): This one occurs close to the well-known and very dominant first Saturn Return and is actually inseparable from it. As we exit youth and enter midlife, this semi-sextile adds a "clashing" note, as we must embrace the reality that our youth is over and our dreams must become actualities, or die on the vine.

Sun semi-square Sun (about age 45): "Fighting for freedom" is the aspectual theme. Inevitably, at this stage of life, we find ourselves enmeshed in the circumstances we have created, caught up in all the little compromises—both necessary and unnecessary—that we have made on the way to mid-life. Can we still find any space for our dreams or any room for our souls to breathe?

Sun sextile Sun (about age 60): "Stimulation" arises here, as this aspect augments our second Saturn return. The power held over us by all the things that have made us crazy over the years is markedly diminished; the hold the world has on us has lessened. We feel free to be ourselves—and couldn't care less about other people's opinions. A certain "urgency to live while we can" enters the equation.

Sun quintile Sun (about age 72): "Creativity and inspiration" are the themes here. The liberating existential changes that typically arise as we enter our 70s create an opening into the consciousness into which two treasures pour "from the other side." One is a pulse of creativity, as we are freed from the more youthful need for approval and the appearance of dignity. The second is a palpable sense of the spirit world, as it begins to call us.

Sun square Sun (about age 90): Typically, we are "challenged" in obvious physical ways, and "blocked" in many of our intentions by the realities of aging. We stand back from our lives, contemplating and evaluating them with a critical objectivity unavailable to younger people. One theme now is "That which does not destroy us makes us stronger."

THE SUN CONTACTING THE MOON

What Must Be Integrated: Try a little tenderness, both with others and with yourself. It is time to ask your body and your soul where they are hurting and what they need. You need more *soulfulness* in your life; that is partly about cherishing the company of people you love and partly about being a little softer with yourself. Let's add spending time in your soul's natural home: physical locations that comfort you, feel familiar, and help sustain your spirit. A lake? A certain city? A magical canyon?

The Price of Failure: A chill enters your spirit and becomes an accepted part of it. You become accustomed to feeling mechanical. You ignore early-warning signals of impending dysfunction in every category of life. Numbness.

Synchronistic Correlates: Strong moods arise, as do external situations that stimulate your emotions. Domestic and familial dramas loom. Changes of address or changes in the physical situation of the home. Medical situations; circumstances that require caregiving—or receiving care.

When Ego Grabs the Steering Wheel: Here we see the Drama King or the Drama Queen taking center stage. Hypochondria. Whining. Irrational decisions made in the emotional heat of the moment.

THE SUN CONTACTING MERCURY

What Must Be Integrated: Your voice; it is time to speak up and be heard. Confidence that you are correct sometimes, even when people think you are incorrect—or have treated you dismissively. Your right to learn and to educate yourself. Your openness to a wider palette of experience and a wider world.

The Price of Failure: Boredom. The futile feeling of having been silenced. Your wisdom "rotting on the vine." The book you did not write. The things you "should have said"—but now it is too late to say them. The moment has passed.

Synchronistic Correlates: Opportunities to learn and generally to widen your horizons. Opportunities to speak; people turning to you for your opinion or your views. Contact with media. Contact with educational institutions. Signs and omens arising synchronistically to guide you, if only you heed them.

When Ego Grabs the Steering Wheel: Compulsive chatter. Speech as a defensive tactic. Rationalization. Speaking in order to avoid listening. Nervousness; frittering away your energies in pointless, fussy busyness.

THE SUN CONTACTING VENUS

What Must Be Integrated: A willingness to be touched by other people; interdependency and mutual support. A recognition that no human being is truly self-sufficient, neither in practical nor in evolutionary terms. Aesthetic sensitivity. Potentially, the emergence or development of artistic skill. Deeper peace and serenity of spirit.

The Price of Failure: Loneliness. Playing with half a deck—and never finding anyone with the other half of the cards. Tragic, self-defeating romanticism. Bad love. Mounting tension, unrelieved—which leads quickly to self-numbing escapism becoming increasingly tempting.

Synchronistic Correlates: Meeting familiar souls. "I feel like I have known you before" (and you probably have). Life-changing encounters with other human beings. Significant intimate developments: marriage, divorce. Contact with art and artists. The development of a creative outlet.

When Ego Grabs the Steering Wheel: Vanity. A lazy sense of personal entitlement. Catastrophic intimate choices driven by ego poisons such as insecurity, desperation, self-importance, or an obsession with appearances. Manipulative behavior towards others. Lying without knowing that you are lying.

THE SUN CONTACTING MARS

What Must Be Integrated: Your ability to stand up for yourself. Courage. A tolerance for risk. Assertiveness. The defensive skills that are required if you are going to protect yourself, those whom you love, and your legitimate territory. Directness; fierceness. The honest reality of your sexuality.

The Price of Failure: Becoming a victim. A diminishment of your life. The loss of precious things. Swallowing injustice. A loss of elemental dignity. Resentments accumulated. Sexual frustration. Misdirected expressions of frustration: "kicking the dog," slamming doors, fights that are not about what they seem to be about, but rather are ineffective, indirect means of simply venting.

Synchronistic Correlates: Conflict. Argument. Crisis. The arrival in your life of rivals and enemies. The appearance of worthy opponents who bring out the best in you. Opportunities for adventure and stretching the boundaries of your courage. Sexy situations.

When Ego Grabs the Steering Wheel: Violence—possibly physical, possibly emotional. The use of unnecessary or inappropriate force. Bloody-minded contrariness. A trail of blood behind you, half of it your own.

THE SUN CONTACTING JUPITER

What Must Be Integrated: Faith in yourself. Higher ambition. A commitment to fulfilling your potential. Faith in your dreams. Hope recovered, despite any previous failures. A willingness to gamble. A lessened fear of failure; confidence in your ability to bounce back. Humor; expansiveness; generosity of spirit.

The Price of Failure: Lying on your deathbed realizing that you missed the boat and that it was your own fault; your main chance came and you let the opportunity slip through your fingers.

Synchronistic Correlates: Opportunity. Your lucky day. A chance to bet the house. Patrons appear, along with other people who believe in you. Resources become available. Doors open. Accolades; applause. Sometimes there are losses that seem dreadful at the time, but which make way for higher possibilities in the long run.

When Ego Grabs the Steering Wheel: Arrogance and over-extension dominate. Brittle pride makes the decisions. Inflated self-importance leads to folly. We get what we want—and it turns out to be a calamity.

THE SUN CONTACTING SATURN

What Must Be Integrated: Self-discipline. Integrity and morality, however we personally define those terms. Maturity; whatever your age. Your next developmental stage. The recognition that you have outgrown yourself and that you are bored with yourself, that it is time to move onward to the next chapter of your life. An ability to face reality clearly and coldly. Making peace with solitude.

The Price of Failure: Becoming stuck in the past, caught in a personality and a set of circumstances that we should have let go a long time ago. Meaningless responsibilities. Profound boredom with ourselves. Frustration; depression; time-serving. Tiredness. Soul-fatigue.

Synchronistic Correlates: The mountain looms before you; climb it—or wither away in the valley below. The Great Work of your life is upon you, and the "journey of a thousand miles starts with a single step." Sacrifices are required. Solitary effort; healthy, gratifying exhaustion. A pattern of delays. Swimming upstream in a river of molasses.

When Ego Grabs the Steering Wheel: Everything is defined as impossible. The feeling that the universe was created to frustrate and annoy you. Self-pitying loneliness. Militantly defending your right to never change or grow. A defeated attitude that works as a magnet for further misfortune.

THE SUN CONTACTING URANUS

What Must Be Integrated: Individuality. True self-knowledge, free from the distortions of socialization: family, society, and so on. Your right to be yourself and to follow your own heart. An indifference to the approval or disapproval of other people.

The Price of Failure: A schism arising between the nature of your soul and your biographical circumstances; living a life that is not your own. Alienation; dissociation. Giving up on following your true path; instead, following "orders" issued by others.

Synchronistic Correlates: Unusual and unpredictable events. On the higher path, these events open doors—against all probability and reason—for the expression of your recently-claimed individuality. Rebellion; break-ups. Breakthrough—or breakdown.

When Ego Grabs the Steering Wheel: Simple contrariness. The "rebel without a clue," compulsively saying no to anyone who says yes. Ostentatious idiosyncrasy masquerading as individuality. The utterly pitiful spectacle of someone trying to "look cool."

THE SUN CONTACTING NEPTUNE

What Must Be Integrated: True mystical spirituality. The next step on your inner path. Increased psychic sensitivity. Faith in the intuition. A flowering of the creative imagination. A vision arises for the next stage of your journey; you must surrender to it in order to receive it..

The Price of Failure: Escapism, as you fail to deal integratively with your increased psychic sensitivity. Falling prey to delusion and illusion. Ignoring the inspiration that is knocking on your door. Lassitude of spirit. Tuning out.

Synchronistic Correlates: Encounters with spiritual teachings and teachers. Bizarre, inexplicable dreams and psychic experiences. Seeing ghosts; feeling energies. Books you need to read falling off bookshelves and landing at your feet. Kisses from angels. Communication with the "dead."

When Ego Grabs the Steering Wheel: Headstrong commitment to delusional states, chimerical goals, and an inflated sense of one's evolutionary condition. Being seduced by the glamour of the world: fame, money, or power. Dumb decisions, often unbelievable in retrospect.

THE SUN CONTACTING PLUTO

What Must Be Integrated: Truth—typically of an uncomfortable or threatening nature. The raw, honest reality of the nature of your psychological wounds and your defects of character. The past you do not remember. An inventory of what is of true "deathbed" importance in your life—and what is not. Dramatic existential adjustments which reflect your fidelity to that inventory.

The Price of Failure: Continuing life as a crazy person, having turned your back on the opportunity to heal. Psychological projection; blaming and victimizing others because they resemble our own unhealed wounds. Acting out. Re-enacting old destructive patterns and experiences. The repetition compulsion.

Synchronistic Correlates: Situations arise which trigger memories of ancient wounds, perhaps from childhood, perhaps from prior lifetimes. Encounters with healers, shamans, and psychotherapists—and maybe an evolutionary astrologer or two.

When Ego Grabs the Steering Wheel: The dark side of the psyche looms large in the life. The child who was once hit now hits his own son or daughter. We become cruel and tyrannical; bottom line, whether or not we know it, we want everyone else to hurt as badly as we ourselves do.

ENTERING LEO

When a planet enters Leo by transit, progression or by solar arc, we're again faced with the need to integrate two archetypes: the specific nature of the planet and the Fiery agenda of Leo. Let's set the stage: the Moon, for example, might be passing through the sign Cancer, indicating a time of inward reflectiveness. From the outward point of view, with everything else being equal, probably this progression is not a particularly eventful time. Better said, the truly interesting events are occurring inwardly. Something has indeed been created—but the realm in which it has been created is invisible to any outward observer. That's the nature of Cancer.

But when that Moon progresses across the Leo frontier, it's time to make the popcorn. The movie is about to get going. Whatever has been created during the Cancer time now roars like a lion. As we learned earlier, the aim of Leo is self-expression. That "agenda" now animates the Moon. It is time for the heart to take the risk of being judged. Evolution now depends on our *volunteering for vulnerability.* Whatever grew in the safety of the Crab's shell needs to step out on the stage of life.

It's time to rock 'n roll.

We have just finished exploring what it means for the Sun to progress through its various aspects with all the planets. Now let's investigate the meaning of each planet entering Leo the Lion—the sign ruled by the Sun.

THE SUN ENTERING LEO

The Risk You Need To Take: Performance, in some sense of the word. There is a part of you that is colorful and interesting, worthy of taking up some space, worthy of claiming time and attention from other people. You are the hero in your own story and that story is worth hearing—take the risk of acting as if you believe that. You have done the inner work; it is time to let others have the benefit of it.

Helpful Behaviors: Cultivating a creative outlet. Public speaking—which might mean expressing an opinion in front of four or five people. Or telling a joke. Or singing loudly, even if it is only in the shower—that's at least a start. Time to dance as if no one were looking. Expressing yourself dramatically or passionately about some belief that you hold deeply.

When Ego and Insecurity Steal the Show: Mere display or ostentation. A neurotic need for the approval of others. Copying your heroes in order to be perceived as cool or impressive. Name-dropping. Conspicuous consumption. Becoming a "dancing monkey."

THE MOON ENTERING LEO

The Risk You Need To Take: Expressing your feelings—and taking the chance that you might get hurt in so doing. Crying. Asking for help. Saying I love you. Expressing tenderness; inviting tenderness in return.

Helpful Behaviors: Spontaneity. Immediacy. Trusting whimsy. Revealing your heart. Attracting attention—and being worthy of it. Acting in ways that trigger applause and appreciation. Walking away from fruitless situations or from people who do not appreciate you.

When Ego and Insecurity Steal the Show: a frustrated need for attention manifests as over-the-top, overbearing, and inappropriate loudness or as histrionic, overly-dramatic behavior. Presumptuousness. Apparent obliviousness to the needs and stories of other people.

MERCURY ENTERING LEO

The Risk You Need To Take: Speaking up. Acting as if you have something to say which you truly believe could be of benefit to others. Making the assumption that you are interesting. Speaking in paragraphs rather than in sound bites. Not muttering. Not apologizing before you open your mouth. Looking people directly in the eye as you speak.

Helpful Behaviors: Oratorical possibilities; holding forth. Telling a story colorfully and with drama. Expressing yourself in writing—and being brave enough to show what you have written to at least one other human being. Posting your feelings to Facebook. Submitting a letter to the editor.

When Ego and Insecurity Steal the Show: Speaking when you have nothing to say. Speaking simply so others hear your voice. Obvious posturing. Plagiarism and copy-cat behavior. Tediously taking too much time to make a point. Compulsive chatter. A pattern of conversations in which you did most of the talking. Mistaking others' silence for interest in what you have to say.

VENUS ENTERING LEO

The Risk You Need To Take: Making a bid to be seen as attractive. Presenting yourself handsomely or beautifully. Putting yourself out there. Giving expression to your inner Aphrodite or Dionysus. Revealing and underscoring the parts of your personality that are attractive in non-physical ways.

Helpful Behaviors: Listening to others and conveying interest in them. Responding to people rather than simply reacting to them. Upgrading your clothing, your grooming, or your hairstyle. Being willing to attract attention.

When Ego and Insecurity Steal the Show: Vanity raises its embarrassing head. We can become ridiculous in ways obvious to everyone except ourselves. A terrible loop ensues, and we are caught in it: people withdraw attention from us, which further fuels our desperation for their attention.

MARS ENTERING LEO

The Risk You Need To Take: Mars is a hot planet; that is why the subjects it represents are hedged about with social constraints and taboos. It is time to stretch those repressive boundaries, to challenge them. If you are angry, express it. If you are passionate about something, do not pretend otherwise. Do not let anyone shame your sexuality into invisibility; put it out there and let people deal with it. You have a right to take up some space. You have a right to have your needs met.

Helpful Behaviors: Embracing some measured degree of drama in your self-presentation. Expressing desire (in any of its categories). Taking emotional risks. Stepping out on the stage. Singing like you mean it. Making some noise and not apologizing for it. Actively protecting yourself or anyone you love.

When Ego and Insecurity Steal the Show: Bombast replaces sincerity; exaggeration eclipses vulnerability. As an example, what does it tell us about a person when he or she uses the famous "F-word" too frequently? While that word might not be the exact issue here, that particular verbal dysfunction gives us insight into the dark side of this potentially bombastic configuration. When ego and insecurity steal the show, Mars in Leo becomes simply offensive.

JUPITER ENTERING LEO

The Risk You Need To Take: There are two ways to say "King" in astrology—Jupiter, the king of the gods, and Leo the lion, the king of the beasts. When the two come together, it is definitely time to think big. To think like a King. To walk with your head held high. There is emotional risk inherent in positive thinking—some would say that you are setting yourself up for disappointment. Do it anyway. Claim a kingdom. Create a reason to feel that life has blessed you abundantly.

Helpful Behaviors: You have already dreamed—it is time to actively do something with those dreams. Bet the house. Make your move. Step up to the plate. Just remember to think carefully about what you really want and what is actually good for you. Then aim for that prize.

When Ego and Insecurity Steal the Show: High-handed moves lead to "pride goeth before a fall" scenarios. Off-putting grandiosity and entitlement arise. We get what we thought we want and it turns to cotton candy in the mouth. The applause of fools.

SATURN ENTERING LEO

The Risk You Need To Take: What would your masterpiece look like? What is the exact nature of your "best shot?" If, in contemplating these two questions, you are not frightened by the prospect of failure, you are not taking the right risk. The stakes need to be that high. Going for the gold means letting ourselves want something so badly that the prospect of not achieving it becomes anathema. Your potential for a Great Work has entered the sign of the King—do the math on that one!

Helpful Behaviors: Look in the mirror, and try to embrace and celebrate the evidence of aging that you see on your face. Even if doing that is tough on your ego, that outward behavior leads to a liberating inward realization: you are ready to move to the next level of unfoldment in your maturational journey. Claim the powers and the dignity that you have earned.

When Ego and Insecurity Steal the Show: Fear wins. Afraid of failure, we turn away from our potential Great Work. Afraid of aging—whatever our age—we turn away from its golden cousin: maturation.

URANUS ENTERING LEO

The Risk You Need To Take: No one likes to be mocked, marginalized, or dismissed—but all geniuses have faced exactly that. To be true to your own existential genius, that is the risk you now need to take. It is time to walk on the wild side. Do not even bother to read your reviews.

Helpful Behaviors: Dressing "inappropriately." Embracing whatever weirdness arises naturally in you; expressing it unabashedly. Seeking the company of cultural dissidents. Exploring unfamiliar creative outlets, ones where your ego makes no claim to excellence—and therefore your inner child can express itself with absolute spontaneity.

When Ego and Insecurity Steal the Show: Quirkishness arises. Such odd or contrary behaviors do not have any real roots in the deep self; they are aimed only at creating scandalous theatrical effect. Instead of expressing true individuality, we try to manipulate others, tricking them into thinking that we have found our true individuality. We may fool them—and even worse, we may fool ourselves.

NEPTUNE ENTERING LEO

The Risk You Need To Take: There is always a certain tension between ego and spirituality. It is time to risk embracing them both simultaneously. Act as if you believed—grandly—in your spiritual potential. In your shoes, what would a saint's next move be? Make your boldest move in a mystical or imaginative direction—just be careful not to lose your sense of humor about yourself in the process.

Helpful Behaviors: If you were that great saint, what would the next chapter of your life look like? Do that! Is it time to take a sabbatical? Time for a trek to some holy land? Time to accept some role of spiritual leadership or to head up some public act of charity or compassion toward your community?

When Ego and Insecurity Steal the Show: Spiritual grandstanding, spiritual pride, inflated spiritual claims—all can arise in such a convincing delusional form that even you fail to understand their true natures. Your ego can masquerade quite effectively as your soul.

PLUTO ENTERING LEO

The Risk You Need To Take: Nothing can be healed until we own the wound and admit its existence. Expressing your most daunting, humiliating, embarrassing inner realities out loud to at least one other human being is the risk you need to take. The only virtue you need here is absolute sincerity. Own your imperfections out loud.

Helpful Behaviors: Always with Leo, one critical ingredient is an audience that applauds your vulnerability. In this case, you need to be scrupulously selective: who can hear your deepest, and perhaps most embarrassing, truths without flinching or shaming you? Seek these people—and avoid judgmental, shaming ones as if they were a terrible virus for which there was no cure.

When Ego and Insecurity Steal the Show: As my psychotherapist friends say, "that which we do not work out, we must act out." In responding weakly to this configuration, a person can behave in spectacularly, extravagantly, flagrantly crazy ways. Instead of being squarely faced, the wound is simply revealed. The irony is, everyone except you understands that fact.

THE SUN CHANGING HOUSES

Of all the developments that might arise with the progressed Sun, house changes are very near the top of the list in terms of their life-altering significance. With the progressed Sun moving only 1° per year, it doesn't change from one house to another very often. When it does, it is not sufficient to say that "a new chapter" has begun in your life. A better term would be a new volume.

Let's quickly go around the circle of houses. The sketches that follow are an attempt to get to the bones of each solar house transition; the signs and aspects involved are of course major modifying factors. We ignore them here and focus on the essence of the circumstantial (house) changes.

When the Sun progresses out of the first house and into the second house...
it is time to act in a way that concretizes and supports your dreams and intentions. You have solid ideas and a clear vision; experience has deepened you. But now you must prove yourself to yourself in the real world through self-affirming, observable action. You know that you need to do something about those ideas and visions, but you're probably feeling blocked and frustrated. What *resources* do you need in order to go forward from where you are now in life? The second house is connected with money, so maybe those resources are financial—but the second house deals with many questions that have nothing to do with money: it can be about anything that supports the development of a *realistic, practical basis for confidence in yourself*—allies, skills, credentials. Your self-doubt is at least partly rational; take those doubts seriously and follow them down into yourself—you will often realize that they have an authentic basis in your actual limitations. Just remember that those limitations are correctable with enough effort and humility. That's how you solve the problem and go forward.

When the Sun progresses out of the second house and into the third house...
it's time to celebrate and express your own true voice. You've been through a long period of intensive self-questioning and probably self-improvement. You are wiser for it. You have *proven yourself to yourself.* The seed of that confidence must now blossom. The required action lies in empowering and enriching your ability to be heard and to be taken seriously. Perhaps you seek education. Perhaps you broaden your horizons through travel. Synchronistically, opportunities arise to speak or to write or to express yourself through some other medium, such as photography or film. The Internet might begin to figure more prominently in your life. The archetypal field of the third house also reflects unexpected or emergent circumstances: get ready for a wild ride, in other words. This is a busy time, fraught with detours and distractions, all of which have something to teach you. Trust your curiosity and your ability to improvise as you surf the waves of chaos and endless change. Far more than you realize, you are being guided.

When the Sun progresses out of the third house and into the fourth house...
it is time to put down roots. The recent decades of your life have been a wild ride; you have learned a lot and figured out how to see life from many perspectives. You have embraced a wide range of experience. Now it is time

to *digest* all of that experience, to turn it into quiet wisdom—something so precious that you can actually take it with you when it comes time to leave this physical world. To do that, you need to establish yourself in a safe and stable situation. You need to be free of the endless outward distractions that have been the characteristic signature of much of your recent life. You are entering a deeper, quieter time in your journey, and your spirit is crying out for it. When we speak of "roots," one dimension of the idea is a physical residence—your home. A question you must ask your soul now is, *where is your true home?* That might mean a house—but it also probably means something more broadly geographical. Do you need to live by the sea or in the mountains? Has Austria always felt like your true home, even though you were born in Chicago? Physical moves are not unusual at this time. But the word "home" also means *human relationships* at least as much as it means a place. Where is your *spiritual family*? Who are they? You need them now—and they probably need you too. Find them; everything depends on it.

When the Sun progresses out of the fourth house and into the fifth house...
it is time to put the fruits of your rich inner life out there in the world. Don't be the flower that never opened. It is a time of creativity and self-expression. Whatever your outward circumstances have been, the truth is that the recent decades of your life have primarily been about inner work. Perhaps you have accomplished that invisible victory psychologically or spiritually. Perhaps you have accomplished it through that ancient, profoundly effective method of facing ourselves: *family life.* In any case, we celebrate the insights and inner victories of your recent experience—but now those realizations need to take a form in which they can be shared. Opportunities to step up to the plate and express yourself become abundant now. They may manifest as some kind of *artistic creativity,* but they can take other forms too, such as social activism, stepping out on the stage of community life, or perhaps simply in the form of a more colorful—and possibly more controversial—lifestyle. The Fiery Sun meets the Fiery nature of the fifth house: with two Life-Givers coming together this way, the bottom line is that it is time for you to renew your passionate engagement with the *joy of being alive.* The inner work you have done has provided you with the treasure, but it has also tired you out. Bottom line, you really need to have some fun.

When the Sun progresses out of the fifth house and into the sixth house... it is time to engage energetically with meaningful responsibilities and meaningful work. A "calling" is arising in your life now. Circumstances *in which you are needed* emerge. You may not welcome them—but you cannot deny them without losing your own moral compass. You have been through a period of enormous evolutionary creativity; you really have something precious to offer other people now. That is what this "calling" is all about. Despite the language I am using here, there is no depressing "party's over, now back to work" feeling about this solar progression: deep down, you know you have been preparing all your life for this moment. People—often people younger than yourself—will enter your life, benefitting from the quiet guidance you offer them as a role model. Similarly, teachers and mentors are likely to come into your own life, triggering the manifestation of necessary skills in you. Situations in which you must submerge your own needs enough to respond to the needs of others appear at this time. You are playing a pivotal teaching role in some collective healing process far bigger than yourself. If you look for it, evidence of that reality will be existentially abundant . It is time to accept your place in a larger lineage.

When the Sun progresses out of the sixth house and into the seventh house... it is time to recognize that your next evolutionary steps must take place in the context of *partnership*—and immediately, remember that "partnership" here is not limited to conventional coupling relationships. Those kinds of connections are definitely one possibility; you will probably meet "significant others" at this time. But these partners—these living, breathing evolutionary triggers—might very well appear in other ways. For example, as creative partnership, business partnership, or profound friendship. In any case, the point is that *you cannot go forward without some help.* You are learning *whom to trust*—and, once you have learned that one, then it's time to learn *how to trust.* Also significant here is the fact that ever since you were born, the progressed Sun has been below the horizon. Now that is changing: you are experiencing *progressed sunrise.* So far, much of your growth and evolution has occurred in the inner, subjective realm where no one except you can fully see and appreciate it. Now you are called to emerge into the larger world of your community, making a difference there, and touching the lives of people whom you do not know in a personal way. That condition will persist for the rest of your life.

When the Sun progresses out of the seventh house and into the eighth house... it is time for a change in the tenor of your relationships. Everything grows deeper now; your capacity for genuine psychological intimacy has broken through to a new level. You are capable of more profound honesty, both with others and with yourself. As a result of the dance you have been doing with other souls for the past few decades, you are simply more self-aware than you were in the past. This deepening of your own nature can put tension on your existing relationships. The synchronistic question is simple to ask, but often hard or even painful to answer: *of all the people currently in your life, who among them are capable of joining you in these deeper waters?* Let us underscore that while you are now capable of handling this intensity, it has arisen synchronistically with a need to explore some charged and probably wounded places in your own consciousness—and *you cannot do that alone.* You need help of the highest quality. Who can help you—and who is standing between you and that help?

When the Sun progresses out of the eighth house and into the ninth house... it is time to stop gazing at your navel, time to embrace life, and to sally forth on an adventurous reboot of your identity. Characterizing the previous decades of your life as "navel-gazing" is unfair—we honor what you have accomplished psychologically so far in life—but it is time, in the words of poet Leonard Cohen, "to put your hat on your headache and dance." How can you break the hypnotic gaze of your inner dragons? There is only one effective answer: your outer life must become beguilingly, fascinatingly amazing. Opportunities to travel are on the horizon; take advantage of them. There are abundant opportunities to break up the predictable patterns in your life—and some of those opportunities might take the form of the chaotic intrusion of unexpected events. Trust them; they are a gift from the gods. Educational opportunities loom. You may take classes based on personal interests or enroll in some institution of higher education. The bottom line is that you have been mesmerized by a deep mood for many years; the mood is losing its hold. It was a necessary stage in your development, but it has served its purpose. Most likely, your life is about to feel easier than it has for a long time. Good news—but don't sleep through the looming adventures! They are soul-food too.

When the Sun progresses out of the ninth house and into the tenth house...
it is time to *get a job*. That simple phrase—"get a job"—is of course a simplification, but it is approximately correct. You just have to look at the word "job" through the eyes of angels rather than through the eyes of the tax man. You have been through decades of what we can rightly call "spiritual education"—and that education has been more about life and experience than about "school," even if you've earned a PhD. That "forging of character in the cauldrons of experience" has been the significance of the Sun's recent progression through your ninth house. Here is the key: after receiving "education," a natural desire arises somehow to make it relevant to the larger community. Part of this desire lies in your righteous sense that you deserve to be rewarded for your efforts. Fair enough. Some of it is connected to a more altruistic desire to make a difference in the world. Circumstances arise now that can be understood as *a Calling*; in other words, a readiness in you and a readiness in the world come together synergistically, leading to doors opening at the professional level—or, to put it more modestly, at least at the level of "the hat you are wearing" in your community.

When the Sun progresses out of the tenth house and into the eleventh house...
it is time to "take your place at the feasting table of the gods." Admittedly, that is a rather grand way of expressing it—so here is the same idea expressed in more mundane terms: your hard work over the past decades has drawn the attention of people more powerful, accomplished, or privileged than yourself. They are now beginning to recognize you as one of them: a *peer*. It is graduation day. You are harvesting the legitimate fruits of efforts that you have already made; this social recognition is one of them. Strategic, long-term planning is appropriate now. What are your priorities? What are your goals for the rest of your life? Historically, the eleventh house was called the house of friends—although "friends" is the wrong word. It actually has more to do with *teamwork, alliances, organizations*, and *networking*. These collective enterprises loom large in your life now. The reality that will become increasingly evident is that your destiny is tied to the destiny of a soul-tribe—to a group of people, in other words. Within that clan, you are now invited to play a solar role: leadership, or at least that of a role model.

When the Sun progresses out of the eleventh house and into the twelfth house... it is time to turn away from many of your worldly entanglements. Synchronistically, like magic, some of those entanglements now fall away of their own accord. You may experience that falling away as *a threatening loss of structure*—but trust the process. Your mind is naturally more engaged with eternal questions at this point in your journey. Outward circumstances arise that support your spiritual life: friends with a mystical bent appear in your life, opportunities for more silence and less distraction arise. Sometimes—not always—there are what appear to be outward losses; typically, as time goes by, these losses are understood as necessary blessings, clearing away obstacles to your soul's evolution. Psychic phenomena abound; spiritual teachers appear. There is a general sense of your *previous social identity unraveling*; there are, in fact, strong analogies between the twelfth house process and the process of dying—and let me hasten to add that *dying is a prerequisite for rebirth.* As your old life falls apart, a new vision, based on an emerging higher state of consciousness, is slowly crystallizing in the subterranean caverns far beneath your rational mind. This leads us directly to one of the most epochal astrological events that can ever happen to anyone: the progressed Sun's arrival at the Ascendant...

When the Sun progresses out of the twelfth house and into the first house... it is time to take charge of your life, to move forward decisively, and to begin again. Remember that vision crystallizing in your subterranean caverns when the Sun was in the twelfth house? That process took decades, but if you played it right, it was worth it. Now is the time for that vision to come into bold manifestation in this three-dimensional world—time to *actually do something about it*, in other words. The switch of orientation is edgy: for the past decades, you have been learning lessons of non-attachment; that means that the results of your actions have been unpredictable and often disappointing, and that, in order to survive, you have developed an attitude of acceptance—perhaps even an attitude about being somehow "jinxed." That attitude must change now because the lessons of the first house are of an entirely different nature. If the twelfth house is about *mystics,* the first house is about *magicians.* The power of your Will and your Intentions is dominant now: make daring decisions, trust your first instincts, do not be afraid of being called selfish, and move forward boldly. Remember that the progressed Sun would require 365 years to get all the way around your chart. That means that, in terms of "cosmic statistics," the progressed Sun forming a conjunction with the Ascendant comes along once every five or six lifetimes. It is a very big deal, in other words. At the metaphysical level, it is fair to say that this event marks the completion of an entire *cycle of lifetimes*—and the beginning of a new, more evolved, and more conscious cycle of lives.

This completes our look at the transits, progressions, and solar arcs connected with the second family of Life-Givers: the Sun and the sign Leo. We have one more to go: Jupiter and Sagittarius, the Philosopher Kings of the zodiac.

21

CELESTIAL NAVIGATION III: JUPITER TIMES, SAGITTARIAN TIMES

The gods never die, they just change their names every couple of dozen centuries. In Greece, Jupiter was called Zeus. When I was getting my bachelor's degree in Religion many years ago, I learned that long before the Greeks and the Romans, the principle god in the Indo-Aryan hierarchy was named *Dyaus Pitar.* Say it fast, and you can hear both "Zeus" and "Jupiter" in it. I was taught that that was where both names originated.

But I guess no one knows where "Dyaus Pitar" originated. Or what Jupiter was called before then.

Today, in the Western world, many of us know Jupiter by another name: *Santa Claus.* Good old St. Nicholas, or Father Christmas—just say their names in front of the five-year-old child and you will learn more in thirty seconds about the archetypal reality of Jupiter than you are likely to learn from five hours spent pondering an astrology textbook.

A young woman is laboriously making her way through law school, preparing to become an attorney specializing in commercial real estate transactions. She actually does not enjoy the subject very much, but she wants to be "practical." She knows that there is serious money to be made in that field—and "of course" with those bucks in her bank account, she assumes that happiness will arise automatically in her life. That is a popular illusion! She passes the bar exam, and gets a position with a big downtown law firm, starting salary: $200,000 a year.

What she does not know is that this big professional moment is the peak of her happiness. From there on, it's all downhill.

A decade later, she feels lost, phony—and somehow cheated. In the sad version of this story, she might even cling defensively to the illusion that she is "happy" with her choices. But for the rest of her life, she is grumpy, and of contrary mood, and not quite able to put her finger on exactly what happened.

Santa Claus left a glitzy piece of plastic with flashing lights under her Christmas tree. And she fell for it.

Naïve astrologers often describe Jupiter as "lucky." And indeed, when we do in fact get lucky—when we win the contest, or meet our true love, or when we find a perfect parking space on a rainy day—take a peek at your chart: transiting Jupiter is trining your Ascendant or something like that. In my astrological apprenticeship program, we typically put the names of all fifty or eighty of the students in "The Sorting Hat" and then pull two or three of them to use as chart examples. Naturally, there is a prevalent sentiment of, "I hope he picks me..." More often than not, the person whose name is pulled "at random" is currently experiencing some kind of Jupiter event.

To say that Jupiter is "lucky" is not incorrect, but it leaves quite a lot of reality out of the equations. Just think of that woman starting her high-dollar career in a field about which she does not really care.

She was having a Jupiter transit too.

ALL THAT GLITTERS IS NOT GOLD

You have, of course, heard that aphorism many times. Here's another one: *be careful what you pray for, you might get it.* Sayings such as those two reflect the collective human wisdom about failed Jupiter events. Again, Jupiter boils down to Santa Claus—we just have to add one more critical insight: this particular Santa Claus does not come equipped with a brain. The "brains" are something we have to supply for ourselves. During times of Jupiter stimulation, most of us encounter a distinct pattern of getting what we *think* we want. But do we actually want it? We will soon find out...

How would you feel about hitting a state lottery and suddenly having $127 million in the bank? For most of us, the question is rhetorical—that is to say, it's really not a question at all. Of course all that money would make us happy... but would it really?

Put on your wizard's hat and think about it: are wealthy people automatically in a state of perpetual ecstasy? Are there no miserably depressed rich people? We know the answers.

Let's say that you did suddenly win that $127 million prize. Might that windfall trigger a predatory gleam in the eyes of your friends? How is your family going to react to this sudden vast surplus of wealth? Are you ready for some guilt trips from various worthy charities? There's a new set of questions in your life now: which children from disadvantaged countries do you choose to allow to starve to death? Which species will you let die just so you can buy that ranch in Montana? Which noble politician will go unfunded?

Perhaps even worse, how will that money interact with your own vices and your appetites?

Inside of six months, you might wish that you'd never won that contest.

There's a laugh-or-cry paradox here: if you're wise enough to be reading this book, you already understand all of this. But if you're anything like me, you're also rather confident that you *personally* would be just fine with that $127 million...

Jupiter's glitter can be very seductive.

IF YOU KNOW WHAT'S GOOD FOR YOU...

That line is often used by extortionate thugs and gangsters as they threaten you with dreadful consequences if you don't knuckle under to their will. But let's take the words more neutrally: do you, actually and honestly, *know what would be good for you?* We all believe that we do—that pile of money looks pretty good to all of us—but what kinds of developments would *truly* put you in a happier place? What would actually bring you joy?

Knowing where Jupiter is currently located by transit or by solar arc in your chart can help guide you toward a wise answer to that question. That's how we put some brains into the head of Santa Claus.

We will explore all of Jupiter's planetary aspects and house passages in cookbook detail in the next chapter. In a nutshell, here's how to think about all this: money might actually be what is good for you at a given moment—but to confirm that, I'd want to see, for example, Jupiter contacting a planet in your second house. Were Jupiter instead interacting with a twelfth house Neptune, the distraction created by a large sum of money might rob you of a far greater prize—a spiritual one that you can actually keep when the time comes to leave this world.

Remember: once again, Jupiter is indeed Santa Claus, but the brains are not included. You need to supply them yourself.

A QUICK NOTE ABOUT JUPITER'S PROGRESSIONS

By progression, Jupiter moves so slowly that it is not particularly useful. Remember that with progressions, days become years. Everything therefore slows down dramatically. By transit, Jupiter takes about twelve years to make a circuit of the zodiac—11.862 years, to be exact. What if those days turn into years? Patience, patience, patience...

Here's the math: expressed in days instead of years, Jupiter takes 4,332.6 days to circle the Sun. With progressions, days become years—so it would take Jupiter *over four millennia* to progress completely around anyone's chart. That's about twelve years to progress by a single degree.

You get the picture.

If you were born anywhere near a Jupiter station, its motion by progression will be even slower.

It's not that the progressed Jupiter lacks meaning; the issue is that it moves so slowly that human consciousness doesn't seem capable of distinguishing its influences. In the first half of life, progressed Jupiter and natal Jupiter generally remain within the orbs of a conjunction. Subjectively, we can't tell them apart.

No worry though: transiting Jupiter moves fast enough to keep you busy. You never have to wait long for a Jupiter event. And of course by solar arc, Jupiter moves at the universal pace of about 1° per year. It stays pretty busy too.

HOW HAVE YOU BEEN UNDERESTIMATING YOURSELF?

That is my favorite single Jupiter question. I love it for its dynamism—the way it invites active participation in the transit or the solar arc. Instead of passively waiting for dumb luck to hit us over the head, under the impetus of that question, we go *looking* for the luck.

Even better, questioning how we might've underestimated ourselves encourages us to look for "the luck" in the right places. Those places are always a little higher on the food chain than where we've been previously looking. That's what underestimating yourself means. You are better than you think you are.

Sometimes people underestimate themselves because they've been fed psychological poison. They have been shamed or disrespected, and they have internalized it.

Maybe you're female and you got a near-lethal dose of "girls can't do that." Maybe you're male and you were taught not to feel. Maybe it's the poison of racism or social inequity. Maybe it is the poison of the ghetto—or the poison of the country club.

In any case, such shaming, when internalized, constrains our imagination about our own potentials. During a Jupiter time, the evolutionary aim is to break free of those toxic boundaries. We can soar. Our hour has arrived.

I would quickly add that a Jupiter period is not really about meditating on our woundedness. That's a noble process, but far more under the domain of Pluto than of Jupiter. As we saw earlier, Lord Jupiter "don't need no stinking psychology." Lord Jupiter says, "just do it." He might even add "fake it until you make it," if that's what it takes.

There's another form of underestimation which you might need to address during a Jupiter time. We need to consider the limiting effect of a *previously-accurate* estimation of ourselves—but one which no longer applies to us. Bottom line: we've gotten better, but we haven't fully integrated that realization. Here's an illustration: we have a friend who's seventeen years old. She shares with us that, even though she loves her boyfriend, she really doesn't feel ready for marriage. How do we react? We of course applaud her wisdom—at that young age, she probably isn't ready to make such a choice or to maintain such a commitment. In this moment of her life, she's right about her limitation, in other words. She is truly *not* ready for marriage.

We can all boldly tweet zippy, encouraging statements such as "Doubt Everything But Your Limits"—but in reality, operating that way is rarely the wisest policy. We are finite; we all have limits and weaknesses that need to be respected. Paying mindful attention to them contributes significantly to our longevity—and also to our potential for developing wisdom in the long run.

Swimming naked across the Pacific Ocean would definitely get you on the cover of *Time* magazine—but it's still a monumentally stupid idea.

Our seventeen-year-old friend grows up, fed by her intimate experiences. In common with most young people, along the way she has experienced different relationships. She has spread her wings. She has probably made some interesting and "instructive" mistakes. She has explored various facets of her sexuality. At some point, she probably crosses a familiar line: now, after digesting all of that wide experience, she is in fact ready for a committed partnership. She is ready to recognize her natural partner and wisely to fulfill her own responsibilities in a committed bond.

The underlying idea is that she was indeed "not ready" at age seventeen—but today that same attitude would constitute a form of underestimating herself.

Where is her Jupiter at this pivotal moment of realization? Perhaps it is transiting through her seventh house. Maybe, by solar arc, it is conjuncting her Venus. There are many possible astrological configurations that might be in play. Let's add that, because of the way synchronicity works, her inner readiness for an intimate breakthrough correlates concretely with her meeting someone with whom she could imagine spending her life.

As ever, consciousness mirrors reality, while reality mirrors consciousness. That profoundly reliable synchronistic principle is the blood in the veins of our craft.

YOU NEED A VICTORY

I often deliver that line to a client experiencing some kind of Jupiter event. Almost invariably, the person lights up. The words "you need a victory" confirm and validate the inner state that naturally dawns during a Jupiter time.

The implication is not that everything is so terrible; the implication might as easily be that things need to be *even* better. Always, deep down inside, during a Jupiter time, we sense a hunger for something more than we currently have. There's wisdom in that hunger—but it typically faces some cunning enemies before Santa Claus can come down our chimney.

Here's one enemy: you might hear voices in your own head or in the world around you suggesting that you *not get your hopes up because hope only leads to disappointment.*

Ignore that depressing counsel; you really do need a victory. Admit it—and recognize that it's time to roll the dice.

Here's another enemy: misguided conscience might block the evolutionary impulse with noble sentiments such as "you already have so much to be grateful for." As true as those lofty words might be, they don't cancel the evolutionary impulse of Jupiter: it is indeed the right time to "hope for more."

Here's an illustration: a female client of mine, happily married, was experiencing Jupiter transiting toward the cusp of her seventh house. I asked her how things were in her marriage. She said everything was fine. She was content with her husband.

Now watch me sprout horns, a tail, and sulfurous breath: I said to this happily married woman, "So, are things *perfect* in your marriage?"

We both laughed, of course.

Like me, this woman understood that marriage was the most human of institutions, never truly perfect. Encouraged to complain, she went on to describe a minor issue she had with her husband. It was a small thing; definitely not divorce material, not even really "therapy" material. I suggested that a session or two with a counselor would probably break the logjam and that both she and her husband would be happier for doing it. She quickly agreed—but added that her husband would never agree to do anything like that. Talking with a counselor wasn't his style.

I said, "Ask him on Tuesday."

That's tactical astrology; Tuesday was when Jupiter entered her seventh house.

You know the rest, or I wouldn't be telling the story: she asked her husband if he would be willing for them to get some help. Much to her surprise, he agreed. They did a session or two with a counselor I recommended—and their marriage, which was already quite good, became even better.

She *needed a victory*, she asked for one, and she got one. Her "wanting was wise." She knew what was good for her, and she didn't underestimate herself or settle for too little. In a nutshell, she pleased Lord Jupiter and he rained down blessings upon her.

That's how Jupiter works when a person gets it right.

THE ARCHITECTURE OF HOPE

Would you rather be hopeful or hopeless? The question seems tediously obvious. Who would choose to be hopeless? But there are far deeper layers to the issue; the answer isn't nearly as obvious as it seems.

Earlier, we quoted a familiar line: "don't get your hopes up, you will only be disappointed." Clearly, those are not encouraging words. But we've all experienced times when that proverb rang true, at least in retrospect—times when we wished that we had been more cautious and not set ourselves up for heartbreak.

Harboring hope in our hearts represents an extravagant expenditure of energy. Here's why: the architecture of hope is always the same—*tomorrow can be better than today*. And as soon as we begin thinking that way, a certain discontent with our present conditions arises. We want that tomorrow so much that we can taste it.

Meanwhile, our present reality loses its savor.

In spiritual circles, we're often encouraged to be fully engaged with the present moment. Worrying about tomorrow is taboo. Wishing and longing are viewed as distractions from the more immediate psychic realities, which is where the real magic always happens. Many of us reading this book have probably also read Eckhart Tolle's *The Power of Now*—or, some years ago, *Be Here Now*, by the great Ram Dass.

If we fancy ourselves to be on the spiritual path, focusing our consciousness on the present moment is right up there with compassion, charity, and organic vegetables.

I was quite startled when I came to the obvious conclusion that hope—the belief that tomorrow can be better than today—runs counter to much of the world's profoundest spiritual teachings.

But Jupiter is emphatically the planet of hope, and all the planets represent spiritual pathways. There is a time for hope, despite all its pitfalls.

Somehow we have to weave a right relationship with this very risky psychic condition into the evolutionary instruction manual we call astrology.

When Jupiter steps into the spotlight, Santa Claus is coming to town. From an evolutionary point of view, it is time for you to *dare to hope*—and to knowingly pay the extravagant price that goes along with it. The time is right for that process; get it right and your soul will learn a necessary lesson. There's a good chance that you'll get what you want—and thus learn whether your wanting was wise or foolish.

A TIME FOR EVERY SPIRITUAL CLICHÉ

In contrast to Jupiter, when Saturn steps into the spotlight, you might discover that lack, difficulty, and constraint can potentially offer you profound blessings. We'll delve deeply into that when we get to *The Book of Earth*. That's definitely not Jupiter's attitude. Similarly, when the Moon progresses into the twelfth house, you might be presented with a chance to learn about letting go and sustaining yourself on a diet of very little but faith. Those are lofty lessons too—and very different from what you're potentially learning during solar arcs and transits of Jupiter. *The Book of Water* will carry us into that territory.

One of my favorite playful definitions of astrology is that it is "the study of the seasonal applicability of clichés." In other words, for each cliché, there is a season—which is to say, a time when it will really work. And of course, the converse is also true: astrology can warn us about which clichés we should definitely not trust at any given crossroads.

Think of all the New Age clichés about Positive Thinking, the Law of Attraction, and the power of optimistic Affirmations to create the realities we experience. Together, they represent the distillation of human wisdom and human experience in Jupiter times.

At other times in life, a different Bible might serve you better. Astrology holds the mirror of truth before that ever-changing kaleidoscope.

THREE LEVELS OF RESPONSE TO JUPITER

Looking rigorously at the action of transiting or solar arc Jupiter, we can distinguish three possibilities for what to expect. One of them is truly lucky, one of them is not—and one of them is a subject astrologers typically like to avoid: that is, sometimes Jupiter seems to do nothing at all.

Level One: Armed with hard-won self-knowledge and grounded faith in the notion that we're ready to move onward to greater victories and higher levels of self-actualization, we are aware of what is actually good for us. We move boldly and decisively to claim it, remembering always that Lord Jupiter does not like to see small bets on the table. We make a genuinely triumphant breakthrough, both inwardly and existentially. Synchronistically, reality responds to our wise and audacious heart with a big dose of what the world calls good fortune. We indeed "get lucky."

Level Two: Bamboozled by the world into mistaking mere glitter for gold, we set our sights on seizing a mirage. The "mirage" is actually real enough in the physical sense—but when we attempt to dine on it, it turns to sawdust in our mouths. As Bono and the boys in U2 put it in their brilliant song *Stuck in a Moment*, "You can't get enough of what you don't really need." Remember that kid on Christmas morning, with that longed-for piece of plastic pushed aside? Remember our real estate attorney and her big salary? Perhaps a lesson is learned. It is fair to ask ourselves, is there ever really any such thing as a mistake? And yet, what might have happened if we had used that Jupiter energy with more wisdom and genuine self-awareness…

Level Three: This is the one astrologers often don't like to talk about: the client complains that "nothing happened"—that those bright Jupiter promises we made fizzled down to zero. The primary point I would underscore here is that astrology never fails; it is astrologers who fail. In this case, very likely the astrologer fell into the materialist fallacy—that is, the idea that astrological events must always be materially visible. The reality is that astrological events can sometimes operate purely on internal and intrapsychic planes. In the case of the apparently failed Jupiter transit, here's what very likely happened: the client was self-aware enough not to be beguiled by mere glitter—but not bold or audacious enough to actively claim the victory she needed and deserved.

Illustration: imagine a bright woman in her forties with a high school education. To pay her bills, she's a waitress. During a Jupiter transit to her midheaven, hope arises in her—she thus allows herself to feel discontent with the present realities of her job.

So far, so good.

One day at lunch, she's looking at the Want Ads in the local newspaper. She circles a job she knows she would love: better pay, more dignity—not to mention a better fit with her actual capabilities. For a moment, she considers the possibility of applying for the position. Then she decides not to do that; she "knows" that they "would never hire anyone like her," with her history of waitressing and only a high school education.

Wistfully, she closes the newspaper and goes back to work. Why get her hopes up only to have them dashed?

In reality, if she had called about that job, she'd have been reporting for work there on Monday morning.

But "nothing happened."

Or did it?

Her Guardian Angels are weeping. They know that indeed "something happened." What happened was that our waitress gave up hope.

And the sound a dream makes when it is dying is barely a whimper.

LOSS

Jupiter rules Sagittarius and, by extension, the ninth house; turn a few pages, and we'll be exploring those Fire energies individually and in detail. But Jupiter is also classically the ruler of Pisces and the twelfth house. Much later in this series, when I finally get to writing *The Book of Water*, we'll explore those Jupiter connections more deeply. But here, in quickly reflecting on those two watery symbols, we need to mention one more property of Jupiter's action by transit or by solar arc: *it can correlate with loss.*

This heavier face of Jupiter doesn't get much astrological press; astrologers today seem more focused on what we might call the Sagittarian-side of the planet. That "Life-Giving" dimension of Jupiter is real enough—and very much our subject here in this book. But no discussion of Jupiter is complete without a reference to this more "Piscean" expression of the planet's archetypal field.

Let me start with a darkly cartoonish exaggeration, one which will give us a stark sense of the basic Jupiter principles in play.

You and your partner are on your merry way to the airport, bound for your dream vacation in Thailand. Halfway there, you get a flat tire. AAA says they can be there in ninety minutes—which is twenty minutes before your flight departs. You try to change the flat yourself, but the tire iron seems to have gone missing—undoubtedly the fault of your partner—and you can't budge the lug bolts with a pair of pliers.

In a spirit of anger, frustration, and futility, you watch the time pass. The flight takes off without you. You feel martyred; this might be the worst day of your life.

Later you learn that the airplane disappeared somewhere over the Indian Ocean.

I promised "darkly cartoonish," didn't I? But events such as this one do indeed happen under Jupiter influences. The core principle is simple: that which seems like misfortune at the time later turns out to be a blessing.

If you're going to "Google search" your cranium for illustrations of this principle in your own personal history, try this formula:

Losing that_______ was the best thing that ever happened to me.

Your partner "meets someone else." How do you feel? Lousy. Betrayed. Homicidal, perhaps. But if it weren't for that humiliating, heartbreaking loss, you never would have met your present partner, who has given you far more joy than his or her predecessor.

You lose your job. Perhaps you're forced into bankruptcy. It's obviously not the best year of your life—but soon enough you recover and thrive in a new, more meaningful position.

You are hit by a drunken driver as you cross a street. You are in hospital, in traction, for three months. During that time, you begin to read astrology books. Five years later, you are a practicing professional astrologer—and grateful for that accident.

Many years ago, with transiting Jupiter squaring my own Sun, I quit my job to write my first astrology book. This wasn't *The Inner Sky*, which was only published nine years later. This book, which I titled *New Evidence for an Old Art*, was a statistical study based (semi-legally, I guess) on data from a National Institute of Mental Health project on which I'd worked. I was able statistically to correlate people's Sun signs with their psychological profiles as they emerged in a survey of about 1,200 people. The data proved that astrology, even of the simple sort, could pass the science test. The correlations weren't spectacular, but they were mathematically significant.

In Jupiter-fashion—not to mention, in "twenty-something" fashion—I had grandly envisioned myself personally revolutionizing the public attitude toward astrology, all the while dining with rock stars and lining my own pockets rather handsomely.

It didn't turn out that way.

That manuscript was rejected by a dozen mainline publishers. One of their acquisitions editors memorably wrote me a note that I wish I'd saved and framed. It read, "The thrust of astrological publishing is egocentric and I expect it will remain that way."

He was, of course, basically correct in that assessment.

The failure of that first book of mine was a painful defeat. I absorbed it. I found another job. In the evenings and on weekends, I continued to develop my astrological practice, which soon grew pretty large. Eventually I bought a 22-foot sloop named *Puffin* and, along with my first wife, sailed one summer from New York harbor down to the Virginia line in the Chesapeake Bay. After that cruise, praise God, I never had another job. My astrological practice took off; four years later, I got a contract with Bantam Books to write what would eventually become *The Inner Sky*.

Was the failure of *New Evidence for an Old Art* truly a misfortune? I don't think so—and I don't mean simply that I bounced back from the defeat. What I mean is that I now see that Jupiter's better angels were looking out for me. I'm not a statistician, nor a scientist, nor do I have any interest in becoming an academic. I respect those paths; I just know that they're not mine.

Had that first book been published, I would've been pigeonholed in a life I didn't want to live. That "luck" would have been like taking the wrong fork at a highway junction—and realizing that the next exit was fifty miles ahead.

Losing that particular dream is on the short list of the best things that ever happened to me—and remember: Jupiter was squaring my Sun at the time.

Sweet are Jupiter's victories. Sweet are its losses too—at least in retrospect. That perspective—enjoyed in the present tense—can give us great comfort in times of apparent difficulty.

ENTER SAGITTARIUS

The Jupiter-ruled Fire sign Sagittarius is the third Life-Giver. What happens when a planet enters it via transit, progression, or solar arc? If the planet is moving slowly enough to have time to develop depth and complexity of meaning—as is always the case with progressions and solar arcs, and never the case with the transits of the faster planets—such a Sagittarian event can radically expand the horizons of your life. It's certainly time to blow out the cobwebs. You need some fresh air and some fresh perspective—and the laws of synchronicity will support you in finding them.

In the next chapter, we will look in detail at the specific meaning of each of the planets, one by one, as they pass through this third Fire sign. For now, let's explore the underlying principles.

Remember that signs always represent basic needs and drives, each with its own core agenda of unique values. As a planet passes from one sign to another, its orientation changes according to the tone of the new sign. To understand the transition of a planet into Sagittarius, it's helpful to start with a brief look at Scorpio, the previous sign. It is what sets the stage.

The values that animate Scorpio are essentially psychological; Scorpio seeks the interior significance and deeper meaning of everything. Scorpio, by reflex, questions what's *really* going on. What's happening beneath the surface?

Think of the attitude of an effective police detective, or a skillful psychoanalyst, or even a good murder mystery writer—that's what interests and motivates Scorpio.

Maybe one Tuesday night, you have a difficult heart-to-heart talk with your partner. Good for you both, that's how you keep a relationship alive—*but how do you feel about having another such discussion on Wednesday night?* Rightly and wisely, the idea probably makes you want to gag. How much growth and intensity can you take in a given week? Perhaps instead you both agree to rent a funny movie and order takeout pizza.

Welcome to Sagittarius. After your Scorpionic growth period, you need a good laugh. In the words of Bob Marley, you need to "Lively Up Yourself." We need to grow—and we need to recover from growth too. It's time to stop gazing at your navel and take in the mesmerizing, miraculous, eminently entertaining glory of the undiscovered world around you. Sagittarius helps us recover from Scorpio, just as Scorpio helped us recover from Libra, and Libra helped us recover from Virgo, and so on backwards around the circle.

Most of us know the Greek myth of the *Gorgon Medusa.* Anyone who looked at her directly would immediately be turned to stone. The hero,

Perseus, was charged with the task of beheading her—a difficult feat to accomplish without her catching his eye. He polished up his shield until it was as reflective as a mirror. Thus, he could look at her *indirectly*, and he managed to whack off her head in pretty much the same way that the dentist cleans the back of your teeth.

I don't think this will ever make much of a movie; the choreography works better in writing than it would in real action.

But the myth is still valid and powerful. The danger with Scorpio lies in our tendency to sometimes challenge the Gorgon Medusa to staring contests. She can quickly "turn us to stone"—which is to say, cripple us with depression—or with so much psychological self-absorption that we become disengaged from the restorative joys of life.

Sagittarius represents a set of skills for breaking the gaze of the Gorgon Medusa. To balance the seductively mesmerizing fascination of the Scorpionic inner worlds, we need to make sure that the outer world is equally fascinating.

That's Sagittarius in a nutshell—at least, from the evolutionary point of view.

In practice, in Sagittarius we see an orientation to *travel* and *adventure*, along with *educational opportunities* and *philosophical quests*—these are the familiar keywords normally associated with the sign. All of them are connected with the process of enlivening and invigorating our experience of the world.

In the next chapter, we'll explore the signature qualities of each planet's passage through Sagittarius. All drink from the same adventurous, boundary-bursting well. All reflect the evolutionary need to break out of the tyranny of repetitive—and killingly boring—patterns of thought, attitude, and experience. In so doing, all restore us to full vitality—and all present some hint of the presence of that ultimate Holy Grail: the meaning and purpose of our existence.

22

SAGITTARIAN TIMES, JUPITER TIMES: THE BUILDING BLOCKS

Via transit and solar arc, Jupiter is a powerhouse. As befits the most massive planet in our solar system, its "gravity" can reshape your life. Good news or bad? As ever, it's the quality of your own self-awareness that determines the answer.

With Jupiter's solar arcs, we are of course talking about the standard pace of approximately one degree per year, held in common by all the solar arcs. As we saw in the previous chapter, by transit Jupiter spends about one year in each sign. There's a trick to evaluating the amperage of a Jupiter transit. As we learned earlier, the meaningfulness of any moving astrological event is very much a function of how slowly it unfolds; the slower event has time to develop "depth and complexity of meaning." The trick with Jupiter's transits is to realize that they actually operate in both of those modes, fast and slow.

Jupiter is the swiftest among the slower planets. For that reason, its pendulum-swings between stations cover a lot of ground. When Jupiter turns retrograde, it typically takes three or four months to back up by about ten degrees—then it zooms forward by 40° or 45° over the next eight or nine months.

When Jupiter is moving at maximum speed in the midst of those direct periods, it might cut through a sensitive zone in a week or two—and, poof, be gone. You might hardly notice it, in other words. On the other hand, if Jupiter makes a station anywhere near a critical zone of your chart, it's a good time to make your boldest move—Jupiter's "amperage" is at maximum power then. As Jupiter approaches a station, it slows down gradually, stops, and then speeds up—again, very slowly. The effect of that turning of the tide might be that Jupiter remains within at least wide orbs of a given aspect for nearly a year—plenty of time for it to become a significant milestone in your life.

In this chapter, we'll detail what happens when Jupiter moves through an aspect with each one of the other planets individually—what it means, for example, when it squares Mercury or trines Neptune. As we saw in Chapter Seventeen, the main point with aspects is the integration of two archetypal energies. Jupiter squaring Mercury is certainly different from Jupiter trining Mercury, but the two archetypes are the same. That basic integration is what we consider here in this "cookbook" chapter. Adding the exact nature of the aspect is something you will need to do for yourself—it would take too many pages to spell out each of them, one by one. As ever, understanding the specific nature of the aspect gives you a sense of how best to handle the integrative process.

What we focus on here is the integrative process itself.

We can make helpful remarks about any such astrological event, but, as usual, there is much more granular information available in the actual birthchart. What if that transiting Jupiter is entering Pisces while making a trine to a Scorpio Sun in the twelfth house? That's a different beast than Jupiter entering Aries and trining a Leo Sun in the tenth house, even though it's still "Jupiter trine the Sun" in both cases.

With twelve signs and twelve houses, there are a vast number of such possible configurations, each with its own meaning. As ever, it would require a library of books, all of them much fatter than this one, to spell out all the possibilities. My hope is that the simple formulas that follow will get you started.

As we did with Mars and the Sun, we'll look at three areas:

* Jupiter forming aspects by transit or solar arc to each one of the planets.

* Jupiter's entry into each of the twelve houses.
* The passage of each of the planets through our third Fire sign, Sagittarius.

JUPITER CONTACTING THE SUN

Look for Opportunities... to act boldly on your authentic dreams—but make sure that you define those dreams wisely too. The "wisely" part boils down, at the technical astrological level, to honoring the actual evolutionary intentions implicit in your natal Sun's sign, house, and aspects. That is the goal you want to aim for during this period. Once you have established that focus, look around—the laws of synchronicity guarantee that you will see exactly those kinds of opportunities materializing right before your eyes. Grab them before Jupiter moves on and they evaporate!

Never Underestimate: what you have accomplished already in your life in terms of self-realization and empowerment. Update your self-image. You'll like the result. You are in a stronger position than you have previously imagined, ready for a big breakthrough. That evolutionary victory depends on your having faith enough in yourself to seize the moment.

The Prize: A first-class upgrade in your existential circumstances. You have earned it and the time is right to claim it. You need a victory now, but not just any victory—it needs to be a lasting one, and one that will still ring true and beautiful as you look back on things at the end of your life. That is the prize that lies before you now. Make sure that you discern it accurately.

The Price of Misguided Pride: An empty victory that leaves you feeling that life has broken a promise to you. "You get what you want"— only what you thought you wanted turns to sawdust or cotton candy in your mouth. It was someone else's dream which you mistook for your own.

JUPITER CONTACTING THE MOON

Look for Opportunities... to quietly tune into your own heart. To care for yourself. To listen to your body. To take a look into the mirror of your soul before you make any big decisions. To make your physical home more of a haven for your heart. To address family or domestic questions in a healing, generous way.

Never Underestimate: The wisdom of your heart's first impressions in any situation. The validity of your instincts. The sustaining power of any supportive circle you might call "family." The illuminating impact of silence. The beneficial, illuminating, consciousness-expanding impact of candlelight, moonlight, and twilight.

The Prize: A deeper sense of well-being. Happiness. An accurate sense of what kinds of aims and developments will actually, truly lead to greater contentment. Improvements in your home-life and inner life. Better sleep. Attitudinal supports for good physical health.

The Price of Misguided Pride: Irrationality grabs the steering wheel. Pompous behavior. Dumb choices made impulsively. Compulsive spending. Saying things you wish you could take back. Expensive self-indulgence.

JUPITER CONTACTING MERCURY

Look for Opportunities... to expand the base of knowledge and experience that fuels your intelligence. Because of the principle of synchronicity, critical facts you have never considered lie openly before you now, appearing as if by magic. Educational opportunities in every sense of the term abound. Anticipate chances to speak up and to be heard; also, to write. People need to hear your voice.

Never Underestimate: The value of ongoing, ever-expanding, learning. That education can come from classes—but it can also be found in books, conversations, and media.

Don't underestimate the synergy between your unconscious mind and what comes out of your mouth—that is to say, trust your voice; just open your mouth and speak, with faith that you will say the right things and that you will be heard.

The Prize: A better alignment between what you believe and the actual truths of the world. A well-nourished intelligence. More confidence in your voice; more recognition and appreciation for your thoughts.

The Price of Misguided Pride: Bloviating, pompous, presumptuous chatter. Talking too much. Opinions that stand between you and the truth. Decisions based on wishful thinking and fanciful, self-serving information. Building views on fallacious assumptions.

JUPITER CONTACTING VENUS

Look for Opportunities... to move your closest relationships toward higher ground. To ask your partner, friends and family for what you really want. To freshen and update your circle of intimacy. To make new friends. To comfort your soul with aesthetic experience: buy art, attend concerts, enjoy film. To claim islands of peace in your life. To improve your appearance, both physically and socially.

Never Underestimate: The magic of simply asking people in your life for what you want or need. The time is right for doing that. Never underestimate the infectious quality of your own generosity of spirit and sense of humor; they will be mirrored back to you now. Never underestimate the way having some quiet time elevates the level of your animal magnetism.

The Prize: Deeper intimacy and a more profound sense of connection with the people in your life. New friends who prove to be precious to you. If you are single and don't want to be, perhaps a partner appears. Contacts with people who open doors for you.

The Price of Misguided Pride: Vanity. Relationships established on the inauthentic ground of improved status or getting ahead. Hurting existing relationships through high-handed, presumptuous or arrogant behavior. Overplaying your hand.

JUPITER CONTACTING MARS

Look for Opportunities... for meaningful victories. It is your hour; seize it. Use as much force as you need, but no more. Recognize that life can manifest as situations where someone wins and someone loses; it is your turn to win. Be decisive, defend what is rightfully yours, and claim some fresh territory.

Never Underestimate: What you can accomplish with courage and audacity on your side when the time is right—and that time is now. The wisdom inherent in your passions. Never underestimate the warrior's ancient secret: there is magical power in clear intention and in *not even imagining* the possibility of failure.

The Prize: A genuine, meaningful improvement in your circumstances or in the circumstances of those whom you love and protect. The victory you need. Progress on the path. Breakthroughs. Deeper courage, confidence, and charisma integrated into the fabric of your being.

The Price of Misguided Pride: A trail of pointless emotional bloodshed behind you. An empty, meaningless victory for which you pay a hefty karmic price. Damage you cannot easily undo. A missed opportunity—the chance that slipped through your fingers.

JUPITER CONTACTING JUPITER

Look for Opportunities... that align symbolically with the sign and house position of your natal Jupiter. A "doorway to opportunity" is opening in connection with that fundamental soul-contract. Is the opportunity creative? Spiritual? Professional? Again, we answer those questions with a question: where is your natal Jupiter? There is your answer. You signed up to do something big in that area of your life. This moment represents one of your chances to accomplish that.

Never Underestimate: The "luck" that materializes automatically when you are acting venturesomely in alignment with your soul's actual purpose in this world. Recognize that you have now surpassed some old limits. They were once real, but they no longer apply. Don't live a minute longer under the yoke of who you used to be.

The Prize: Breakthroughs that arise at the happy confluence of faith, opportunity, and a willingness to roll the dice. Navigated wisely, memories of these breakthroughs can still feel sweet as you look back on your years in this world from the perspective of the end of life. You were born for them—but they were your high "destiny" rather than your reflexive "fate."

The Price of Misguided Pride: Cocksure moves in precisely the wrong direction. Mistaking social advancement for spiritual advancement. Pride going before a fall. Feeding the ego while ignoring the soul.

JUPITER CONTACTING SATURN

Look for Opportunities... to take on some Great Work, one which has previously been unthinkable. To discern, celebrate, and embrace the good things that have come to you with the process of aging. To accept the kinds of new responsibilities that enhance your self-respect and dignity—and which outwardly reflect the wiser, more tempered person you have already become inwardly.

Never Underestimate: the productive power of relentless determination. Genius is "1 percent inspiration and 99 percent perspiration"—and it is time for you to perspire. Never underestimate the beneficial result of mistakes you have already made, however costly; it is time to turn old failures to good uses. You've paid for that wisdom; it is time to put it to good use.

The Prize: Seeing what your "best" actually looks like when it is manifest in this physical world. Making your vision real. Self-respect; a sense that you are *really doing something meaningful* with your life; genuine, lasting accomplishment.

The Price of Misguided Pride: Choosing a lesser path because you are daunted at the prospect of your true one. Caution, hesitation, and "second guesses" crushing a dream that might actually have become reality. Other people's judgments, fears, and values grab the steering wheel of your life.

JUPITER CONTACTING URANUS

Look for Opportunities... that arise suddenly out of the blue—but which happen to resonate powerfully with what you sense that you are becoming. The true key to the apparent magic here lies with two specific self-realizations: you are a) not the person you have been socialized into believing you are, and b) you are better than you imagine. Trust that pair of feelings and insights, and orient your choices around them; they are the magnet that is attracting these seemingly magical opportunities to you.

Never Underestimate: The synchronistic magnetism of true self-knowledge, allied with active faith, plus a willingness to take a risk. To win, you must play—and you miss 100 percent of the shots you do not take.

The Prize: The world would call it "luck," but it is not nearly so random. The prize is the out-of-the-blue disruption of an old set of limiting circumstances and self-imagery coinciding with the opening of a doorway that no one would have rationally anticipated—all triggered by your willingness to be true to what you have discovered that you truly are.

The Price of Misguided Pride: Silly rebellion. Contrariness. Breaking rules just to prove that you can. Turning left because people tell you to turn right. Headstrong idiocy. Desperate gambles aimed at chimerical prizes.

JUPITER CONTACTING NEPTUNE

Look for Opportunities... to care for your soul. There is much that is good and beautiful in this physical world, but now is the time to reach toward good and beautiful things you can carry with you as you journey beyond it. Teachers and teachings present themselves; avail yourself of them. Ditto for transitory opportunities to ditch your responsibilities, get away from all worldly demands, and have a chance to peacefully reflect, meditate, pray, and contemplate.

Never Underestimate: Your level of spiritual attainment. Update the inventory of your soul-life: you are further along than you were the last time you checked. Make sure you are not serving yourself cheap "religious" candy when what will actually nourish you is two hours alone on a mountaintop in the presence of the great mystery.

The Prize: A significant spiritual revelation; a breakthrough that comes as the result of previous acts of devotion and kindness towards others, whether in this life or in previous ones. Genuine insight into consciousness. Deeper generosity of spirit and a more compassionate engagement with humanity.

The Price of Misguided Pride: Spiritual posturing and posing. Delusional and inflated "psychic powers" and a too-rosy evolutionary self-assessment. Putting "Guru" or "Saint" on your business card.

JUPITER CONTACTING PLUTO

Look for Opportunities... to bring a positive attitude to bear upon some difficult but ultimately liberating psychological work. You are ready to heal some old wounds—and the universe wants to help. Watch for omens: three friends mention the same helpful book to you in the same month; circumstances mirror your wounds back at you; you connect with a counselor—who may be a "shrink," but just as easily could be an evolutionary astrologer, a good psychic, or just a friend with whom you can talk things out. Look for financial opportunities too—this aspect is good for money!

Never Underestimate: Your ability to change and grow. No problem is too great to be lessened—and no positive action on your part goes unrewarded with "cosmic matching funds" at this crossroads.

The Prize: Energy previously locked up in denial, rationalization, or even legitimate and necessary self-defense is now liberated. What will you do with it? *Anything you want!* It is your energy; it is only unfamiliar because you haven't seen it for a while.

The Price of Misguided Pride: Unresolved anger and hurt start making extravagant and foolish choices for you. The demon grabs the steering wheel. You project the parts of yourself that are bleeding onto other people, treating them the same way you are treating yourself—badly.

ENTERING SAGITTARIUS

Always remember that signs add fresh motivations and attitudes to the planets, significantly changing their natures. When, for example, Jupiter enters Capricorn, it takes on a seriousness of purpose we might not normally associate with Jupiter. By contrast, put Jupiter in Aquarius, and its famous enthusiasm focuses on the joyful Aquarian mayhem that comes from breaking all the rules.

When any of the planets enters Sagittarius, it swallows a big, intoxicating dose of raw enthusiasm, faith, and tolerance for risk. In other words, any planet—even dour Saturn—moving into Sagittarius temporarily becomes Jupiter's second cousin. Even Saturn orders a second martini.

With all that follows, remember our basic principle: slowness equals significance, while speed indicates transitory triggers. Thus the Sun transiting into Sagittarius is a far less momentous event than the Sun *progressing* into Sagittarius. The former might liven things up a bit—but the latter will shift the very foundations of your existence and identity.

Here are some practical tips for actually applying the sketches we provide in what follows:

* All of these descriptions are actively relevant to every solar arc—although some of them will not happen in the lifetimes of my current readers or myself. None of us, for example, are very likely to see Pluto entering Cancer by solar arc—if you are living now, early in the twenty-first century, that event lies roughly two centuries into the future. Short of cryogenic suspension, that solar arc is only an abstraction for us.
* The analysis of the Sun, Moon, Mercury, Venus, and Mars entering Sagittarius applies most actively to their progressions and

solar arcs. My words below would prove inflated and hyperbolic if we took them in reference to the mere transits of those fast-moving bodies. The basic ideas are sound enough, but throttle them back a bit if you are applying them to transits.

* The analysis of the entry of Jupiter, Saturn, Uranus, Neptune, and Pluto into Sagittarius refers both to their transits and their solar arcs. Their progressions are too slow to have practical relevance.

THE SUN ENTERING SAGITTARIUS

Your New Frontier: A wider world now looms before you. The deep inner work you have been doing for so long is finally paying off; many of the wounds and complexes with which you were born are now, due to your healing efforts, resolved. Today, you are on a road of discovery, seeking a richer sense of meaning and purpose in your life. Opportunities to travel and learn present themselves; take advantage of them. Live boldly; do not be afraid of making mistakes—you are resilient enough now to survive them and to thrive.

The Prison You Must Escape: The inner work you have done was honorable and necessary, but it is time to release yourself from any fascination it holds for you. Stop gazing at your navel and behold instead the miracle of the world, especially the world that lies beyond the tyranny of your familiar horizons. Realize that you are hypnotized by your own inner dragons; it's time to break that spell. It has served its purpose.

The Terrible Toll of the Dark Road: Slipping into boredom and predictability as a lifestyle. Locking yourself in an existential jail and throwing the keys out through the barred window, down to the streets below. Giving up on hope, dreams, and the fire of life.

THE MOON ENTERING SAGITTARIUS

Your New Frontier: Cultivating an attitude more conducive to embracing adventure, the fortunes of the road, and a general openness to the experience of life, come what may. This is actually a wonderful time to apply every cliché you have ever heard about positive thinking. Right now, those kinds of "gamblers' attitudes" will serve you well. An added benefit is that they will, through synchronicity, trigger the appearance of genuine, concrete opportunities for expansion.

The Prison You Must Escape: Conservative, overly-cautious thinking. A too-narrow focus on your inward, psychological life, coming at the expense of the full richness of human experience. Ultimately, what could possibly be more practical than trying to figure out why you are here and what it's all about?

The Terrible Toll of the Dark Road: A looming sense of life slipping away from you—or one of watching the fulfilling and fascinating lives of other people through a barred window. Life happening on the other side of the glass. Watching life on television.

MERCURY ENTERING SAGITTARIUS

Your New Frontier: Education!—but going to school is only one possibility here. Life itself can be an education, but only if you are willing to truly dive in and live it. Trust your intuition about what fascinates you and stimulates your interest. Follow the guidance of your own natural curiosity, even if it seems impractical or irrelevant. If you know in advance what you are going to learn, you are probably not learning anything new at all. It is time to break out of your own mental boxes.

The Prison You Must Escape: Mental fugues. The tyranny of endlessly repeating, mentally or out loud, your own pre-recorded position papers on every subject. Beware of the trap of becoming "the resident expert." Even if you are truly skillful at what you do, that is a dead-end road. It is time to learn something fresh and new.

The Terrible Toll of the Dark Road: Listening to your own boring lectures every day for the rest of your life. Never becoming any wiser than you are in this present moment. Unwittingly turning this moment of time into the point at which you ceased to learn anything new.

VENUS ENTERING SAGITTARIUS

Your New Frontier: A bolder and more experimental exploration of the meaning of intimacy. Allowing yourself to be touched and changed by other people; learning from them and letting them help you stretch your boundaries. Risking your heart in novel or daring ways. Connecting with different kinds of people than the ones with whom you have customarily connected. Bonding across lines of class, ethnicity, age, nationality—and the rest of these stupid border walls people seem to love to build.

The Prison You Must Escape: Stodginess and inhibition; predictability in the expression of affection or sexuality. If you are single, reflect upon a too-narrow definition of "your type"—which is to say, the kind of person to whom you are habitually attracted. If you are in a relationship, together you must explore some new directions now, or the bond is at risk for running out of fuel down the road.

The Terrible Toll of the Dark Road: Many cynical people hold the belief that passion and romance must always be short-lived. Even though there is a lot of human evidence that their gloomy view is correct, your challenge now is to prove them wrong. How? By doing the things we described in the "New Frontier" section above. If you fail in that, the price you pay is that you alone—or you and your partner, if you are in a relationship—become more evidence for that cynical view.

MARS ENTERING SAGITTARIUS

Your New Frontier: Fear is a survival-positive emotion: most of us would fear attempting to swim with hungry sharks, for example. Wisdom! But how would your world expand if you pushed that fear-boundary back a few inches? What possibilities would dawn in your awareness if you realized that you *had become competent enough safely to tolerate more risk in your life*—and furthermore, that you could do that without crossing the line into actual recklessness? That expanded horizon is your new frontier.

The Prison You Must Escape: A world defined too much by caution. A world unwittingly based on the groundless fantasy that, if you are careful enough, you will live forever. A world defined by the narrow horizons of your cultural, familial, or ethnic training.

The Terrible Toll of the Dark Road: The fire goes out of your blood and your heart. You begin to "get old" in the flat, unpleasant sense of that term. A feeling that you somehow "missed your chance in life" takes center stage in your own inner narrative.

JUPITER ENTERING SAGITTARIUS

Your New Frontier: Everything hinges on one critical realization: across the board, you have been underestimating yourself in every category. It may be that your faith in yourself was damaged by other people somehow or perhaps via some genuine misfortune; even if that is so, quit whining about it and recognize that you are now sufficiently healed to get on with your life. Alternatively, it may simply be that you have reached a stage of development and maturation in which you are capable of doing more than you had ever previously imagined. Either way, this is an excellent time to simply take a chance—and to expect a miracle as surely as you expect an echo if you shout in a canyon.

The Prison You Must Escape: A constricted, unimaginative vision of your actual potentials. You are better than you think you are; that pattern of limiting or negative ideation is your prison. Your social and cultural horizons are too restricted; *you have been trained to be less than you are capable of being*. Rise up! Do not accept a life wasted in those shackles.

The Terrible Toll of the Dark Road: The chance not taken, the opportunity missed. Standing slack-jawed and paralyzed before the gateway to the Golden City—then watching the gate swing shut in your face.

SATURN ENTERING SAGITTARIUS

Your New Frontier: Integrating realism and self-discipline with a more expansive vision of your possibilities. It is as if you already have the vehicle, but you lack a map. Where can you acquire one? To find the answer, here is what you need to add to your mental mix: hope, aspiration, and a sense of the existence of more exciting possibilities than you have ever before imagined. Standing on that foundation, scan the far horizon. There is your destination—and the journey of a thousand miles starts with a single step.

The Prison You Must Escape: The crippling power of words such as "No," "Impossible," and "Unlikely." Remember that when the meteorologist says there is a fifty percent chance of rain, that means that there is also a fifty percent chance that it will *not* rain. There is no shame in exercising due caution—bring an umbrella, but head out anyway. Add one more pivotal point: the mysterious, magical impact upon the shape of reality that comes from faith and a positive attitude. Do not be afraid to imagine everything working out fine.

The Terrible Toll of the Dark Road: The unwitting triumph of bitterness or cynicism over faith and hope, all in the holy names of "reasonable caution" and "realism." A fundamentally depressing philosophical slant begins to permeate your sense of reality. An almost xenophobic fear of anything exotic or different drives imagination into a dark, damp dungeon of fear masquerading as reason.

URANUS ENTERING SAGITTARIUS

Your New Frontier: Self-discovery, in a word—but we are talking about a specific method for attaining it. Put someone in a terrifying situation and he or she often realizes previously unimagined reserves of courage. The process here is similar, except it does not have to be terrifying—only exotic and unfamiliar. Perhaps you need to travel or to risk experiencing something completely outside your normal orbit. Step outside your familiar world. The point is that by exposing yourself to circumstances which you've never seen before, you invoke aspects of your true individuality which otherwise would remain buried. If you are American, go to China. If you are Chinese, come to America.

The Prison You Must Escape: Unwittingly becoming a generic caricature of your culture or family of origin. The insidious part of this prison is that if you fall into that trap, you will not know it. You would believe that you were simply being yourself without the slightest idea that you had been conditioned into accepting only a partial expression of your true potential.

The Terrible Toll of the Dark Road: A weird and seemingly inexplicable sense of alienation from your own life, as if you are playing a scripted part in a film someone else wrote. The lingering sense that "if you had only taken that one chance," your life would have turned out differently—and you are probably right about that.

NEPTUNE ENTERING SAGITTARIUS

Your New Frontier: A transformation in the nature of your spiritual experience and your imaginative life. To trigger this magical alchemical process in the core of your consciousness, you need only to add one single ingredient: a willingness to step outside your philosophical comfort zone. If you are Presbyterian, it is time to learn about Buddhist meditation. If you are Buddhist, undertake Jungian analysis. If you are a professor of astronomy, get an astrological reading. Pilgrimage—which is to say, traveling with spiritual intention—is a particularly powerful catalyst at this time.

The Prison You Must Escape: Mistaking your belief system for reality. Even if your belief system is free from serious errors, it is still ultimately only an idea in your head. Reality in the larger sense of the word is always far vaster; the trigger you need to pull lies somewhere out in that vastness.

The Terrible Toll of the Dark Road: Religiosity replaces the direct experience of the Great Mystery. "Religion" here is not restricted to the obvious meaning of the word; it includes all belief systems—materialism, cynicism, or the idea that life happens at random. All can be compelling once we accept their basic premises; therefore each can result in terminal blindness.

PLUTO ENTERING SAGITTARIUS

Your New Frontier: Everyone is at least a little bit crazy. To make the same point more formally, most of us embody at least a few seemingly intractable patterns of minor psychological dysfunction. Now let me say it a third way, more lightly, although my meaning remains the same: there are lessons that I have "learned" hundreds of times—in other words, I have not learned them at all. However you choose to phrase it, realize that you are faced with a fresh opportunity to successfully wrestle those personal dysfunctions now. A cure is presenting itself—but the cure lies outside your present belief system. If you have been trying to heal yourself with meditation, it is time to try psychotherapy—or vice versa. Are you intellectual? Hire a deep body-worker. You need to shake up your approach to maintaining your own mental health.

The Prison You Must Escape: Famously, Freudians declare us "cured" when we begin to think like Freudians, just as Fundamentalists declare us "saved" when we begin to think like Fundamentalists. For you, now, being truly saved and truly cured depends upon your escaping the limiting boundaries of the beliefs that you have unwittingly swallowed. It is time to critique your basic assumptions.

The Terrible Toll of the Dark Road: Making a religion out of your own madness. Self-justifying beliefs can create an impervious boundary, stopping evolution in its tracks. A nearly infallible sign that you have slipped into that trap is a compelling need to convert other people to your beliefs.

JUPITER MOVING THROUGH THE HOUSES

By transit, Jupiter takes approximately a year to pass through a house. During that time, real opportunities typically arise in the areas of life symbolized by the house. These opportunities come in two flavors: opportunities to genuinely better your circumstances, along with opportunities for spectacular pratfalls. As ever, knowing what is truly good for you is the key to getting to the higher ground.

Generally speaking, the entire period of Jupiter's passage through a house actively reflects the symbolism, often punctuated by peaks of activity that correlate with transiting Jupiter's contact with the house cusp and any aspectual contacts it makes during its passage.

Solar arcs move much more slowly than transits. In broadly average terms, Jupiter will take about three decades to pass through a house via solar arc, although houses vary widely in width. Look about a year on either side of Jupiter's passage *by solar arc* over a house cusp for a flurry of characteristic activity. For the rest of the time Jupiter is moving by solar arc through the house, there are likely to be some long dormant periods—years in which Jupiter is not making any significant aspects to the rest of the chart and is thus mostly quiet.

When Jupiter moves out of the twelfth house and into the first house... the transition signals a major green light in your evolutionary journey. It's time to "bet the house," as they say—although it would be more accurate to say that it's time to bet on yourself. The wind is in your sails; if you drop your morning toast off the table, it will now land butter-side up almost every time. Angels are watching over you. Literally entering contests is actually a good idea; the odds of winning are markedly improved. Your luck will be even better if you "enter contests" in areas of your existing life that are ripe for improvement—that is to say, it is time to take chances in areas where you are actively, personally engaged, such as your home, your profession, your relationships and so forth. We can't help but be a bit vague here. That is because, while the other eleven houses tend to refer to specific areas of life, the first house operates in a more generalized way. Ultimately, this transit is about developing faith in the magical, life-shaping power of your *will* and *intentions*. Every arena of life provides an effective laboratory for that evolutionary work. Dare to hope, and put your money where your mouth is..

When Jupiter moves out of the first house and into the second house... the focus of expansive activity moves to the *resource base* necessary for the support and continuation of the intentions you set moving back when Jupiter was in the first house. Classically, the second house is about money, and finding ways to cash out your dreams might be part of what is happening here. Do you need to ask for money? Do you need to be bold enough to take out a loan? Those are definite possibilities. But the second house is not only about money—there are many other kinds of resources in the world. They can take the form of *skills* you need to acquire or strategic *alliances* you need to create. In all cases, the key is to ask for what you need. You're building confidence in yourself now, but it's important not to frame that process in narrowly psychological terms. It is not as much about "giving yourself a big hug" as it is about providing yourself with concrete, objective reasons to have faith in your dream.

When Jupiter moves out of the second house and into the third house... your voice needs to be heard. You really do have something important to say; you are a fountain of good ideas. Have faith in all that. Hold your head high and speak up. If you're shy, join a discussion group or take part in a theatrical performance or join Toastmasters—during this period, it is imperative not to let shyness control you. For your journey through life to continue unfolding on its natural path, you must realize that you have been underestimating your intelligence, your level of articulation, and the helpful relevance of your ideas. Is it time to write a letter to the editor or to start that book you have always wanted to write? There's always an element of *learning* connected with the third house. With Jupiter there, precious educational opportunities arise. These are characterized by the right teachers arriving, armed with the right teachings—which is to say the teachings that are most relevant to putting some polish on your own thoughts. This is typically a busy time, and it might make you feel like a billiard ball bouncing around a pool table. Underlying the chaos, the universe is communicating unexpected information to you via omens, repeated messages, and synchronicities.

When Jupiter moves out of the third house and into the fourth house... it is time to slow down and take stock of who you have become. If you settle down enough to do that, you will probably like what you discover. You are better than you thought you were. That is true in many categories; each one of those breakthroughs is a natural side effect of the work you have been doing on yourself. Beware, though—if you fail to slow down and take stock, you will not realize what you have accomplished. You won't claim the prize you have earned. More is at stake here than missing a chance to pat yourself on the back: your dreams and intentions in life need to be placed on a more ambitious foundation. Right now, you are like the seed of a beautiful flower germinating invisibly under the ground. Water that seed! In order to experience the necessary quiet at this phase of your journey, you may need to make some changes in your domestic situation. You might need to move, for example, to a more pleasant home. You might need to rethink some of your family responsibilities in a way that leaves you more quiet, fertile time. As ever with Jupiter, it's time to bet on yourself. Ask for what you need and there is an excellent chance it will come your way.

When Jupiter moves out of the fourth house and into the fifth house... the seed you planted in the fourth house is ready to blossom into that beautiful flower. This is a time of creative self-expression—and probably a time of being recognized and appreciated for it. Of course for any of that to happen, you really need to take the risk of somehow stepping out on the stage of life. Face those butterflies in your stomach and put yourself out there. Inwardly you will feel vulnerable, while outwardly you will probably look a lot more confident than you feel. Life, for all of us, can sometimes be a battering experience. Our ability to hope and to have faith is often challenged. During this period of your life, opportunities arise for you to renew your basic animal joy. It is imperative now, from the evolutionary point of view, that you *have a really good time*. That statement might sound lightweight—until you reflect on the impact of all the disappointments and hard things you have experienced. We are not asking you to whine about anything; we are only saying that there is an art to recovering from all of that disappointment and heartbreak. Now is the time to practice it. So: celebrate! Dance! Spend some money on yourself. Why do you think God gave you that *Visa* card?

When Jupiter moves out of the fifth house and into the sixth house... the focus shifts to an increased workload and inflated responsibilities. That prophecy can sound gloomy until we reflect more deeply on it. Work and responsibility do not necessarily equate with misery—although of course sometimes they do exactly that. What makes the difference? The dull routine of "doing what we have to do" rarely brings anyone much joy, especially when we feel that we could train an intelligent chimpanzee to do the same job. But what about doing work that actually matters to you? What about being really good at something that gives you true pleasure and fulfillment—and probably adds something wonderful to another person's life in the bargain? Your evolutionary effort now lies in realizing that you have been underestimating your capacity for *joyful competence*. Here's an illustration: since you are reading this book, I know that you are interested in astrology. I can tell you from personal experience that some of the most fun you will ever have sitting down is surfing the waves of an intense astrological consultation with a deeply engaged client. Is it time to "hang out your shingle" as an astrologer? Not all of us need to become professional astrologers, but the foregoing scenario illustrates the point: there are forms of work and responsibility in this world that are worthy of you and would give you a lot of joy. All the laws of synchronicity suggest that such opportunities now lie before you. What if you don't see them? Then instead look for mentors, role models, and teachers who are ahead of you on that road. Follow in their footsteps; those footsteps will soon be your own.

When Jupiter moves out of the sixth house and into the seventh house… help and support are on the way. Even though the seventh house is conventionally framed as the house of marriage, we need to cast our nets more widely. How much, for example, do you value your treasured friendships? They are precious seventh house gifts too. Jupiter entering the seventh house can bring you new friends. It can also bring you catalytic allies in your creative or professional life. None of this is to say that romantic or intimate developments are unlikely at this time; they are common as well. Maybe you will "meet someone." What if you are already in a good relationship? Jupiter's question then becomes how can you make that relationship even better? To lift these statements above the narrow context of fortune-telling, we have to add the active ingredient: a recognition that, in your intimate circle, it's time to stop settling for too little. To find these precious soul-friends, you need to elevate your vision. How have you shortchanged yourself in terms of the people you have attracted into your life—or in terms of the existing "contracts" with them? You have come to a time in your life when you need some help; the help is there, somewhere right before your eyes. Look *up* and you will see it.

When Jupiter moves out of the seventh house and into the eighth house... opportunities arise that, while emotionally daunting, can lay the foundation for many satisfying developments down the road. Facing your own woundedness and the systems of reflexive defense that have grown up around it can put a knot in your stomach and a lump in your throat; anyone who has done any psychological work on themselves knows exactly what I'm talking about. But once accomplished, that kind of inner healing liberates us from looping patterns of self-limiting or self-destructive behavior. That's a fast track to deeper aliveness. Opportunities to do exactly that kind of healing are abundant now: pivotal conversations happen, counselors appear, secrets are revealed. Try to accept these treasures gratefully, even if they hurt at the time. Often the triggers for these breakthroughs involve sexual energy, the impact of sexual soul-mates, and the unique—and soul-revealing—intimacy of such bonds. Sometimes the cathartic dramas involve someone passing through that mysterious doorway we call death. It sounds strange to think of death as a gift—but someone sharing their end-of-life experience with you can be a treasure that you will hold precious for the rest of your own days.

When Jupiter moves out of the eighth house and into the ninth house... at the simplest and most concrete level of astrology, this event tells us that we can expect a *travel opportunity* to materialize. We can predict the appearance of opportunities to expand your horizons in other ways too: classes, lectures, conversations with people who have something exotic and valuable to teach you. A lofty philosophical note makes itself felt in your life. At a deeper level, you are harvesting the fruit of the inner work you have already done—at least we hope so—while Jupiter was passing through the eighth house. The underlying point is that the saner you become, the more clearly you see reality and the more boldly you participate in it. You have made some significant breakthroughs over the past year or two; these breakthroughs have cleaned your windows—your understanding of life is less distorted. In a sense, your intellect is now trying to catch up with what your deeper psyche has already learned. You are rewriting your philosophy of life so that it reflects your hard-won wisdom. To add some fresh air to this valuable process, it is helpful for you to experience an outward change of scenery, along with some unfamiliar educational input. All of that simply serves the purpose of breaking up stubborn patterns in your existing mental and existential routines.

When Jupiter moves out of the ninth house and into the tenth house... it is time for all the inner efforts you have been making to translate into an improvement in your worldly status. Career is the classic focus of the tenth house, and it is common for professional opportunities to open up at this time: new jobs, increases in pay, promotions, and so on. But the scope of the symbolism is far broader: Jupiter passing through the tenth house also refers to elevations in your *status in your community*—including your general reputation and how you look to people who do not actually know you personally. As always, the underlying evolutionary question is, how have you been underestimating yourself? It is time to actively make a bid for more recognition, recompense, and a chance to show the world the full extent of your capabilities. Synchronistically, worldly doors open now—the laws of the universe guarantee that. Here is what they do not guarantee: that you recognize these doors and march through them with your head held high.

When Jupiter moves out of the tenth house and into the eleventh house... the question becomes one of updating your *priorities* and your *goals* in life. You have achieved a position of some strength in your community. Chances are that from an exterior point of view, things are looking pretty decent in your life now—maybe even enviable. Weirdly, underlying those appearances, there is an insidious sense of tedium. *Is this all there is?* The time has come to look ahead and to reflect upon a more enlivening set of long-term dreams and ambitions—ones worthy of the person you have actually become. In a nutshell, it is time to think big and to plan accordingly. This is not about impressing other people; it is about recognizing that you are capable of doing more than you have ever done. Speculate freely about that possibility; let your imagination conjure up a future you would be grateful and proud to live. As you do that, look around you: you will find *allies*, which is to say people who can be helpful to you. *Network* with them; you will find that their goals and their strengths are convergent with your own. It is a time of *social synergy*. Traditionally, the eleventh house was called the house of friends. It is more accurate to think of it as a house of networking and alliances. The key here is realizing that in order to choose them appropriately, you must first have framed a direction in life that inspires you. *Without a goal, how can you possibly recognize the people who might help you achieve it?*

When Jupiter moves out of the eleventh house and into the twelfth house... what the wisest part of you truly desires at this point is only a quiet mountaintop, away from the craziness of the world—a place where you can reflect and listen to the "still, small voice within." You are actually preparing the ground for a colorful, life-changing new start as Jupiter crosses your Ascendant, although you might not be thinking in those terms at the moment. No worry; doors will open for you then. To put it vividly, some of them are doors to heaven, some are doors to hell—and all of them look pretty good on the surface. How are you going to know which doors are the right ones? The answer brings us back to that "quiet mountaintop"—which might not be a mountaintop at all; it is really a reference to your making space in your life now for inspiration, surrender, and divine guidance to arise in your consciousness. If you have made time to receive the vision, your actions and decisions as Jupiter crosses your Ascendant will be the right ones for you. Because of the laws of synchronicity, opportunities for that kind of precious quiet are arising now. They may come into your life packaged as contact with spiritual teachings or teachers—or they may be as simple as a friend offering you the use of a cabin somewhere far from the madding crowd. Whatever form the gift takes, *angels are trying to whisper in your ear.* Take time to listen—those angels are a lot smarter than you. It takes a real fool to ignore them.

23

AFTERWORD: THE FIRE OF LIFE

And so we come to the end... of the beginning. This is the Fire Family—as essential to your mental, physical, and spiritual health as calcium is to the health of the teeth in your mouth. Without a strong response to these nine Life-Givers, human existence is simply too much for us. Disappointment, heartbreak, and tragedy, finding nothing to counter them, gradually erode the human spirit.

But none of us have to go down that sad, dark road. Built into our souls is a potential source of such indomitable, transrational, exuberant vitality that our spirits cannot be broken.

Think of the love and faith and hope in the eyes of a man walking down the aisle to be married for the third time.

Think of an old woman laughing and beaming on her deathbed.

Think of a young woman giving birth, in triumph over all the pain of that ultimate life-giving process.

With the good angels of Fire on our side, this vibrant affirmation of the sweetness and resilience of life is part of our spiritual heritage as human beings. It is a treasure we have all been given as our birthright—but it is a treasure that must be nourished, lest we lose it. Failing that, every day we awaken to find it slightly diminished, a little bit less shiny with the glow of faith, and a little bit less capable of sustaining us as we pursue our long and sometimes arduous journey to ultimate freedom.

My hope for *The Book of Fire* is that it can serve as a user's manual for the care and feeding of these nine Life-Givers. Each one of them, as we have seen, has its own nature and its own idiosyncrasies. Each one can be an invaluable friend, but only if we learn its particular dance steps. The dance can be joyful—that's the entire point. We just have to be careful not to step on anyone's toes, including our own.

As we weave our tangled paths through life, astrology can be such a precious ally. In common with every astrologer with whom I've ever spoken, I wish our craft were more widely accepted by the general public. It could potentially help so many people. But we quickly encounter a major hurdle—and I'm not thinking of the massive wall of ignorance we face. I am thinking of a more practical problem: while anyone can read a magazine prediction for Taurus or Gemini, to garner anything like the real power of astrology, people need to go down one of two possible roads: either they sit with a skilled astrologer for a personal consultation, or they take a six-week course and learn the basic language for themselves.

There are obvious emotional and practical hurdles connected with each of those paths, but I am not pessimistic here at all. In the course of my lifetime, I feel that I have seen major progress on both fronts. The level of public acceptance of astrology has probably slowly doubled before my eyes. Many communities are now graced with fine, competent astrologers. Many of them teach classes, and so there are ever-increasing numbers of people in the general public who, while not astrologers themselves, can find their way around a birthchart.

I celebrate all this, and I hope that *The Book of Fire*—along with the next three volumes in this "Elements" series—contribute to that cultural sea change.

Obviously, this hasn't been a book aimed at beginners. For that, I would recommend my first book, *The Inner Sky*. In writing *The Book of Fire*, I have tried to keep two audiences in mind. One of them comprises people who, while lacking any real ambition to practice astrology, have simply been fascinated with it long enough to have internalized the basics. They use astrology for reasons of personal growth—and I suspect that most of them have been inveigled to help out their friends with some informal astrological counsel from time to time.

I hope that this volume has sharpened their skills on both of those fronts.

The second audience for whom I have written *The Book of Fire* is composed of serious students of the system—individuals who are actively working with astrological clients or who have aspirations in that direction.

By the way, if you'll forgive me for mounting the pulpit for a moment, any sharp distinction between students and professionals is counterproductive: I personally would never trust any astrologer who was not committed to being an astrological *student* for the rest of his or her life. Every astrologer is different; it probably borders on fair to say that each one of us has seen something that no astrologer has ever seen before. We can, in other words, all find something to learn from each other. And my prayer is that even among my professional colleagues in the field, there are a few who have read this book and taken something from it that they find valuable, which they can then pass on to their own clients and students.

We are all one family, all living under one mysterious sky.

My tonsils came out when I was a senior in high school. While I was in bed at home recovering, my mother asked me if she might bring me a book to read. Somewhat to her surprise, I asked for an astrology book. I lucked out: the one she brought me was *Write Your Own Horoscope* by Joseph F. Goodavage. The great thing about that book was the way it went, planet by planet, through each of the twelve signs. I learned how my Mars in Aquarius was different from my sister's Mars in Taurus, and so on. That book was really my first introduction to the nuts and bolts of how astrology worked. Goodavage's language was accurate enough, even though it was old-style astrology, more descriptive than prescriptive. I'd quibble with him today, but I'm grateful for the astrological foundation his little "cookbook" paragraphs gave me about each sign/planet combination. It was through them that I began to acquaint myself with the basic symbolism of our craft.

With the astrological hook firmly in my mouth, I soon began to read voraciously. I was particularly enthusiastic about a slim volume by an Englishman named Ronald C. Davison simply called *Astrology.* It too was full of tables detailing the meanings of the individual planets in each of the signs—but Davison introduced me to houses as well. From him, I learned that, with my Mars in the third house, I was "alert" and "determined"—but that I could also be "stubborn and headstrong."

Fair enough—but in *Astrology*, Davison also warned me that because of my third house placement of Mars, my neighbors could be "disputatious and annoying."

Those three words gave me goosebumps. Just five years earlier, a psychotic next-door neighbor in the urban apartment building where we lived told my mother that he was planning to kill me. I was only thirteen. He was specific: he was going to run me over with a car. He meant it too.

Needless to say, this was a major family drama. Obviously, I survived.

We never fully understood what the whole thing was about. I suspect he imagined some sexual involvement between me and one of his daughters, who was my own age. There was no truth in that allegation; I was just thirteen and still a blushing virgin. Looking back, I suspect my crazy neighbor was, in the language of psychology, *projecting*. My intuition is that he had himself probably been sexually abusing both of his daughters. My only evidence for that belief is that a few years later, his younger daughter was busted for solicitation for prostitution—a common enough result of early sexual violation.

Anyway, Davison telling me that my neighbors could be "disputatious and annoying" really rung a bell in me. From that moment onward, I was incurable: I knew that astrology would be a big part of the rest of my life.

It worked!

As my skills developed, I came to believe that "cookbook" interpretations such as those I'd learned from Goodavage and Davison, were a dead-end, sort of like resorting to heroin as a way of dealing with life in a ghetto. When, some years later, I was writing *The Inner Sky*, I was determined to try to teach my readers how to "think astrologically" rather than how to parrot memorized paragraphs from some book. I had come to realize that astrological competence required an integrative, intuitive approach: messages from signs, planets, houses, aspects, not to mention the entirety of the chart, need to be blended together in your heart before you open your mouth.

At first that process sounds dauntingly difficult, but I realized that it's something we all do every day. Think of how many thousands of individual facts blend together seamlessly when you contemplate the nature of someone you love. The process happens in your heart, not in your intellect. It's that part of your consciousness which can succeed at astrology; it's very different sets of neurons and synapses than the ones that do mathematics or balance a checkbook.

I still believe all that.

But I couldn't have developed that integrative style without first internalizing Joseph F. Goodavage's contrasting paragraphs about the meaning of Mars in Aquarius versus Mars in Taurus, and so forth. I might not have persisted in my astrological studies without the boost that came from Ronald C. Davison's near-miraculous observation that my Mars in the third house warned me of neighbors who might prove "disputatious and annoying."

In laying my original plans for *The Book of Fire*, I intended a series of essays about each of the nine words in the Fire vocabulary. I planned on going deeply into a few specific examples of synthesis, with the aim of demonstrating the integrative process.

As you've seen, I actually did quite a lot of that in the foregoing pages—but writing a book is a mysterious process. The unconscious—call it the soul or even the angels—always casts a deciding vote. Somehow, early in the writing process, I realized that *The Book of Fire*, along with everything else I had intended for it, needed to be a "cookbook" too.

I needed to write a book which might accomplish for students of evolutionary astrology what Goodavage and Davison had accomplished for me so many years ago.

What exactly was that?

The best answer I can come up with is that they provided me with a *starting point.* Intuitive, integrative analysis is the ultimate aim—but even to have a shot at getting there, we all need to burn the midnight oil. There's much that we simply need to memorize. We need to study astrology in an academic way, internalizing the nuts and bolts. That's how we master the basic building blocks of the system. The process starts with absorbing the core definitions of each of the signs, houses, and planets. It proceeds from there into learning how to put them together in pairs. How is Mars flavored by Aquarius different from Mars flavored by Taurus? How does Mars express itself through the third house as distinct from the twelfth or the fifth?

Eventually, we cross the astrological Rubicon: we learn how to put them together in triads: a planet in both a sign and house.

When I was first learning how to answer those foundational questions, I turned to the "cookbook" pages written by Goodavage and Davison, along with a few other authors. They really helped. I don't think I could have learned astrology without them. And yet, at the same time, I meant what I said earlier about memorizing stock paragraphs being an astrological dead- end. It is essential along with everything else I had intended but, alone, it is not enough.

What I'm saying is that first we must build our wings, and then we must fly.

In *The Book of Fire*, I have attempted to do a little bit of both. There are many pages of stock paragraphs—I suspect they will be well-thumbed before long, just as were my copies of *Write Your Own Horoscope* and *Astrology*. I do hope that you will benefit from the cookbook material and find it useful.

I also hope that you will soar beyond it.

The realization that writing the present volume would involve generating a great number of rather formulaic paragraphs was daunting to me. I'm a Capricorn, so I am wired for that sort of nose-to-the-grindstone project—but my fiery Moon, Venus, and Pluto all balked at the proposition. They are not so patient. I also had to break the news to my inner chorus of Fire planets that there would be three more volumes in this series. Each one would have to dance to the same "cookbook" tune.

I bit the bullet and wrote those stock paragraphs. If you have read this far, you already know that. I'm glad I did. By the time this set of books is complete, my hope is that it will supply to my readers and students the same kind of helpful support I received from Goodavage and Davison, but that it will do so more in accord with the open-ended philosophy of evolutionary astrology.

I also hope that these cookbook paragraphs will help to flesh out the more integrated picture I tried to describe in *The Inner Sky* and *The Changing Sky* many years ago. In fact, I've come to think of this present series as companion volumes to those two, my original books.

I was able to give my poor Fire planets some minor solace. Inevitably, as I move on to write *The Book of Earth, The Book of Air* and *The Book of Water,* there will be some overlap among them. Jupiter, for example, rules

Sagittarius, and so it has figured prominently here in this volume. But we must never forget that there is another face to Jupiter: it co-rules Pisces, sharing that role with Neptune. Jupiter will, in other words, make a second appearance in *The Book of Water*. In these present Fire pages we have already detailed the meaning of Jupiter in each of the signs and houses. Its rulership of Pisces does not change a syllable there—those same paragraphs will therefore also appear again in the final volume of the series.

The repetition is a bit awkward—but leaving Jupiter out of *The Book of Water* would be a disaster.

For exactly the same reasons, Mercury, Venus, and Saturn will make appearances in both *The Book of Earth* and *The Book of Air*, while Mars will appear again in *The Book of Water*. In the long run, I hope the convenience of the "completeness" of each volume enhances the "toolbox" utility of all four volumes, rather than afflicting anyone with a bad case of *déjà vu*—or, worse, a sense of having bought the same book twice.

Thank you all for giving me the life I have been able to live. The older I get, the more deeply I appreciate that generous gift of Fire you have given me.

Stay tuned. Next up—*The Book of Earth*.

—Steven Forrest
Borrego Springs, California

LEARN ASTROLOGY WITH STEVEN FORREST

Interested in learning more about Steven's unique approach to astrology? For a listing of lectures and workshops that are available in a variety of audio and video formats, go to: **http://www.forrestastrology.com/store**.

Better yet, join the many successful students who have completed Steven's Astrological Apprenticeship Program, where he teaches both the specific techniques of interpretation and the style of presentation that have made him one of the most successful and influential astrologers in the world. Steven takes great joy in passing on the teachings and strategies that have worked for him over the years through his Apprenticeship Program.

The Apprenticeship Program presents students with a rare opportunity to learn astrology in a supportive environment of like-minded individuals, who together create a feeling of community and connection, leading to bonds that last throughout life. Some come to the program to train professionally, while others come for personal or spiritual enrichment.

Learn more at www.forrestastrology.com

Made in United States
North Haven, CT
11 June 2023

37625804R00173